The HOUSE-WIVES

The HOUSE-WIVES

THE REAL STORY BEHIND
THE REAL HOUSEWIVES

BRIAN MOYLAN

FLATIRON
BOOKS
NEW YORK

www.flatironbooks.com

Design by Meryl Sussman Levavi

The Library of Congress Cataloging-in-Publication Data is available upon request.

ISBN 978-1-250-80760-1 (hardcover)
ISBN 978-1-250-80761-8 (ebook)

Our books may be purchased in bulk for promotional, educational, or business use. Please contact your local bookseller or the Macmillan Corporate and Premium Sales Department at 1-800-221-7945, extension 5442, or by email at MacmillanSpecialMarkets@macmillan.com.

First Edition: 2021

1   3   5   7   9   10   8   6   4   2

*For the woman who gave me life and is
the greatest person I've ever known:
Jill Zarin, I couldn't have done it without you.
You really do travel with a fabulous circle of people.*

CONTENTS

The HOUSE-WIVES

INTRODUCTION

THE SKY TOP'S THE LIMIT

Rewatch the very first episode of *The Real Housewives of Orange County* (*RHOC*) and you'll notice a few things. Like Vicki Gunvalson taking pictures before her daughter's prom on a camera with actual film. What will really stick with you, though, are the Sky Tops.

Manufactured in LA and designed by a husband-and-wife team, these were tank top or halter top blouses cut to accentuate the ample chests of the "85% of women who have fake boobs" in the area, as a quote running over the *RHOC* opening credits informs us. They were always embellished with sequins, rhinestones, or even giant medallions around the wearer's silicone-enhanced décolletage. Vicki wears several in the first episode, including a canary-yellow number with ruching just below the boobs that flares out toward the waistband of her low-rise denim. She looks like she's dressed as Britney Spears while chaperoning her kids to the pop star's concert. Later, she rocks a baby-pink top where the straps are chains of sequins that travel along the neckline to meet in the middle as if kissing her breasts good night.

In the artwork used to promote the show's premiere—March 21,

2006, on Bravo—all five cast members are wearing Sky Tops. Vicki wears her most spectacular version of all, a champagne-colored satin halter with a keyhole cut out near the neckline and a print of a vase with flowers exploding across her chest.

Looking back on this episode as a snapshot of the George W. Bush administration with America on the precipice of a financial crash, it's easy to look at this like a relic, like some sort of cave painting depicting the fall before a terrifying future. We should think of it more like the mosquito frozen in amber in *Jurassic Park,* because this strange little episode, barely watched in its premiere, contained all the DNA—women baring it all, a look inside an affluent lifestyle, a bit of interpersonal conflict—to create a menagerie of monsters who would take over the world.

For me, it didn't start with Sky Tops but a topless man. I was sitting on the floor of my sparse apartment when the lithe, sculpted body of eighteen-year-old baseball player Shane Keough appeared on my combination TV/VCR. Shane was square-jawed with at least as many visible abs as the leanest Hemsworth brother, and just the kind of guy who would have been an asshole to me in high school. Exactly my type. *My, my, what is this?* I thought, suddenly paying attention to the screen. Turns out it was *The Real Housewives of Orange County,* and it would change my life.

My love for the Real Housewives wasn't immediate. When I started watching the show in 2006, it was simply because Bravo was my go-to channel. *Queer Eye for the Straight Guy* and *Project Runway* had debuted three and two years earlier, respectively, starting Bravo's golden age along with shows like *Top Chef, Kathy Griffin: My Life on the D-List, Flipping Out, Being Bobby Brown,* and *Blow Out.*

Real Housewives of Orange County wasn't "appointment television," as we would call it at the time. I would catch it during weekend marathons, while putzing about the apartment, folding the laundry, or just lounging on my twin mattress on the floor, chain-smoking Marlboro Menthol Lights.

The show grew on me, little by little, until it was an all-consuming passion. It was a perfect trap for me at the time, toiling away as I was at two low-paying jobs in Washington, D.C. Instead of focusing on making ends meet, I could watch Vicki and her crew prowl their sprawling, antiseptic homes, shouting at their children, their spouses, each other.

It wasn't that I wanted to live like these middle-aged women across the country, so much as I felt a certain kinship with them. There couldn't have been a more opposite lifestyle from mine—and yet. They traveled in a pack, fighting and gossiping among themselves, just like I did with my crew. As mothers of a certain age before *MILF* was the most popular Pornhub search term, they were also marginalized from society in a similar way that gay men were. If they were not aware of giving a camp performance of American affluence, they were still giving it to us with both manicured fists.

My career as a professional *Real Housewives* chronicler started shortly after I started at the gossip blog *Gawker* (RIP) in 2009. I filled in for my colleague Richard Lawson when he couldn't do the recaps and then took over entirely once he left the site. In 2013, my recaps landed at Vulture, *New York* magazine's pop culture website, and have been there ever since. As the president and founder of the (entirely fictional) Real Housewives Institute, I've written about the franchise for *The New York Times, The Guardian,* and other publications I was surprised were interested.

When I started recapping, I thought people just wanted to have their opinions confirmed. I imagined my readers wanted an "expert" to tell them that, yes, this season Jill Zarin was behaving like a crazy person, or maybe we shouldn't make too much fun of Gia Giudice's songwriting ability because she's only a minor. (Though her birthday song for her sister is an all-time classic.)

But the more I interacted with fans in the comments sections, on social media, and for hours cornered by gays in bars, the more I learned that they didn't want to agree; they didn't want to be told. People just wanted to talk about the Housewives. These women were like the popular girls in high school that everyone hated and were jealous of at the same time. We all wanted their version of privilege, and we all wanted to grind it under the boots of our Doc Martens. (I obviously went to high school in the '90s.)

I like to call the Housewives, even those I don't particularly care for, my "TV friends." I'll never meet most of them in real life, but I talk about their latest tantrums, dating habits, business failures, and outfit choices at brunch as if each is a part of my extended circle. We all know when Luann filed for divorce from Tom or when she headed into rehab—both times. It's not just passing the news along; it's sharing concern, or joy, for the experiences the rest of us are living vicariously.

There is no one with whom I talk more *Real Housewives* than my partner, Christian. We met at a *Gawker* party back when I worked on the site. Christian, newly single, was a friend of a friend and liked my recaps enough that he decided to introduce himself. He started by telling me about some project he was working on that, honestly, sounded like a huge bore. I was about to exit the conversation politely when he said, "But I really love the Housewives." He didn't have me at hello, but he did have me at "Sonja Morgan is my favorite."

In all our time together, the Real Housewives are a constant source of conversation. Christian loves to watch along with me, making jokes and keen observations that he hopes I'll repurpose for the recap. Without credit, of course.

I decided to write this book mostly for selfish reasons, to answer all the questions that keep me awake at night. How does casting work? How does the show get made? Does Andy Cohen really have as much power as we think he does? Who on earth actually pays for these trips? I wanted to call up insiders for some other reason than being a nosy reality fan.

I also knew that if I had these questions, other fans did, too. Bravo will let a certain amount of behind-the-scenes info out into the world, but they always control the message. I wanted to know—and report—answers without filter. The result is in these very pages, where you'll find answers to all the questions I had going in, and more.

As I dug deeper into the making of the franchise, I started to wonder about us fans, too. Who are we, and how have these shows become so important to so many of us? What does that say about us and our TV friends both? I spent over two years trying to figure all of this out so no one will have to lose sleep over the Housewives again. (I'm sure we will, but we don't *have* to.)

I talked to Real Housewives, some on the record and some off. I tracked down former Bravo executives and current employees. And I spoke to dozens of the real soldiers on the ground—the producers, editors, sound technicians, and production assistants that really get things done. I found these people, often more than the Housewives themselves, truly insightful about how the show gets made and why we love it. Almost everyone who worked on the show, past or present, requested that their names not be used for fear of retribution from Bravo, which can ruin a career faster than Ramona Singer can order a pinot grigio.

My *Housewives* journey might have started with Shane Keough as a piece of meat somewhere in the background, but it has become entirely immersive. I literally owe everything to this franchise: my career, my partner, and having the phrase *Make it nice* to throw out willy-nilly even when people don't entirely understand the implications. Maybe not every fan has been so richly rewarded, but I think there's something in *The Real Housewives* for everyone. And for anyone who thinks that's not worth writing a book about, well, I probably don't want to know you anyway.

1

MENTION IT ALL

THE MAKING OF A HOUSEWIFE

There is nothing that annoys a Real Housewife, former or otherwise, more than a woman who says to her, "They asked me to be on *The Real Housewives,* and I told them no." Nearly a dozen Real Housewives I talked to (both on and off the record) mentioned this during her interview. I didn't even have to go digging for it. This is a pet peeve they all divulged voluntarily. And if they all mentioned it . . . it must happen all the time.

"When that person at the dinner party is like, 'They considered me.' I'm always like, 'All right,'" says Kristen Taekman, who was on seasons 6 and 7 of *The Real Housewives of New York City.* "It's one thing to get the contracts, and then it's another thing to be considered, because there's a ton of people that are considered."

Who is a Housewife? Demographically, she should be in her mid-thirties to late forties, rich, and with a family. Bravo now wants all new Housewives to have a job, but if they don't, production isn't above creating one for them. (Just ask a certain "accountability coach.")

As for personality, it's a bit less cookie-cutter, but there is one essential: a woman must be willing to put her entire life on camera for four to six months of filming. She must be unafraid to talk about the cracks in her marriage, the disappointment of not being able to conceive, the heartbreak of being snubbed by someone she thought was her friend, or the devastation of her divorce. She needs to be willing to, in the words of Bethenny Frankel talking about her past as an actress in erotic Skinemax-style movies, "mention it all!"

Speaking of Bethenny, look at everything we've seen her go through on camera. She started off as a poor second fiddle with a boyfriend and a one-room apartment in season 1. Then we saw her start a business, get engaged, and take a pregnancy test with the door ajar and a cameraman outside. We saw her wedding special (where she peed in a bucket rather than get out of her wedding dress) and the sale of her little company for a cool $100 million. Then we saw the quick dissolution of that marriage, her ex turn into a stalker, and a protracted custody battle. Then she was the leader of the pack, in a succession of sleek SoHo apartments and Hamptons houses where she would invite the girls over. Just as she started getting serious about charity work and reeling from the sudden death by drug overdose of her fiancé, Dennis, she left the show for good. What will life be without Bethenny? (Oh, I'm sure we'll be fine. After all, we have the in-jail-out-of-jail-deportation-dating-again life of Teresa Giudice to keep us occupied.)

〽 〽 〽

If movies are a director's medium and scripted TV is a writer's medium, then reality TV is a casting director's medium. Any reality show—whether it's *Survivor* or *Here Comes Honey Boo Boo*—lives or dies by its cast, and *The Real Housewives* is no exception. Before any of the above happened, someone decided Ms. Frankel was worth following around for a while.

Housewives casting directors, usually freelancers who work on multiple reality shows, start their search with the women they've already booked. "We found the number-one thing for every season I cast, and still do for that type of format, is you want to find someone that's organically in the group," says a director who worked on many early seasons of the show.

Barrie Bernstein, who has been working on *RHONY* since its start, agrees. "What makes the best cast member is someone who knows the current cast," she told an audience at BravoCon, Bravo's first fan convention in 2019.

"They will suggest friends of theirs that they want to be on the show with them," says a casting director who has worked on several different franchises. "Nine times out of ten, they're not good. But you have to kind of go through the motions and interview them and pretend you're going to put them on the show knowing they're probably not the best choice."

This tactic has worked, however. Erika Jayne says in her memoir *Pretty Mess* (which I coauthored, so you know it's good) that during lunch one day her friend Yolanda Hadid (then Yolanda Foster) asked if she was interested in *Housewives* and texted an executive on the spot to recommend her.

Cary Deuber says that she brought her friends Kameron Westcott and Kary Brittingham to the attention of those casting *The Real Housewives of Dallas*. She insists it wasn't awkward when she was demoted to "friend of" the cast while Kary was asked to sign a contract for the show's fourth season.

Kristen Taekman found her way to the producers thanks to a Real Housewife, but not one on the franchise that she eventually joined. She is old friends with *RHOBH*'s Brandi Glanville, who invited her out to a party in New York. It turned out to be the after-party for Bravo's upfront presentation, a splashy affair where networks present advertisers with the shows they have for the upcoming year.

Packed into a Manhattan event space full of white couches, tropical florals, and a bar as open as NeNe Leakes would say Kim Zolciak's legs are to married men, if it wasn't a meeting of the Bravo minds, it was at least a meeting of the Bravo Botox. Original Housewives Vicki Gunvalson and Ramona Singer posed for pictures while Heather Thomson of *Real Housewives of New York* chatted to *Real Housewives of Atlanta*'s

Kandi Burruss and a very pregnant Phaedra Parks in front of a bar made up to look like a tiki hut. The party was like one of those old "Summer by Bravo" commercials, where Jeff Lewis from *Flipping Out,* Reza Farahan from *Shahs of Sunset,* and Cynthia Bailey from *Real Housewives of Atlanta* could be together playing the same drinking game.

After the prodigious step and repeat (if a Real Housewife has a party without a step and repeat, did it make a sound?), Andy Cohen made his way toward Glanville and Taekman. "Literally, Brandi and I never spoke a word about it," Kristen says. "Brandi blurts out, 'Andy, this is Kristen, your next New York Housewife.' Out of nowhere!

"Andy was kind of getting mobbed, and he stopped and looked at me, and then looked at Brandi, and looked at me, and then just kept going. Then I went and ended up connecting with a bunch of other New York girls that night, and Heather Thomson and I know each other, and then met Carole [Radziwill] that night, and Carole and I had so many mutual friends, it's insane. A week later, I get this phone call from production saying, 'I just got off the phone with Andy, and he wants to put you on tape.' And I was like, what!?" On the show, Kristen would be introduced as a friend of Heather Thomson's, since Thomson and Kristen's husband, Josh, worked together.

Those women who don't come through the Housewives directly are found through research. "We start looking at who they know, because we want these connections to seem organic even though we all know a lot of them aren't," a casting director says. "If you can tie them together—maybe they're part of the same charity group or maybe they live on the same street or their husbands work together—it helps."

Another agent has a similar strategy. "It's just doing outreach. It's asking: Where are they getting their nails done? Where are they buying their cars? Where are they buying their jewelry? I'm contacting those people, getting referrals that way."

In the early days, there were even some open casting calls in Orange County and New York. A typical scene took place in 2009 at the marble-dappled South Coast Plaza mall in Orange County, where about seventy women turned up to the 5:00 p.m. casting to stand penned behind a velvet rope. Each was given a name tag with a big Sharpied number to put on her probably printed, probably bright pink top. The sea of blond hair was high, and the boobs were higher.

When it was her turn, each woman approached a table with three casting producers, each with a huge bowl of oranges in front of them, and stopped for a brief chat before getting her picture taken on a digital camera. One hopeful, the spitting image of eventual Real Housewife of Orange County Shannon Beador, approached the table holding out an old copy of *The Coto de Caza News* that featured her on the cover after her win in the Mrs. United Nation International Pageant. Naturally, she wanted world peace.

"It was definitely what you think it is going to be," sums up a casting director who was there. "Done up and overdone."

Often, the women who want the show the most are the most unsuitable. Casting directors complain that they're just trying to play a part or behave like they're something they're not. The audience can sense inauthenticity like a vegan can sense a break in the conversation to talk about their dietary habits. It's a hard balance to find the women who are willing to do the show, but aren't foaming at the mouth for it. I mean, do we need another Aviva Drescher situation—so craven to keep her apple that she hurled her fake leg across a restaurant? It's a tough balance to strike, women who will be open and vulnerable for the viewers, but aren't throwing their imperfections (or limbs) in our faces.

That said, Cindy Barshop was one of the women who wanted it really badly. Cindy, for those who remember her one season on *RHONY,* was the owner of Completely Bare, a chain of hair-removal spas in the Big Apple that also specialized in vajazzling. She had a publicist get her business in *Vogue, Elle,* and even on *Live with Regis and Kelly,* but it hadn't made a huge impact.

Then she got on reality TV. She was friendly with Kimora Lee Simmons, who then had her own reality show and Cindy was featured on an episode getting the supermodel completely bare (and probably vajazzled). "I got bombarded with business," Barshop says. She had never seen *Housewives,* but called her publicist right away to ask what was the biggest reality show at the time. When the publicist said *RHONY,* Barshop told her, "Get me an interview."

The first stage for a promising candidate these days is a phone screen. A casting director will ask about her family, her jobs, where she lives, if she watches the show, and generally probes whether she's suitable and interesting enough to make it to the next round. They try to push and prod her into saying things that might be unflattering, like they would in one of the "confessional" interviews the Housewives film each season. One former Housewife told me it was the closest she ever felt to being in an actual interrogation.

For those who pass the smell test (they must smell like La'Dame by Karen Huger), a video interview is next. Nowadays, these are mostly done over Skype, but in the olden days, casting agents would visit each potential woman's house with a video camera.

With the exception of *RHONY,* the typical Housewife home is going to be a suburban McMansion, but details do vary. The *RHOC* house can have a bit of a beachy feel, whereas the *RHONJ* house is a faux château as assembled by Home Depot. The *RHOA* women live in the kind of houses that have brick fronts but white siding around the rest of the house. There are almost always columns. On *The Real Housewives of Potomac,* the houses are much the same except the lawns are drier. It's only *RHOBH* where the homes are sleek and architectural or understatedly homey, the kind of thing you'd see in *Architectural Digest.* It must be said that most of these are in the San Fernando Valley, rather than Beverly Hills proper.

The video interviews are an exercise in provocation, as the casting agents try to see how a candidate would act or react in certain situations—whether or not she's going to be fiery and quick enough for the free-for-all that is *The Real Housewives.* "For example," says Taekman, "how would you feel if a girlfriend threw a glass in your face at a dinner party? Like what would you do? It's that kind of stuff, just to kind of razz you a little, to kind of spark who is this person, and how is she going to react."

Alex Baskin, the co-president of Evolution Media which oversees

RHOC and *RHOBH,* will never forget his first meeting with *RHOC's* Shannon Beador. "She told me a story about an issue she had with someone at Medieval Times. Someone was asking for it," he said on the podcast *Reality Life with Kate Casey.* "She is a regular person who happens to be compelling television."

The interviews are recorded and edited together with pictures of the women, their families, their businesses, and their homes and presented to the execs at the production company. Of the twenty to fifty women who start the process each year, about a dozen make it this far. The casting directors and producers then do a background check on the women—what their husbands do, what their net worth is, whether or not they have a criminal record. We all know that last one wouldn't get a potential Housewife stricken from the list, necessarily, but it is good to know.

From that group, about five are chosen for the final round, which is a home visit with a full camera crew simulating what it would be like filming for the show.

"This is where a lot of women fail," one casting director says. "Like a lot of women get to the last stage and then just completely shit the bed." The reason for the shitty bed is not parasites, unlike when Luann shit the bed on a cast trip to Cartagena. They just can't deal with the cameras being there, directors say. They freeze up, they overperform, or they otherwise don't come off as natural.

NeNe Leakes, then working as a real estate agent, says that she had a meeting planned with producers from Bravo at her house to talk about casting her on the show, and she was so nervous that she decided she was going to have only wine for breakfast. "I was drinking, and when she rang the doorbell and I opened it, I said, 'Helloooo and welcome, honey,'" she revealed in an interview with E!

Of course, NeNe can't help but be real. In her casting tape, she has the long hair she sported in the first season, covered in a camouflage baseball cap. She also has on a pair of distressed camouflage cargo pants, and a white-on-white tank top and cardigan set you could buy at any Marshalls. But she had the demeanor of the star she'd become. "I am

NeNe Leakes, and I'm forty years old," she says. "I'm bougie. I'm ghetto. I'm hood. I'll cuss you out. You know, whatever I gotta do, and I know how to go out and handle my business, and flip properties, and open up a hotel. I can do all that. But, at the same time, I'm not gonna take your [bleep]." No, she is not going to take anyone's [bleep] indeed. The producers loved her so much, they asked to be introduced to her friends.

Ana Quincoces, who did two seasons on *The Real Housewives of Miami,* will never forget her home visit. "My youngest daughter in particular, she's completely unfiltered, and I'm always worried about what she says," she admits. As she tells it, her daughter was taken outside for an interview, and when she returned, she said to Quincoces, "Don't worry, you got it. I Bravo-sized it."

"What do you mean you 'Bravo-sized' it?" said Quincoces. "What did you tell them?"

"I might've mentioned something about you giving me, like, step-by-step instruction on how to engage in anal sex," said her daughter.

"Why the fuck would you make that shit up?"

"Don't you want this?"

"Yes, but . . ."

"Okay," said her daughter. "I'm pretty sure you're going to get it."

Sometimes, especially with new casts, producers will get some of the finalists together to see how they interact. Chris Oliver-Taylor, who developed *The Real Housewives of Melbourne,* invited that show's candidates to lunch in different configurations and gave them conversation-starting note cards to preview who would emerge as what type. Producers may be looking for the next breakout reality star, but the cast of each city also has to be balanced out among different roles: the alpha, the drunk, the voice of reason, the comic relief, and, most importantly, the villain. If you have all alphas, things are too contentious; all voices of reason, things are too boring; all drunks, they're *The Real Housewives of New York City.*

Cindy Barshop was ostensibly being considered to "replace" Bethenny on *RHONY,* but taking the spot of an alpha is easier said than done. She made it through the interviews and a home visit, but there was one more hurdle: she had to meet Ramona Singer, the notoriously difficult origi-nal cast member who fancies herself the top dog of the New York group. Known as much for her bulging eyes and her inappropriate mouth as her flagrant narcissism, she has pissed off nearly every woman in her ensem-ble at one time or another.

"They wanted me to interview with Ramona, and Ramona didn't want me in the show," Barshop says, adding that the interaction was filmed like it would be a potential scene on the show. "So I walked into her apartment . . . and the woman just wouldn't talk to me. So we are just staring at the walls. It was like a cat scratching sandpaper. You could just hear tension."

Luckily for her, she got trapped in an elevator with a producer and a cameraman on the way out of Ramona's. "I started doing this whole thing from *Natural Born Killers*. I was like Robert Downey Jr.: 'All right, here we are,'" she says, launching into an impersonation of the TV news host from the movie. "I was doing this whole thing, and we were laugh-ing. I had no idea he filmed the whole thing. But I know I got it from that. They said it was the clip that they sent to Bravo."

Housewife casting has not been without controversy. "They're very harsh on look. Very harsh on look," one casting director said about Bra-vo's choices. They said that it's been hard to get people of color on shows other than *Real Housewives of Atlanta* and *Real Housewives of Potomac*—each of which is majority black—or openly queer women cast on any of the shows. Racial segregation has been so distinct that it was the sub-ject of a *New York Times* exposé in 2019, after *RHOBH* added Garcelle Beauvais, the second Black woman on any show other than *RHOA* or *RHOP*. In the article, *RHONY*'s Heather Thomson says she advocated for more diversity in her cast and volunteered some of her friends who are people of color, but they did not make it through the casting process.

Bravo is also more concerned with the trappings of wealth than in the past. In the early seasons, *RHOC* women like Gretchen Rossi and Lauri Waring weren't living in the gated palaces that are so familiar on the show. They both lived in sad little town houses that might actually be attainable for the viewers; in fact, Lauri's story line in the first season is about finding a way to support herself after a gutting divorce. One former producer says that neither of these women would probably be cast now. A recent potential hire was nixed because she only owned a bungalow (albeit seaside), and production complained it was too small to film in.

Naturally, Evolution's Baskin has a more egalitarian view of the casting. "The whole process is designed to weed out people who just want to be on television because they want to be famous, people who are not who they say they are, who are full of shit, people who are too, frankly, fragile to . . . end up on television."

There is one way around most of this, however, and that's women with enough fame or notoriety that Bravo ends up looking for them. Denise Richards had been interviewed by casting agents numerous times and declared too stoic for television, until Bravo ended up asking for her specifically and casting her. Based on her talking about her husband's penis size on camera and her possible affair with Brandi Glanville, she's a whole different breed of stoic.

After Lisa Rinna, Eileen Davidson, and Richards all joined *RHOBH*, fans often speculate on which former actresses or stars should join the show. Nicollette Sheridan, the ex of both Richards's husband, Aaron Phypers, and Rinna's husband, Harry Hamlin, is a frequent request, as are the now-disgraced former *Full House* star Lori Loughlin and Rinna's *Melrose Place* costar Heather Locklear.

"Heather Locklear, she's blacklisted. She's interviewed several times, but she's in all this legal trouble and doing drugs and shit," one casting producer says, referring to her back-to-back arrests in 2018 for assaulting police officers, both while "extremely intoxicated and very uncooperative."

"Most of those women that [fans] want on *Housewives* have been interviewed and/or approached, and either Bravo doesn't want them because they're a mess, or they don't want to do it for whatever reason," she goes on. "There's a huge list of everyone they've talked to, that's pretty much like every woman alive in Beverly Hills and Orange County. I mean, the extent that we go to find new people is crazy 'cause everyone's been approached." I asked who else was on the Do Not Call list. "A ton of women. A ton of women," the agent says. "Actresses, musicians, it's literally, it's like a grid. There's a tab on it that says 'Forever No.' That's what it's called. The Forever No List."

For those who get the elusive *yes,* they're thrown to the wolves pretty quickly. There is little introduction to what life on camera is going to be like; Housewives are just invited to their first events, and the lights are on them. "It's always weird the first season for anybody," a veteran producer says. "They're being miked up, there's cameras with strangers they don't know and that's kind of weird, but it's amazing how quickly they get used to it and forget."

◊ ◊ ◊

Whatever the learning curve is for a Housewife today, let us never forget: before the too-small bungalows and home visits, before the chemistry lunches and mall casting calls, there was a first-ever season of *Real Housewives* and a first-ever group of women under the bedazzled microscope of mid-2000s reality TV. They needed to create something that women would want to brag about at dinner parties: that they were considered for the show, even if they would turn it down.

"Coto," as it is known to the locals, is a gated community of about four thousand homes in the northern part of Wagon Wheel Canyon, in southeastern Orange County, about sixty-five miles south of Los Angeles. Started in 1974 as a joint venture between the Chevron and Arvida Corporations, it's the sort of planned community that would later be spoofed on *Arrested Development.* In 1996, the average cost of a home in the area was $375,000. It is well over $1 million today. According to the 2010 census, the population of the community hovers around fifteen thousand residents, of which 82 percent are white. The average income is $169,000 a year. They are represented in both the state and federal legislatures by Republicans—but they're both women, so maybe they're more progressive than you think.

The genesis of *The Real Housewives* happened there in 1997, when Scott Dunlop was bored at a dinner party. Latter-day *Real Housewives* fans tend to assume the concept sprung out of Andy Cohen's head fully formed, like the goddess Athena cracking open Zeus, but it was actually created by a rather successful dilettante with his fingers in more pies than Sara Lee.

Dunlop grew up in Michigan City, Indiana, about twenty-five miles from Gary. After college, he moved to Los Angeles to pursue a career as a drummer. He eventually found his way into the house band of the famous improv troupe the Groundlings. There he hung around with future stars like Phil Hartman and Paul Reubens, better known as Pee-wee Herman.

Like so many others who have been to even one improv show, he caught the bug and thought he might be able to give it a try as well. He segued into trying his hand at acting, but the biggest credit on his IMDb page, at least before *The Real Housewives,* was playing a Tentacle Alien in the movie *The Last Starfighter.*

With parallel careers in entertainment and music not really panning out, Dunlop became the kind of guy who seems to have every job in the world and no job at all. He worked as a location scout and producer for small films and television projects. He worked in "computerized biomechanics" at Wilson Sporting Goods. He started a "virtual ad agency" in 1991 in Orange County and did a lot of radio spots, sometimes using his improv skills to record several different voices in one commercial.

The confluence of all these different industries would eventually lead to the crazy alchemy of *The Real Housewives of Orange County.* But the real catalyst was Dunlop's home in Coto de Caza.

"I was at a dinner with social friends, and they said, 'Why are you in a bad mood?' I said, 'I'm not in a bad mood, I feel like someone has vacuumed out the sense of humor in Coto,'" Dunlop remembered on an episode of *Inside Orange County* filmed in 2015. Everyone was talking about getting their kids into the best colleges and what it took to get good domestic help these days. "I said, 'What I would like to do is to offer you a small taste of immortality. Because we're all mortal, we're all going to die, I would like to offer you a part in a short film about life in Coto de Caza.'"

The party guests were ambivalent, Dunlop said, until he told them that they would be the film's stars. Suddenly, they were wildly interested. His idea was something like a community theater production where people from the community would act out scenes from their real lives. The short's opening would be a time-lapse video of the neighborhood transitioning from abandoned coastal wilderness to the affluent suburb it had become. He produced it in fits and starts over the years, mostly meeting with rejection along the way.

In 2004, Kevin Kaufman, a longtime friend of Dunlop's based in New York, came to visit him in Coto, and Dunlop told him that he was thinking about doing this project based in the neighborhood. Kaufman had recently started Kaufman Films, a production company that was getting in on the unscripted boom on network and cable television that had started after the runaway success of *Survivor* in 2000. Kaufman had already produced two specials for Bravo: 2002's *The Palladium: Where Mambo Was King,* about Afro-Cuban music in New York, and 2004's *100 Scariest Movie Moments,* which if you can't figure out by the title, then, please, reenlist in public school.

Kaufman talked Dunlop into putting a reality spin on the show, which might make it easier to find a buyer. Also, it would allow Dunlop to dust off his Groundling's improv skills for a round of "yes . . . and"–ing in Coto. Kaufman also brought on his business partner Patrick Moses, and the three formed a production company called Ventana Ventures LLC.

By January 21, 2005, Dunlop was talking publicly about an upcoming project called *Behind the Gates.* He told *The Orange County Register* newspaper it would be a show like HBO's *Curb Your Enthusiasm,* where some people would play themselves and some would play characters and all the dialogue would be improvised based on a detailed outline. "We're changing [the reality TV] genre a bit," he said. "Our point of view is that it can be a reality show, but how do you define a reality show? If we were to do a documentary . . . it's not going to be entertaining."

Robert Bartosh, a longtime Coto resident, was skeptical of the project in the paper, but a little prescient about the direction it would eventually take. "I don't think this is the kind of community like *Desperate*

Housewives, and it probably doesn't fit with the Larry David format, but I'm probably too long in the tooth up here to understand what the younger crowd would like to see, and that's probably what [Dunlop] cares about," he said.

Jeana Keough was in from the beginning. A former *Playboy* Playmate turned Realtor, she was married to Matt Keough, a former Oakland A's pitcher and major league all-star. Jeana had dabbled in acting in the past, playing bit parts in a number of 1980s TV staples like *T. J. Hooker, St. Elsewhere, The A-Team,* and *Cheers.* She is also one of the models in ZZ Top's music video for the objectifying hit song "Legs." As any former actress still in the orbit of LA, her attractive children also got in on the game. Kara, her middle daughter, was in the 1995 movie *Outbreak* as Kate, a little girl who befriends a monkey spreading a killer disease. (Kate eventually helps Rene Russo's character, oddly named Dr. Keough.)

The Keoughs lived in Coto and were close friends with the Dunlops. They had children about the same age and often went on joint vacations together. Jeana, and her family, were perfect for what Dunlop had planned. Sadly, the rest of the community wasn't as enthused, and a month after the original article in *The Register,* there was another article covering a meeting of residents angry about the incipient TV program. "Many people worried the show would be an exposé or a documentary that would include unwilling participants, but Dunlop and Kaufman said that is not the case," the paper wrote.

Keough, of course, was there to show her support. "I thought they were so un-Coto, so rude," she said of those upset about the show. "All those people had a preconceived opinion, and they didn't even know what the show was about."

Jim Eggold, a local podiatrist, filmed some early footage for the show, along with his college-age son. In their skit, Eggold's son moved home after graduation from USC and is unrealistic about the opportunities life would afford him. "There was a bit of hyperbole, but what was said was not scripted," Eggold said at the time. "Having been raised in a gated community like Coto, [my son's] expectations are skewed in a way and are a reflection of values at Coto, but at the same time, it is a universal theme."

Eggold and son were eventually dropped from the concept. All the men were. Dunlop placed an ad in *The Register* looking to recruit kids coming home from college who lived in privilege. Michael Wolfsmith, Vicki Gunvalson's son, responded to the ad with a two-page letter about why he would be great for the show. He did this while Vicki and her second husband, Donn, were on vacation at her second home in Puerto Vallarta, probably drinking a ton at her favorite bar, Andale's.

When Dunlop got in touch, Vicki, who happened to be Jeana's neighbor at the time, had no idea it was coming. "I really want you to be on this show," Dunlop said to Vicki, as he later told *Inside Orange County*. "She said, 'Why? I don't know anything about television. I don't look the right part for television.' I said, 'Look, let's take a jump off the diving board and have fun this summer.'" Thank god she did, or we would have been denied the OG of the OC.

At the time, Vicki was running her insurance brokerage from a room in her McMansion. She employed Lauri Waring, a friend of Gunvalson's whose husband had recently left her and, she claimed, took all the money—leaving Waring to raise three of her four children in the sad town house nearby.

"It was mainly Jeana. She was really the one that really did a lot of the work for the show and getting the girls together," says Tammy Knickerbocker, a friend of both Jeana's and Scott's who would appear on the second and third seasons of *RHOC*. "She tried to get me to go on the show, but I was so busy the first year, so I just didn't do it."

Kimberly Bryant, the one who delivered the line about how many women have fake boobs in the OC, had just moved to Coto a few years earlier from Baltimore. A working mom married to a finance exec, she had gotten her own 34D augmentation after six months in the area.

The final addition to the cast was Jo De La Rosa, the twenty-four-year-old girlfriend of the soon-to-be-infamous, thirty-six-year-old mortgage broker Slade Smiley. He bid $2,500 in a charity silent auction for Jo to be cast in the show before they even knew what it was going to be.

With their Housewives assembled, Dunlop and company filmed a sizzle reel to sell the show concept to networks. "I remember it very vividly . . . we had, like, this little camera setup with a couple guys coming in," Shane Keough, Jeana's oldest, who was eighteen at the time, told me almost fifteen years later over brunch. (Yes, he's just as handsome as ever. Yes, I could barely contain myself.) "It was very crude."

Through his previous relationship with Bravo, Kaufman got the tape into the hands of Amy Introcaso-Davis, then head of development at the network. She passed the tape off to Andy Cohen, who was then the vice president of original programming. Introcaso-Davis, Cohen, and Frances Berwick, then executive vice president of programming and production, had Dunlop and company make a pilot, or a "development reel." They wanted a better idea of what the series would look like. Based on that, Berwick ordered a first season. Dunlop was named executive producer, and he, along with Moses and Kaufman, got to work with their coterie of women.

"If we got this right, I thought it could be a *Knots Landing* for the millennium: hot women in an aspirational town living the high life, marked by drama both extraordinary and ordinary," Cohen writes in his memoir. "ABC's *Desperate Housewives* was the biggest show on television at the time. Clearly, people loved watching a show about fictional fabulous friends and frenemies living in the same neighborhood. Wouldn't they love the real thing, too? We changed the name from *Behind the Gates* to *The Real Housewives,* and we were off."

No one knew what to make of the cameras around the neighborhood at first. Rumors started circulating that the crews were shooting a porno, though that would be hard to do at some of the more public venues the cast visited.

"All of a sudden it was like, 'Oh, we got picked up,'" Shane Keough says. "Then all of a sudden a bigger producing group came out. They had microphones and lavaliers and a producer with an iPad watching the camera shot. We all thought, 'Whoa, this is cool.' It was like an explosion." But the production still wasn't entirely welcome in Coto. As Dunlop told the New York *Daily News,* "I got an email that said, 'Dunlop, why don't you, Michael Moore, and your crew go to Baghdad and film roadside explosions?'"

In *The Orange County Register* a week before the show's premiere, Vicki, addressing the concerns of some in the community, shows the kind of confrontational density that would eventually make her a star. "We don't talk about anybody else. We're just as self-absorbed as the rest of Orange County."

A bigger problem was that Kaufman Films (or Ventana Ventures, if you're nasty) shot almost all of the first season before Bravo got a look at it—and what they saw, they absolutely hated. "We wanted something very authentic and they started to film something *Curb Your Enthusiasm*–esque," Berwick told *The Hollywood Reporter.* "It required a whole revision, so we came to a point where we had to decide whether to sink more money into it or just pull the plug."

Cohen saw the germ of something there, but what Dunlop had produced wasn't quite right. "The women weren't going deeply into their emotions or being honest about what was happening with their friends," Cohen writes. "And the stories didn't always make sense—what they were saying didn't match the way we saw them acting. Why was Jo bored while Slade was at work? Did Vicki have a love/hate relationship with Jeana, or did she really just hate her?"

In the first episode, you can still see the holdovers from the improv phase of the show, especially in the exact scenario of a kid returning home that Dunlop used when testing material. (Lauri's oldest daughter, Ashley, who had been working retail in Los Angeles, arrives back home with a suitcase and a new dog and tells her mother she's tired of paying her own bills. Lauri tells her she can sleep on the floor in her much-younger sister's room, and Ashley pitches an ungrateful fit.)

Instead of canning the show, Bravo stepped in. They fired Kaufman Films, reshot much of the first season and additional interviews with the women, and sent the footage into a marathon of an edit. Once the network was confident the show would air, they shot the gates of Lou Knickerbocker's house, Tammy's ex-husband, for the opening sequence. Jason Klarman, then head of marketing at Bravo, came up with the idea of having the women hold oranges in the opening sequence, much like the women of *Desperate Housewives* held apples in their intro. The season would fill out at seven episodes.

Just before it went to air, Lauren Zalaznick, then head of Bravo, decided to change the name from *Real Housewives* to *The Real Housewives of Orange County*. Her thinking was that if it worked, though no one at the time thought it would, that they could then branch out to other areas with their own Housewives. Cohen and his colleague Shari Levine hated the name, thinking it was too clunky. In retrospect, it does look like it's trying to combine two fictional dramas, *Desperate Housewives* and the hit teen show *The O.C.*—but maybe that's its genius.

Bravo didn't sink much money or promotion into launching the show, since no one thought it would be a hit. It debuted two weeks after the finale of the third season of *Project Runway,* then the network's biggest show. The prime post-*Runway* finale spot was used to debut *Top Chef,* a cooking competition in the same vein as *Runway. RHOC,* by comparison, was launched on an average Tuesday night at 10:00 p.m.

So how did *The Real Housewives* go from a show that no one wanted to be on, no one wanted to film, and its own network thought no one wanted to watch to a franchise that has people trying so hard to be on it that their daughters are lying about their anal sex education? To answer that will take a deeper trip inside the Bravo machine.

Oh, and Ana Quincoces's daughter is now a reality television producer. She knew what she was doing.

A *REAL HOUSEWIVES* TAXONOMY

Just like our horoscopes, while we all have one main sign, there are aspects of others within us.

The Villain: The ones we love to hate.

>*RHOC:* Kelly Dodd
>*RHONY:* Ramona Singer
>*RHOA:* Kenya Moore
>*RHONJ:* Danielle Staub
>*RHOM:* Karent Sierra
>*RHOBH:* Camille Grammer
>*RHOP:* Candiace Dillard
>*RHOD:* LeeAnne Locken

The Alpha: The one who thinks it's "her" show.

>*RHOC:* Vicki Gunvalson
>*RHONY:* Bethenny Frankel
>*RHOA:* NeNe Leakes
>*RHONJ:* Teresa Giudice
>*RHOM:* Joanna Krupa
>*RHOBH:* Kyle Richards
>*RHOP:* Gizelle Bryant
>*RHOD:* Brandi Redmond

The Voice of Reason: The audience needs a surrogate.

>*RHOC:* Emily Simpson
>*RHONY:* Carole Radziwill

RHOA: Kandi Burruss
RHONJ: Caroline Manzo
RHOM: Ana Quincoces
RHOBH: Eileen Davidson
RHOP: Robyn Dixon
RHOD: Cary Deuber

The Comic Relief: Whether we're laughing with them or at them.

RHOC: Shannon Beador
RHONY: Sonja Morgan
RHOA: Porsha Williams
RHONJ: Margaret Josephs
RHOM: Lisa Hochstein
RHOBH: Lisa Rinna
RHOP: T'Challa
RHOD: Stephanie Hollman

The Kid Sister: The one still trying to earn her place in the group.

RHOC: Gina Kirschenheiter
RHONY: Tinsley Mortimer
RHOA: Eva Marcille
RHONJ: Jacqueline Laurita
RHOM: Marysol Patton
RHOBH: Kim Richards
RHOP: Ashley Darby
RHOD: D'Andra Simmons

The Uptight One: The stick in the mud who may not actually play by her own rules.

RHOC: Heather Dubrow
RHONY: Luann de Lesseps
RHOA: Phaedra Parks
RHONJ: Dolores Catania
RHOM: Lea Black

RHOBH: Lisa Vanderpump
RHOP: Karen Huger
RHOD: Kameron Westcott

The Fighter: What is drama if it doesn't end with a whole lot of shouting?

RHOC: Tamra Judge
RHONY: Dorinda Medley
RHOA: Shereé Whitfield
RHONJ: Jennifer Aydin
RHOM: Adriana de Moura
RHOBH: Brandi Glanville
RHOP: Monique Samuels
RHOD: LeeAnne Locken (yes, again)

2

BRAVO, BRAVO, FUCKING BRAVO

THE FINE ART OF SELLING OUT

Lauren Zalaznick is the person who turned Bravo from a channel into a brand. With most cable channels, say USA or TBS, people tune in to the one or two shows that they like. People tune in to Bravo to watch *Bravo*. Has anyone in the history of the universe ever said, "I'm going home to watch some TBS?" No.

True fans will watch whatever is on because they trust that it's been made with them in mind. There is a dedication to quality and consistency at Bravo, whose only other rival on the dial is HBO. A show being on HBO promises ambitions of critical acclaim. A show being on Bravo promises the oversize, ironic dishiness fans are already addicted to. I didn't watch all of *Around the World in 80 Plates* (and neither did anyone else), but I certainly gave it a shot because it was on Bravo. This everlasting halo is Zalaznick's greatest legacy at the channel.

Her creative vision led to the two key things the network still looks for in any new show: the "Bravo wink" and the "Bravo sheen."

The Bravo wink is something all viewers understand even if they don't have a name for it. It is the acknowledgment to the viewers that, yes, the creators know that this is just as ridiculous as we think it is. The wink shows up when a Real Housewife says one thing and then the camera shows her doing the exact opposite. You know, like when Kyle Richards says, "I never said that," and the editors roll a clip of her saying that exact thing as "17 minutes earlier" appears at the bottom of the screen.

The Bravo sheen is the thing that makes every show look expensive. You're not just watching the loony people at a gym, you're watching the loony people at a gym you can't afford and it looks like it was filmed by a bunch of former USC film majors with top-of-the-line equipment. A Bravo show is never the Zara knockoff; it is a genuine Hermès handbag, shelved precisely and lit to perfection. Yes, it may contain tacky people in gaudy Sky Tops, but the show itself will be as expensive looking as the reality genre has to offer.

Let's let Lauren Zalaznick take a bow. Thank her for the indelible imprint she left on the Bravo brand. But don't grow too attached, since she was eventually pushed out of the network in an act of corporate re-shuffling.

Bravo is the network that made the Housewives, because it is much like *Housewives:* no one is bigger than the enterprise itself, and just when they're getting too comfortable and think they're indispensable, that's when they're shown the door. Just ask Vicki Gunvalson, who was put out after fourteen years on *Real Housewives of Orange County,* in part, I was told, because the amount of plastic surgery she had made her hard to look at for some execs. Nothing she had done for the franchise—the number of personal humiliations endured, from dealing with a grifter boyfriend trying to scam her with a cancer diagnosis to hearing the news of her mother's death on camera—could save her.

The story of the Housewives' rise is in part the story of ruthless corporate decisions like these. It's Bravo's story, rife with compromises and pivots, brilliance and backstabs as messy as the on-camera drama. It is the classic tale of an institution founded on an ideal—bringing the fine arts to the masses!—that turned into a profit machine, willing to celebrate people's creativity but also to get rid of them when they're no longer delivering.

The sheen doesn't come cheap.

◊ ◊ ◊

When Bravo started in 1980, it was basically porn.

Okay, that is a misdirection trying to make it sound more salacious than it really was. But Bravo did share channel space with a porn network when it was founded as a pay station showing highbrow arts entertainment. It was started by Charles "Chuck" Dolan, the cable television visionary (televisionary?) who became a billionaire after starting cable provider Cablevision and wiring a lot of New York City's buildings for cable TV.

In 1970, he founded Home Box Office, the first subscription cable channel, and turned to that model again when he created Rainbow Media (no relation to the rainbow flag) in 1980. A subdivision of Cablevision, Rainbow Media was at first home only to Bravo and SportsChannel New York, which streamed games of the metro area's various and sundry professional teams for a monthly fee. (Rainbow Media would go on to include, at one time or another, channels like AMC, the Independent Film Channel, the Sundance Channel, Showtime, and others.)

Bravo's remit was different from SportsChannel and considerably more highbrow. For between five to ten dollars a month, Gothamites could watch opera, ballet, jazz, and other performances happening at Lincoln Center or the Metropolitan Opera from the comfort of their own Upper East Side enclaves. The initial press announcement touted programming like, "Programs taped at Carnegie Hall and the Aspen Music Festival, performances by the St. Louis and Milwaukee Symphonies, for example, and opera, dance and chamber-music bills."

Where's the porn? you ask. Well, back in the '80s, some cable networks shared channel space. Channel 80 might be one thing during the week and something else on the weekend. That was the arrangement with Bravo, which aired programming only on Sunday and Monday nights from 8:00 p.m. until 4:00 a.m., which seems like a pretty odd time to be sitting at home waiting for the Lyric Opera of Chicago's version of *Don Giovanni*.

Three other days of the week, viewers had access to Escapade, a soft-core porn channel. Watching *The Magic Flute* on Escapade probably took on an entirely different meaning than it did watching it on Bravo. In 1982, Rainbow would join forces with *Playboy* to create the Playboy Channel and never start another arts network. It seems they learned fast where their, ahem, bread was buttered.

Before that, though, everyone was trying to start an arts channel. ABC launched ABC Arts, CBS started CBS Cable, and someone had the idea to launch the almost tautologically named Entertainment Channel. Bravo would be the only one to survive, though it was not initially a roaring success. In 1981, it had 48,000 subscribers, which is probably how many people log on to Netflix every second of the day. By 1985, its ranks had swelled to a whopping 350,000.

By then, about 70 percent of Bravo's programming was reruns of movies, though they showed only independent movies and foreign films that were otherwise hard to find, even in the golden age of VHS. Taking the purist's approach was paying off with the right crowd. To celebrate five years on the air, Martin Scorsese dropped by to host a classic film retrospective—quite a get for a niche channel. Five years later, Bravo was in five million homes, sometimes as part of a basic cable package and sometimes still as a subscription service. It was still mostly arts and movies with subtitles (or at least subtext). It was also gay-friendly way before it was cool. The network spearheaded the "Moment Without Television" on December 1, 1990. To mark World AIDS Day, the channel enlisted almost thirty other stations to air a sixty-second PSA with just a black screen to dramatize the impact that the AIDS pandemic had on the world.

The mid-'90s saw a number of landmarks for Bravo. It went from being a subscription channel to something like PBS, where it was commercial-free but programs had corporate sponsors, like 1992's Texaco Showcase, whose initial offering was an updated version of the ballet *Romeo & Juliet*. By 1998, it became a conventionally ad-supported network for economic reasons. Slowly at first, Bravo was drifting from its highbrow origins and toward market pressures.

In 1994, a proposal from the New School and the Actors Studio found its way across Bravo president Josh Sapan's desk. James Lipton, the dean of the Actors Studio, would interview A-list actors not about being a celebrity but about their *craft*. The show's first guest was Paul Newman, and it was a hit. *Inside the Actors Studio* would be Bravo's signature show for years and would run until 2018, the one holdover of Bravo's hoity-toity past into its present era.

The next phase of Bravo would be shaped by a number of mergers and acquisitions, which is not what you came here to read about, but, hey, TV is a business, and that's how things happen.

In 1996, Frances Berwick moved from Britain's Channel 4 to work at Bravo as the VP of programming at both that channel and the Independent Film Channel, which was spun off from Bravo due to the success of its independent movie screenings. She would be one of the architects of the network's evolution.

By the early 2000s, Bravo was dabbling in pop-culture programming and reality shows, though the latter were more like the cinema verité documentaries it had showed in the '80s. In 2000, Bravo became the television home of Cirque du Soleil, with its silent performers contorting in technicolor costumes. An amazing show called *The It Factor* followed young actors trying to achieve their big break; the New York–set first season was still realistic, but with some extreme personalities. Hey, actors gonna act! The second season, set in LA, featured a pre-fame Jeremy Renner among the cast. And yet, as of 2002, the average age of the Bravo viewer was fifty—ancient in terms of advertising dollars.

Then came *Queer Eye for the Straight Guy*. Berwick acquired the rights to this new makeover show, which would feature five gay experts in fashion, grooming, food, interior design, and culture, turning a hapless straight guy into, well, a straight guy with a new apartment, wardrobe, and haircut. (I guess the culture guy would give him like a ticket to a play or something? Who knows what the culture guy did back then. It would take Netflix, two decades, and Karamo Brown to figure that out in the reboot.)

Berwick oversaw the creation of a pilot for the show, filmed in Boston. The network loved it. But its future was imperiled when, in late

2002, NBC purchased Bravo from Rainbow for $1.25 billion. NBC wanted to get into the cable space and already owned a portion of the network, and there were all these trades of stock and ownership and blah blah blah. Who cares? None of us will ever see $1.25 billion in our lifetimes.

Happily, NBC loved *Queer Eye,* too. It put a huge marketing and advertising push behind the show, including daytime advertising spots on NBC affiliates, which station chiefs in more conservative areas of the country were none too pleased about. The marketing worked, making the July 15, 2003, two-part premiere Bravo's two most-watched programs of all time, at 1.64 and 1.37 million viewers, respectively. Thanks to NBC replaying shortened episodes on the network and great word of mouth, viewership peaked that fall at 3.34 million viewers. Bravo had a zeitgeist-defining hit on its hands. If you know the meaning of the word *metrosexual* (which is basically just a straight dude who showers and uses hair gel), you have *Queer Eye* to thank for that.

"*Queer Eye* changed the network completely, from head to toe," Amy Introcaso-Davis, who worked in original programming at the time, told *Broadcasting & Cable* magazine. "Suddenly, people were pitching us much more forward kinds of shows. Before *Queer Eye,* people weren't even really thinking about us for reality kinds of shows." NBC doubled Bravo's original programming budget.

Just how that programming would play out, however, was determined by another merger. In 2004, NBC acquired Vivendi Universal Entertainment, a portfolio of entertainment companies, including Universal Pictures and a number of cable channels like USA, Syfy, and Trio, an arts network playing in the pop-culture landscape just like Bravo.

Jeff Gaspin, who was president of Bravo at the time, was promoted to oversee all the newly formed NBCUniversal's cable channels. He had worked with Lauren Zalaznick, then head of Trio, when they were both at VH1 and installed her as the new head of Bravo. It seemed like, from the beginning, Trio was on the chopping block due to its mission overlap with Bravo.

Zalaznick had an unexpected rise in the TV business. Known for her haphazard, prematurely gray hair, she graduated from Brown with a degree in semiotics, a field of study so arcane that not even its majors can likely explain it to you. After getting her start in big-budget films, she moved to producing indies, including *Kids,* the gritty 1995 skate punk film that would launch the careers of Rosario Dawson and Chloë Sevigny. From there she moved to VH1, where she was behind the *Pop Up Video* phenomenon, a format where old videos would play with ironic fact bubbles or jokes superimposed. (One in the video for R.E.M.'s "Losing My Religion" asks [Pop Up Video bloop noise], "Q: Which religion is least likely to lose its members?" [pause] "A: Satanism." The treatment of Madonna's "Vogue" video is obsessed with how many nipples are visible [thirty-three].) Zalaznick rose in the network ranks.

An incident from 2000 is telling about her management style. In an essay for the then trendy website Open Letters, Zalaznick wrote about producing a special called *100 Greatest Dance Songs* with the production company World of Wonder, headed by Fenton Bailey and Randy Barbato. "My team of hench-people and I keep going back and going back and going back to them with criticisms," she wrote about the process, which sounds much like how producers and editors describe their rounds of show notes from Bravo: intense and filled with gratuitous snark.

During this drawn-out process, Barbato mistakenly sent Zalaznick an email intended for Bailey, asking him if he made a change to the footage. "I agree with your change—and I think she's a fuckin cunt . . . also, can you believe she crossed out all the writer credits? No one wrote the show? Whatever!" Yeah, even if it's intended for someone else, calling your boss an *F-ing C* in an email is not a great idea.

Zalaznick, known for her dry wit, wrote that she was planning on firing the pair and never working with them again, but began to second-guess that decision. "I'm the second-highest female employee of VH1. I don't take it upon myself to reflect, frequently, on this fact. But I know I'm under an emotional microscope all the time," she wrote. "I'm probably regarded as being tough, fairly hard-hearted, outspoken. I am occasionally criticized for digging in and being less accommodating to other people's ideas and criticisms than I 'should be.' But this is a weird sort of (double) standard to be held to, especially in a 'creative' job where passions are usually what get ideas heard and shows pitched and accepted and produced. This is a place where strong disagreements (among men) are usually taken as a sign of strength and vision and leadership and upward potential."

The essay ends with her concluding that she should stay on good terms with her hecklers because, in her business, you never know when you are going to need someone again. She would continue a fruitful partnership with Bailey and Barbato for years to come, including on Bravo's popular *Million Dollar Listing* franchise.

When Zalaznick arrived at Bravo, she brought some of her own people with her. This included Andy Cohen, a programming exec under her at Trio who had desperately tried to buy *Queer Eye* but couldn't come up with the money. Cohen, a thirty-six-year-old excitable pop-culture fanatic with a thing for soap operas, the B-52s, and an ill-advised mane of curly hair, worked his way up as a segment producer in morning news before transitioning to entertainment. I assume if you shelled out for this book, you've already read his memoir, *Most Talkative,* so you know the full story. In case you didn't, he was young, hungry, and annoyingly energetic.

Zalaznick started her tenure at Bravo with a giant hit served to her on a plate, though *Queer Eye*'s ratings were already starting to sag. A lesser network would have littered their airtime with knockoffs of the show or other makeover programs. Zalaznick did not do that (though zombie show *Queer Eye for the Straight Girl* crashed and burned in 2005). Instead, she decided to focus her programming efforts on the superpowers of the Fab Five on the show: fashion, grooming, food, design, and the always-nebulous culture. Yes, the beating heart of Bravo has always been linked to queer culture and its queer fans.

From the world of grooming, *Blow Out,* a show about the shenanigans at a high-end salon in LA, debuted in June 2004. Fashion brought us *Manhunt,* a male model search in October 2004, which was as much about fashion as about the gentlemen wearing next to nothing. The vague "culture" gave us 2005's *Being Bobby Brown,* a show ostensibly about the life of the R&B singer, was a one-season look into his ridiculous and deteriorating relationship with Whitney Houston. The same year, *My Life on the D-List,* a verité look at the career of comedian Kathy Griffin, proved to be not only a hit but would win an Emmy for Outstanding Reality Program in its second season.

Berwick already had a show in development that fit the new strategy perfectly: Miramax Television's *Project Runway.* It was an offshoot of the company's *Project Greenlight,* a reality show that would give one upstart screenwriter and one fledgling director the chance to make a movie. *Runway* was similar but focused on fashion. Wannabe fashion designers would engage in challenges with the results critiqued by a panel of judges. Each week, one would be eliminated. It was one part *Survivor,* one part *American Idol,* and all *Vogue,* or more aptly *Elle,* who provided editor Nina Garcia as one of the judges.

The December 2004 premiere was hailed by critics but didn't take off with audiences, clocking in only 350,000 viewers after an extensive marketing push. Zalaznick, who had faith in the show, decided that in the week between Christmas and New Year's Day, when people were sitting at home with nothing to do and little to watch, Bravo would rerun the show's first three episodes relentlessly. It was a Hail Mary tactic that worked. Coupled with strong word of mouth, episodes later in the season regularly drew one million viewers. The season finale drew a record two million sets of eyeballs who watched quirky Jay McCarroll—in pink sunglasses, a scruffy goatee, and a magenta winter hat ten years before the Women's March would make them a thing—walk away with the top prize (though he would later refuse to accept it because it came with too many strings).

Similar programing soon followed. *Top Chef* would become another huge success and Emmy winner. The hits came fast and furious after that. *Flipping Out* was a house design show about insane boss Jeff Lewis. *The Rachel Zoe Project* followed the eponymous stylist with a questionable grasp on the English language. (Lit-rally, bananas. I die.) *Work Out* showed us the life of the sexy trainers in a high-end gym. Haircutting competition *Shear Genius* might have been a flop, but it brought us breakout star Tabatha Coffey, who would take over salons and other businesses on Bravo for years to come.

By 2006, with *Runway* drawing in four million viewers and up and Bravo in more than eighty million homes, it was a bona fide cable success story. It still wasn't among the ten highest-rated cable networks—its sister network USA sat upon that particular heap, at ninety million homes. But that year, Bravo had the largest audience growth of any network. Just like Barbra Streisand in *Funny Girl,* get ready world, 'cause she's a comer.

With more than $200 million in ad revenue, Zalaznick was getting most of the credit for the turnaround. She insisted on creating her own research department at Bravo, which would look into not only which shows were performing better than others but which stars on those shows the audience liked best. This team would decide the fate of many a Real Housewife over the years to come.

The thing that advertisers and the NBC overlords loved most were the types of people now starting to watch Bravo. By 2008, it was the fastest growing of the top-twenty cable channels, and its viewers were the most highly educated and highest-earning on television. Bravo initially called them Wills and Graces, after the high-end, urban, female, and gay male demographic that all their programs were drawing in. Eventually, Berwick would combine *affluent* and *influencer* to call them *affluencers.* (Barf.) It was a sweet spot for anyone trying to market everything from luxury cars to hair care products to an audience with disposable income that would then convince their friends to buy the exact same car or shampoo.

Zalaznick, however, wasn't always the easiest boss. She "drove her staff hard, instituting exhaustive meetings and giving input on everything from rough cuts to press releases," a 2006 profile in *Broadcasting & Cable* read. "Although she has a reputation for blunt honesty and a stern demeanor, colleagues say that beneath the veneer of imperiousness is an acute sense of humor."

"Lauren was definitely intimidating," a former Bravo exec told me. "But she listened to everyone, and she knew it could be the coordinator answering phones that could have the next big idea."

An interaction between her and Cohen in 2008 seems telling. During a breakfast meeting at the then ultrahip Meatpacking District eatery Pastis, Cohen told his boss that he had made himself an exercise mixtape featuring new Madonna and Mariah Carey songs ("Fit-n-40"). While the meeting was obviously meant to be about something else, Zalaznick couldn't stop mulling over the mixtape. She let Andy have it, saying that he thought he knew what was going on in the world but he didn't, accusing him of being out of touch and getting older. If he wanted to stay relevant, she said, he'd better expand his worldview.

Though the two quickly got over it, it sounds blistering, and if my boss were that demeaning to me in a meeting in front of other people, I'd be polishing up the old résumé immediately.

Then again, there was plenty for Zalaznick to be tense about in 2008. That year was the highest-rated season of *Runway* yet, its fifth—but also its last season on the network. Miramax Television had changed its name to the Weinstein Company and signed a deal to bring *Runway* to rival cable channel Lifetime. There were lawsuits and countersuits, but the dust had settled, and now *Runway* was on its farewell lap. What would Bravo do without its biggest hit?

⧠ ⧠ ⧠

When *The Housewives* launched in 2006, it was a network anomaly. It didn't neatly fit any of the *Queer Eye* categories; it wasn't a professional ride-along or a competition show. But as we know, Bravo took a chance. There was some vague electricity crackling in the air that its sister network E! also recognized, launching *Keeping Up with the Kardashians* the same year.

The first episode of *Real Housewives of Orange County* is not at all like the show that viewers would eventually come to cherish, full of table flipping, wine throwing, and women navigating their ways through the shark-filled waters of fame together. The women don't interact much at all. Jeana Keough is at home dealing with her spoiled kids. Vicki Gunvalson is trying to get her insurance business off the ground. Lauri Waring is struggling in her town house. Jo De La Rosa is getting drunk with her girlfriends while her older fiancé, Slade Smiley, sits home with his kids. And Kimberly Something-Something (JK, her last name is Bryant) is getting her thirteen-year-old's makeup done for a middle school dance.

Critics were not kind to the show. It "isn't entertaining, exactly—it has none of the wit or style of *Desperate Housewives*. But like so much reality TV, it's both educational and grimly fascinating, and leaves you feeling much better about your own life—if for no other reason than that you would never be so stupid as to appear on a show like this," Charles McGrath wrote in *The New York Times*.

Paul Brownfield in the *Los Angeles Times* had a similar take: "The show is built either to nauseate or fascinate; I myself danced between periods of both, which is probably just what the producers, layering on the scripted scenarios, intend." Wait. He wasn't supposed to know those scenarios were scripted, and they purported not to be.

Most of these reviews came from men and, it must be said, that the critical consensus around reality television back then—and perhaps even now—was skeptical and dismissive of the genre as a whole.

Even the rare rave had to couch itself in the "guilty pleasure" aspects of reality shows. In a piece about his love for the show on NPR, Andrew Wallenstein also interviewed other fans of the show. Still, he ends it with this caustic sign-off: "Maybe it's as simple as I'm a sucker for fancy cars and multimillion-dollar houses. That's what makes me feel guilty about watching *The Real Housewives*. Yeah, I love the show, but now I hate myself."

One of the few women to give her take was Linda Stasi at the *New York Post*. "Whatever it is, Bravo has a genius way of not only finding shallow, desperate-to-be-famous people with inflated egos (and boobs), but then getting these people to expose their boring lives to the world," she says, before taking a knowing turn. "Boring lives, however, can make for fascinating television."

The first episode drew 430,000 viewers, two-thirds of them women. While it was Bravo's best Tuesday night in six months, just a few weeks earlier, the *Project Runway* season three finale had 5.4 million viewers. Yes, that is exactly five million more viewers than the Housewives scored.

The March 26 episode of *Desperate Housewives,* then in its second season, had 21.4 million viewers, exactly 21 million more than *RHOC.*

Among those 430,000 was every single resident of Coto, and they didn't like what they saw. Marcie Mossman described the show in *The Orange County Register* as "embarrassing. Not all people in Coto are like that . . . It's all about looks and beauty and all that. Most of us are about our children. Some of us are real people." Kimberly Bryant said that one of the students in her thirteen-year-old's private school put up an "I hate *Real Housewives of Orange County*" poster and one of her child's teachers pulled her aside and asked if she was ashamed that her mother was on *RHOC.*

Dunlop told the *Los Angeles Times* that he was getting flipped off by passing cars and that people in the supermarket were giving him dirty looks.

Bravo used the Hail Mary strategy that had worked for *Project Runway:* they aired repeats of the first several episodes incessantly. Ratings ticked up week after week as people couldn't look away. "Then suddenly, just before the finale, it started popping," Cohen wrote in his memoir. "Viewers who'd begun watching only to confirm that they found the women repellent somehow became invested in their stories—which proved to be more universal than anybody initially thought."

The highlights of the first season mostly belonged to Vicki, but it wouldn't be until season 2 when she would score some truly iconic moments. The first was when she went to visit her son, Michael, at college and embarrassed the hell out of him. He asked her why she didn't tell him she was coming; she replies that then it wouldn't have been a surprise.

The second was when she ordered a limo for the family to go to the airport for a weeklong cruise. Instead of a limo, a "family van" pulled up, and Vicki—like the world's biggest Karen before the term even existed—wanted to speak to the manager. She cussed out someone on the phone, shouting, "Who sends a family van for six people?" as the rest of the family ambled around the front lawn in embarrassment.

"I don't know why Bravo wanted to be at my house at 6:00 a.m.,"

Vicki now says of the incident. "They put this family van up to it, and they did it. They still say to this day that they didn't but I ordered a stretch limo with mimosas and bagels and . . . we're going to Europe. It was meant to be fun."

Capping off the first season was a reunion special, where each woman talked about her experiences since the show had aired and answered questions fans might have had. (What was in the enormous fishbowl cocktail Jo drank at dinner with Slade? "Three shots of tequila, a couple of shots of rum, a bunch of fruit.") Then all the women minus Kimberly, who had moved her family to Chicago and left the show behind, sat in Vicki's backyard, watching footage of themselves and commenting about it. There was no Andy Cohen.

The season wrapped with an average of 646,000 viewers and a 47 percent increase in the eighteen- to forty-nine-year-old demographic that advertisers crave. With a median age of just over thirty-four years old, the audience was the youngest on Bravo, which might be what saved the show. The network ordered a second season.

Kaufman Films would not be asked back. Bravo tapped Doug Ross of Evolution Film & Tape (2006 isn't that long ago but also seems like the distant past) to be executive producer, which also meant sidelining Scott Dunlop. "Scott did a great job at identifying killer cast members," Doug Ross, who shares his name with George Clooney's *ER* character, told *The Hollywood Reporter*. "But the network thought with the help of some 'grown-ups' this thing could really blossom."

Ross should know what it feels like to be fired after the first season of a reality show. Evolution produced the initial season of *Big Brother* on CBS in 2000, which failed to rank either critically or in the ratings like it had in just about every other country around the globe. In 2001, Evolution was also behind the first season of NBC's all-you-can-eat buffet of rats and snakes, *Fear Factor*, before being replaced.

It was two other shows that had landed Ross and Evolution the job. In 2002, Ross and Kirk Marcolina, both openly gay, had produced the show *Gay Weddings* for Bravo. The eight-part series followed four couples—two gay, two lesbian—as they planned their weddings. In the early 2000s, when gay marriages were still illegal in every state in the union and only a few offered civil unions, the show was revolutionary. It was a modest success, but it gave the network the idea to develop more programing for the LGBT community, including *Queer Eye*.

Bravo also tapped Evolution to make the show *Boy Meets Boy,* which debuted just a few weeks after *Queer Eye.* It was a dating show in the vein of *The Bachelor,* but featuring an extremely handsome gay man, James, who got to choose between fifteen equally ripped suitors, and the happy couple would win a cash prize and a trip for two to New Zealand. The show contained a deadly twist: only eight of the guys in the contestant pool were gay, while the other seven were straight. If James picked one of the gay dudes, they won the money and the trip. If he picked one of the straights, that guy would win $25,000, and James would get nothing but the embarrassment of being a made a patsy on national television. (In the end, James picked a gay guy even though he liked a straight guy more, as he figured out his orientation.)

A spokesman for the Gay & Lesbian Alliance Against Defamation told *The Dallas Morning News* at the time, "GLAAD's wish would be to have a gay dating show without deceptions with twists, but not leaving hurt feelings." While that puts it kindly, a lot of gay viewers, critics, and activists at the time were outraged that a gay person, then something of a rarity on mainstream television, would be treated so shabbily.

With that mottled track record, Bravo gave Evolution the reins of *RHOC.*

On-screen, not much changed in season 2. Kimberly Bryant was replaced by Tammy Knickerbocker somewhat unceremoniously. "They asked me to do it, and I said yes," Knickerbocker said of the casting process. The women still weren't interacting much, but we saw Vicki and Jeana hang out, and all the women, minus Jo, went to an astrologer. Lauri made out with Slade at a nightclub while he and Jo were "on a break"— just like Ross and Rachel! The two broke up for good on camera in the season's ninth and final episode.

There was also another reunion, billed *Housewives Confess: A Watch What Happens Special.* Finally, there was Andy Cohen, then barely known to viewers outside of his Bravo blog and his *Watch What Happens* web series. In the footage, Andy sits in a tall director's chair in a brown velvet suit and unbuttoned shirt, eyes trained on the teleprompter. The women face him in a row in their own director's chairs, wearing their own clothes. There are a lot of shiny fabrics. One of the big discussions is whether or not Jo is hooking up with the oft-shirtless nineteen-year-old Shane. It was, shall we say, a budget enterprise.

After season 2, Bravo confronted drama not with the producers but with the stars.

Jeana and Slade (who isn't technically a Real Housewife, but might as well be) weren't happy with their deals. They accused Bravo of being too heavy-handed with them, trying to control the press they did and the deals they made. Jeana and Vicki had started a website called CotoTravel .com, and Jeana had started a website called TheRealOCBrand.com with three of the other Housewives to sell clothes, jewelry, and other products featured on the show. The women had asked Bravo to partner with them in both ventures and been turned down—but even worse, the network threatened to sue if they didn't remove pictures of more than two of them together and erase all mentions of Bravo. The cast's contracts stipulated that three or more couldn't appear in public together without Bravo's permission and that they could not use the name of the show or network to help sell products, a ban that exists to this day. "We couldn't market products. We couldn't advertise. We could barely say we were on the show," Tammy Knickerbocker tells me. "They were so cautious of their name."

These branding slights, plus her conviction that she could have made more money selling houses than filming the show, rankled Jeana. By all accounts, the salaries were, indeed, low: Tamra Judge, who joined the show starting in season 3, said she made $7,000 her first season—after the show was already a ratings success—while Tammy told me she was too embarrassed to reveal how small her season 2 salary was. And here Bravo was stifling a few small business opportunities, the women trying to exploit their status as local heroes since they were not yet national treasures.

Slade, for his part, says he lost a client because they thought he was too arrogant on the show.

Neither Jeana nor Slade singled out Andy or Lauren or someone else at Bravo. Who knows, it was probably some lawyer they had never met before sending them nasty emails. Slade said that when he did interviews without a Bravo publicist, he was called up and reprimanded, a practice, again, that still persists to this day. "All of us made it happen. I won't let my success be handled by someone else," he said.

The upshot of this tussle was classic Bravo: half milking the drama, half cutting it loose. On the milking-it side, we got to follow the further adventures of Slade in the franchise's first spin-off: *Date My Ex: Jo & Slade,* where Jo tried to choose a suitor with the help of Slade and her two best friends. Slade later came roaring back onto *RHOC*—fame-hungry, slimy, and controlling as ever—when he got into a relationship with Gretchen Rossi after she had spent a few years on the show.

Jeana, meanwhile, would leave the show full-time three episodes into season 5. She says that she demanded what she thought she was worth. Bravo decided that she wasn't worth it after all.

Back in season 3, the November 6, 2007, premiere attracted just over two million viewers. This is when the modern era of *Real Housewives* truly begins. The women start hanging out together a lot more, they all go to San Diego on a cast trip, Vicki and Jeana start having disagreements, and Lauri plans a wedding to a man, George, whom she met after he saw her on TV. Two months after the season 3 finale, a little show originally conceived as *Manhattan Moms* aired for the first time as *The Real Housewives of New York.*

The franchise had officially gone bicoastal. Thanks to Sky Tops, a bit of Larry David fan fiction, and a woman screaming about a family van, a pop-culture phenomenon was born.

〰 〰 〰

By 2009, the Real Housewives were the queens of Bravo. The first-season finale of the *Real Housewives of New Jersey* (a.k.a. the table flip episode) was capturing *Project Runway*–size numbers, with 3.5 million viewers.

Meanwhile, the old *Queer Eye*–style programming wasn't having the impact it once did. *Top Design,* a *Runway*-esque show for interior designers, fizzled after two seasons, and *The Fashion Show,* Bravo's 2009 replacement for *Runway,* proved to be roadkill. As they say on *Runway,* one day you're in and the next day you're on Lifetime.

This aligned with another era of corporate restructuring. In 2009, cable giant Comcast bid to buy a majority of NBCUniversal from its parent company, General Electric. Two years later, with the deal approved, Comcast took control and shuffled the executive deck. Zalaznick was now overseeing not only NBCUniversal channels like Bravo and Oxygen but also Comcast's Style Network and "digital products" like the ticketing site Fandango. A rival executive, Bonnie Hammer, oversaw USA, E!, and Syfy.

As Zalaznick moved up, Berwick was crowned president of Bravo. "Frances is very good at the corporate side of things," a former Bravo employee told me. She is nothing if not a survivor, a bit like the character Littlefinger on *Game of Thrones,* aligning with whatever new monarch might come her way, running things from the shadows. Until she was in charge. (Littlefinger eventually got killed by someone he tried to groom, so maybe it's not that apt of a comparison.) Unlike Zalaznick and Cohen, she has never had profiles in the *Times* or splashy magazine shoots. She is much more of a typical network executive than the other two. Or maybe it's her Britishness that makes her a bad self-promoter.

A former Bravo employee described the Comcast era as data-driven and reliant on the bottom line. While Bravo could model itself as a tastemaker's haven before, delivering a bit of prestige as well as the young, educated female market to advertisers, now it was totally different. "It was like the Mafia," the former employee said. "As long as you made your numbers, they would leave you alone, but if not . . ." Just like with the mob, the threat hangs in the ellipsis.

With Berwick running things and the *Housewives* franchise the post-*Runway* crown jewel, Bravo took on much more of a docusoap sensibility. "*Housewives,* obviously, gave them a new direction that has sustained them since," reality TV historian Andy Dehnart says. "Basically, every single show on Bravo that works is *The Real Housewives* in some form or another, even if it doesn't have that label."

He's not wrong. Just look at their recent hit shows. *Shahs of Sunset,* launched in 2012, is *Real Housewives* but Persian. *Vanderpump Rules, Married to Medicine,* and *Below Deck,* launched in 2013, are *Real Housewives* in a restaurant, doctor's office, and a yacht, respectively. *Southern Charm,* launched in 2014, is a very problematic *Real Housewives* but with people from the South who still party at places unironically called *plantations.* There are still a couple of holdovers from the network's past—notably, *Top Chef* and *Million Dollar Listing*—but now it is essentially a showcase of Housewives and those that aspire to be them. As of 2019, Bravo was the number one prime-time cable network among women aged eighteen to fifty-four, a title it held for three years running.

Two years after Comcast took over, its CEO, Steve Burke, tapped Bonnie Hammer to run all the networks and relegated Zalaznick to head up the company's digital businesses. Zalaznick left the company a little bit more than six months later without a gig lined up. She now works at Boston Consulting and has been an adviser to brands like the millennial women's website Refinery29 and song-finding app Shazam.

Berwick, the longest reigning of the Bravo employees, currently not only oversees Bravo but all of NBCUniversal's "lifestyle" networks, including E! and Oxygen. She has been at Bravo longer than most of the Real Housewives' children have been on the planet.

So who is responsible for the rise of the Housewives, after all? Scott Dunlop receives a "created by" credit; Dunlop Entertainment, with its logo of a TV that looks like it's getting electroshock treatment, still gets a title card at the end of each episode of *RHOC.* (He also gets a slice of every show and all its spin-offs.) But few fans know his name, and he was sidelined long before the franchise reached its final form. Many think that Andy Cohen created the show's heart and soul—but did he? Did Lauren Zalaznick? Did Frances Berwick? No, it was all of them, along with the marketing staff, the EPs at the production companies, and the vicissitudes of corporate mergers. The Housewives have contained multitudes and they were shaped by multitudes, different sets of hands massaging Dunlop's wet hunk of clay like a million Patrick Swayzes guiding Demi Moore in *Ghost*.

Dunlop, for one, is sanguine about the Bravo of it all. "My contract's good," he once told a reporter. "I'm happy."

TEN THINGS A REAL HOUSEWIFE
SHOULD NEVER DO

Renew Her Vows:

Just ask Vicki Gunvalson, Shannon Beador, Braunwyn Windham-Burke, Ramona Singer, and Cynthia Bailey, who were all headed for a breakup shortly after their second walks down the aisle.

Visit a Psychic:

Let us never forget the psychic who told Ramona Singer in Morocco that her husband was cheating, the psychic who started the chain of events that led to Brooks Ayers being caught lying about cancer, or, of course, Allison DuBois, who thinks Kyle Richards's husband will never emotionally fulfill her. Know that.

Get on a Boat:

Brandi Glanville slapped Lisa Vanderpump on a boat. Cynthia kicked Porsha Williams on a boat. Erika Jayne went ape on Dorit Kemsley on a junk, which is a boat, but in Hong Kong. Ramona threw a glass at Kristen Taekman while she was clinging to a canoe, which is a boat in a lake. Scary Island started with a boat trip to a deserted villa. And, of course, there is the Boat Ride from Hell.

Drink Tequila:

There is the tequila that gets Margarita Kyle to do the splits in public, the tequila that got Denise Richards talking about her husband's manhood at dinner, and there is what happened to the *RHONY* ladies when Bethenny took them tequila tasting in Mexico. Actually, maybe they should just always be drinking tequila.

Think about Having One More Baby:

Ramona Singer, Cynthia Bailey, and Melissa Gorga all thought about giving motherhood one more go-round well after their fertility window was barely cracked.

Let Her Man Get Involved in a Woman's Business:

While the husbands and boyfriends of Housewives are always welcome on the show, they shouldn't get too wrapped up in the drama. Just ask John Mahdessian, Simon van Kempen, Michael Darby, Aaron Phypers, or Sean Burke.

Dress Up in Costumes:

Putting on a silly outfit is sure to lead to a fight and an embarrassing, eternal GIF. See: Vicki screaming at an '80s-themed Bunco party, Shannon Beador unraveling at her '70s-themed party, or Lisa Rinna's confrontation with Kim Richards while dressed as Erika Jayne.

Bring Up the Elephant in the Room:

There is no surer way to lead to conflict. Just ask the women of Atlanta, who had a whole elephant room fall around their ears.

Go to Palm Beach:

RHONY's Luann de Lesseps, Tinsley Mortimer, and Jules Wainstein have all been arrested in the Florida town.

Come for Kenya Moore:

Has this ever ended well for anyone? The answer is no.

HE PAID FOR YOUR LIFE

ANDY COHEN AND THE
BRAVOLEBRITY MACHINE

One name you may have found conspicuously sparse so far is Andy Cohen, Bravo's mascot in chief. The popular fan belief is that Andy is behind literally everything that happens with casting, production, development—not just on *The Real Housewives* but on every show that's on Bravo. "Andy must not like her, that's why she's not getting screen time," a fan might tweet about a certain woman. As a high-ranking production and development executive, Cohen was instrumental in many of the decisions that made *Housewives* what it is— but as we've seen, he was never some all-powerful puppet master. That said, he has become not only the figurehead of the franchise but also its most famous member.

He's sort of like RuPaul on *RuPaul's Drag Race.* The drag host is try-ing to find the "next drag superstar" with the caveat that RuPaul will always be the biggest drag star of them all. Andy's public role may be to oversee the Housewives, but he also wants to be more famous than any of them. Long before he was on-air talent, he cultivated his relationships with celebrities like Sarah Jessica Parker and Kelly Ripa. Now his friend Anderson Cooper says that he never saw anyone enjoy the attention of celebrity as much as Andy.

He is at a strange triangulation of power, in that his celebrity was created by and reliant on both Bravo and *The Real Housewives,* though he has increasingly little to do with either. At the same time, he's not above meddling with *The Housewives* when he feels like it.

Cohen's public-facing role started with 2005's *Battle of the Network Reality Stars,* the first project at Bravo for which he was entirely responsible. It was a remake of *Battle of the Network Stars,* which initially aired on ABC from 1976 until 1988, on which the most famous people from different shows would compete in Olympic-style events. Andy was always a huge fan, as were many young, budding homosexuals, mostly for the chance to see the hunks of the day like Mark Harmon, Tom Selleck, and Lorenzo Lamas in their Speedos during the swimming events.

Andy's version of the show would feature former participants from *Survivor, The Apprentice, Project Runway, American Idol,* and other reality shows duking it out in a field day for the wannabe (more) famous. It was a huge flop. However, he would send emails to the executives at the company every day with all the fun goings-on behind the scenes. "Rumor has it that Trishelle from *The Real World* hooked up last night," he wrote. "[*Survivor* winner] Richard Hatch has ideas for how the format of this show could be better—he's oddly competing while suggesting twists to the challenges." Zalaznick told him that these emails were funny enough that he should be blogging for Bravo's website.

He started a regular column, which proved so popular that he started hosting a version of *Watch What Happens Live* online after episodes of *Top Chef* to interview booted contestants. This web series is what led to him being the host of the second *RHOC* reunion. "He has finally made the leap to on-air talent he undoubtedly has been plotting since he typed the first sassy words into his BravoTV.com blog," gossip site (and *Gawker* affiliate) *Defamer* wrote in 2007. "Should audiences warm to Cohen's trademarked name-droppy, anecdote-spinning, kibbitz-from-the-hip conversational style—and really, why shouldn't they?—we imagine it won't be long before network head Lauren Zalaznick (who, says *Variety,* senses a 'brand in the making') gives Andy his own regular slot on the schedule."

Sadly, Andy's blog and most of *Defamer* have been erased from history—the former taken down by the network at some point and the latter taken down by Hulk Hogan.

But *Defamer*'s prediction is basically what happened when Cohen's talk show–cum–*Real Housewives* after-party moved from online to the network in 2009. *Watch What Happens Live* aired on Sundays and Mondays, which gave Cohen plenty of time to fulfill his network duties as SVP of original programming and development . . . until this changed just two years later, in 2011, when *WWHL* was averaging 1.2 million viewers and moved to a Sunday-through-Thursday schedule. Cohen gave up some of his network responsibilities and started focusing on development rather than original programming, a distinction that most of us outside of the free-bagel board meetings at NBCU wouldn't understand. (Basically it means he focused more on creating new programs than dealing with the day-to-day of existing programs.)

"Bravo is all set to announce plans to take *Andy Cohen's Half-Hour Make Me Famous Hour* from its current Sunday and Monday airings to five nights a week," I wrote on *Gawker* at the time. "His plan for global media domination is working!"

In November of 2013, Cohen announced his departure from the network. "Andy has influenced the course and the shape of Bravo tremendously over the past 10 years as a production and development executive, and as creator and host of our flagship late night show, becoming the face of the network," Berwick said in the press release.

He still remains an executive producer of *The Housewives* and has a "first-look" deal with Bravo (they get right of first refusal of any projects he produces through his company, Most Talkative), but he has no say on any shows outside of *WWHL* and the *Housewives* franchise. As he will say on his show on SiriusXM's station Radio Andy, he has nothing to do with the likes of *Vanderpump Rules* or *Southern Charm,* no matter how much fans want him to wave a magic wand and have Jax Taylor fired for not looking as good with his shirt off as he used to.

"He's involved when it comes to the brand as a whole, like decisions about expanding. He was not for expanding the franchise when *Dallas* and *Potomac* started," a former Bravo exec said about his current status at the company. "He has a decent amount of impact on hiring and firing. He doesn't have the final say. Frances [Berwick, the head of NBCU's lifestyle networks] has the final say. Shari [Levine, the current head of production] and Frances. I heard, that he had to be sold on adding Tinsley [Mortimer to *RHONY*], he was not enthusiastic about it. Bethenny [Frankel] and Carole [Radziwill] were really in his ear because they knew her from her socialite days in Page Six."

One producer likened Cohen's role to the Queen of England. If he wants something to change, it will change, but he's really above most decisions. Another former Bravo employee said, "People . . . ask me, 'What's Andy like?' I would say, 'Fine. I see him five minutes a week. I think he knows who I am. But maybe not?'"

When it comes to the on-camera talent, "Andy and I didn't do each other's hair and shit if that's what you're asking," former Real Housewife of Dallas Cary Deuber told me. "I saw him when I filmed stuff with him, when I did *Watch What Happens Live,* and when I did a reunion. He's personable, but it's, like, I don't have him on speed dial." Some of the older stars who were there when Andy was working more heavily in development might actually have him on speed dial, but newer ladies don't have the access.

That said, when the opportunity presents itself, all bets are off. Deuber and others I talked to said that whenever there is a group of House-wives around Andy, the level of ass-kissing is off the charts. Erroneously or not, they still believe his friendship can accrue favors, or at least favoritism. "The wives look at him like the queenmaker," a longtime Bravo exec says. "As it got bigger and as he became a star, [the Housewives] had to lean on the producers. The producers are the real bitch whisperers who control the ladies."

We'll get to the "bitch whisperers" in chapter 5, but for now, let's stay on the, er, bitches. Because the real story of Andy Cohen is also the story of every Housewife: it is the journey of becoming a Bravolebrity. If the rise of *Housewives* is in part a business history, of Bravo as it went from opera and porn to . . . maybe the exact midpoint of those things, it's also a story of personalities. Big personalities, dealing with fame for the first time, in every way imaginable, and not always getting along on their way up (or down).

⊠ ⊠ ⊠

Whenever a new Bravolebrity is cast on a show, they meet with staff from Bravo's digital and publicity teams to get a crash course in how to be internet famous. The teams talk about what is expected in terms of promoting themselves and their shows, and give tips on how to ignore all the chattering on Twitter, not that any of the women pay attention to that. Bravo also furnishes the women with assets like GIFs, video clips, and still images so that they can post about upcoming episodes to get viewers to tune in.

There is nothing free at Bravo. The women get high-quality images for their social media, but Bravo gets free advertising on their social media channels. If the women want to get a link to watch the episode before it airs, then they have to file a blog with Bravo for their website. If you don't blog, you don't get the episode, which means someone like NeNe Leakes, who refuses to blog, never watches the episodes in advance. This is the only incentive to get them to blog; these weekly reports aren't in the women's contracts, and they don't get paid extra to do them.

Some Housewives don't take kindly to the promotion machine, or at least Bravo's control over it. Once, after an editor for the website offered some constructive criticism of professional writer and RHONY Carole Radziwill's blog post, she responded with a terse, "Fuck you."

Several people at Bravo told me about an incident when Ramona called their offices. A brand-new assistant answered the phone. "I'd like to speak to Andy Cohen, please," Ramona asked in her signature rushed and clipped diction. (At least, I imagine it went something like this.)

"Just one moment," the assistant replied. "May I ask who's calling?"

"Ugh, it's Ramona Singer," she said.

When Ramona got on the phone with Andy—or another Bravo exec; I heard she was looking to speak to different people—they got an earful from Ramona. "How can they [the assistant] not know who I am if they're answering the phone?" she asked. "You should fire them immediately."

There was also a harried holiday weekend when Kyle Richards got a death threat from the supposed Twitter account of a terrorist organization. After she called the network for protection, alarmed Bravo execs got NBC's digital security team on the case. It was then that they saw the time stamp on the tweet was two months old. If Kyle had survived that long, the death threat was probably a hoax.

"Any Housewife who gets to the level of feeling like the show needs her more than she needs it, they become unbearable," a former Bravo exec who had dealings with the ladies said. "These are high-drama personalities, and the intensity level is very high, but what they're being intense about is often very silly."

Fair enough, nameless executive. So how do Housewives go from hopefuls and new hires filling out blog posts to asking for bodyguards and demanding the heads of assistants? The Bravolebrity journey. Watch what happens, as it were.

❦ ❦ ❦

"I didn't even know what a tagline was," says Kristen Taekman, who joined *RHONY* in season 6, of the little snippets of personality each woman delivers during the opening credits. Her initial tagline was the much derided, "I may not be the sharpest tool in the shed . . . but I'm pretty!"

"They were like, 'I think your story line's going this way.' I was like, 'Excuse me?' I raised my hand like, 'What's a story line?' So I had no idea. I just literally was like, I'm a model by trade, so I'm going to get a stylist and have my hair and makeup done, and that's what's important to me at this point."

Taekman knew she would be wearing sometimes three outfits a day, five days a week, and couldn't repeat herself. In one of her first scenes on the show, she wears a high-necked peach dress with a short, full skirt and a matching peach chain necklace. She says a bunch of people on social media—who found her social media handles merely because she was cast on the show—asked where she bought it. It was from H&M. No one said they had to be expensive, just look good.

Cary Deuber had a bit of a different experience after being cast as one of the originals on *Real Housewives of Dallas.* "I don't think I really believed it until they showed up at my house with cameras . . . literally had a panic attack," she says. "You know what I panicked about? It was my son, my stepson and my husband were in the bedroom, and I came in there, and I just thought of my kids. I panicked about my life and how great it is, and how much I love my family, and I was like, 'I don't want to fuck this up.'" She obviously thought of her family before making the decision, but it was like she never considered that the show, and its attendant attention, might actually change things.

Deuber did not fuck it up and was asked back on *RHOD* for two more seasons.

For anyone who makes it through her first season (about 80 percent of the cast), watching the results can be very sobering. Taekman says watching herself on television made her realize that her face moves in ways that she never realized before. She also decided she needed to spruce up her apartment a little bit before the crews arrived again in the fall.

Some of the Beverly Hills cast aside, most of these women are experiencing their first taste of fame from being cast on *Housewives,* and you can tell how many get a season 2 makeover. They lose a bit of weight, get a better haircut, start going to the plastic surgeon, and invest in getting a stylist. If you need proof of this, just check out the difference between NeNe's first-season long hair and the shorter bob that became her signature in season 2. If you want an extreme version of this, check out season 1 Kim Zolciak before the new nose, the expensive wigs, and enough lip filler to sink a battleship.

"I think it's really interesting to see when they all come back after their first season," says *RHONY* producer Barrie Bernstein. "Second season they have a different look, hair, they've all watched themselves," she said at BravoCon. "They grow into the role. They really do. I think they grow into it. They thrive with the attention."

A veteran editor who has worked on a number of *Housewives* shows says that attention is the key to them forgetting all the bad things they've seen on TV. "The first-season Housewives don't realize how the manipulation happens in post," the editor says. "They're calling the production office after the first two or three episodes saying, 'How dare you! What the fuck did you do to me?' And then on Friday, they go to the grocery store and people are talking to them and recognizing them. They're on the cover of *People* magazine, and suddenly, they forget how fucking pissed off they were that they never actually said something. They don't care anymore because they're celebrities and they love it and they want more."

Taekman has a theory of her own. "My opinion is I think a girl needs three seasons to really find herself," she says. "I think that the first season, you're kind of like a deer in headlights in a good way. The second season, you're really trying to find your way, like what is my story line, am I going to start a business? I'm aware of the cameras now, so I'm a bit spunkier. Then I think the third season for a girl is like you're all buttoned down. I know I can be snarky and really speak my mind, because that's really good." It's worth noting that Taekman only made it through two seasons before bowing out, she says, of her own accord. I am angry at the perfect third season she kept from us.

Ana Quincoces says that, as soon as the season starts, each Real Housewife has the same aim: "The goal is to get another season." But with that fame and attention, there comes the cost of public scrutiny, and thanks to the advent of social media, that scrutiny has gotten worse and more vicious.

"People are just so mean," Taekman says. "I did this because I thought it'd be a really great experience, and then people are just nasty . . . I think the worst one for me was like, 'I cannot believe you're still with your husband, you need to leave your husband.' I was on a reality show for two years. If we amortized out how much of my marriage you actually saw, like I'm going to throw seventeen years away and two beautiful children, for what?"

No matter how much producers warn the cast not to look at the comments, they're always going to pay attention. Kemar Bassaragh joked at BravoCon that *RHOP*'s Karen Huger calls them the "people in the phone," and that she knows she shouldn't look but she always does. As someone who always tells people on the internet not to read the comments but then reads every single one on all his recaps, I know the struggle is real.

"I think the stuff that the fans say online can actually shape the way that cast member will react on camera," says a producer who has worked with numerous casts. "A lot of times, they will hold back because they don't want to look like this or they don't want to come off this way."

After her fight with Bethenny Frankel went awry and she became the show's villain, Jill Zarin was savaged by fans on Facebook and Twitter. There was a blog at one point called *I Hate Jill Zarin,* which took delight in making fun of every outfit she wore and generally terrorizing her. Darren Bettencourt, Zarin's manager and publicist at the time, said at one point they had to beef up security after receiving pictures of the outside of Jill's house with a threatening email.

"When it gets negative with the comments and social media and things like that, it really does hurt the person, and I think that's when they start to change," Bettencourt says. "I think when they do, it's more about them putting up a wall to protect themselves, which translates as demanding or bitchy or whatever. But it really is just sort of a protective mechanism."

For Cary Deuber, the attacks were a total surprise, as they came from something she wasn't even aware of during filming. When LeeAnne Locken was behind closed doors at a doctor's office, but still with a mic on, she gave a famous speech about Cary, her husband, and what he may or may not do at the Dallas gay bar the Round-Up Saloon. "Why is it so fucking important to Cary to come for me all the time?" she said. "Because I'm gonna do something. She's going to come for me one day and it's not going to be pretty. Her husband gets his dick sucked at the

Round-Up. I know the boys who did it. I didn't grow up with a silver spoon in my mouth, I grew up with a lot of things in my hands, and they're not knives, they're just hands. But they work quite well." All future Juilliard applicants should have to perform this speech for their acceptance.

Jokes aside, though, the Deubers have had to deal with the persistence of gay rumors about her husband. "I mean, it definitely strained our relationship, our marriage, because of the stress," she says. "You can't take it back. You google my husband, you google me, that's what it says. One day I'm going to have to explain this to my daughter." That seems like a ridiculous thing to have to explain to a kid because a castmate made it up.

The Real Housewives of D.C.'s Lynda Erkiletian is one of the lucky few who got something negative about her essentially erased from the internet, and some of that is probably thanks to the fact that her show only lasted one season and she was outshone by those notorious White House party crashers. "I did a fashion show for Burkina Faso [on the show]," Erkiletian, who owns a modeling agency, says. "And I said something about, 'In addition to the department stores and the ad agencies, we cater to embassies and designers that are coming from overseas.' Well, they cut everything except, 'We cater to embassies and ambassadors,' and it made it sound like I was owning a call girl operation."

A local journalist published those allegations, as did several others. I remember back in 2010, when we were both working at *Gawker,* my colleague Richard Lawson made a joke about her being a pimp in a recap of the episode. She goes on, "My publicist locally was like, 'I cannot handle this. There's no way. I'm not qualified.' So I called a publicist in LA who is a crisis manager."

She enlisted the help of Mark Lane and cut him a $50,000 check for his services—almost her entire salary for appearing on the show. "He started writing letters. It was gone. It was really bad for about three weeks, and then once I found him and got him on board, people stopped it," she says. I remember getting a letter at *Gawker* asking us to take the joke out of the recap. The site's attorney at the time told Richard it was easier to just comply than actually fight about it. I also remember the pair of us rolling our eyes.

But it had been "devastating my life, my family, my livelihood," Erkiletian says. "A stupid little rumor that someone started to get followers and get attention . . . it was just unbelievable. If I hadn't been in the position to write that check, God only knows what would have happened to my business."

If a Housewife can weather the harassment, on the other side is the promise of that vaunted "platform": the social media followings in numbers high enough that a cast member can attract endorsement deals or start a business of her own. *RHOA*'s Kandi Burruss has more than eight million Instagram followers as of late 2020, whereas her former (and probably future) castmate NeNe Leakes has the most Twitter followers with just under two million. Most of the biggest Housewives on Instagram are on *RHOA,* but the sixth highest is former *RHOBH* Yolanda Hadid, probably due to the Instagram popularity of her children—supermodels Gigi (sixty million Instagram followers) and Bella (thirty-five million).

Being on the show is no guarantee of these best-case scenarios, however. *RHOC* cast members like Emily Simpson (391,000 Instagram), Braunwyn Windham-Burke (233,000 Instagram), and Gina Kirschenheiter (555,000 Instagram) fare less well. And for other Housewives, the negative effects of Bravolebrity just aren't worth it.

Taekman says she had a bit of an aha moment during one of the Real Housewives' most infamous moments.

It started at the season 6 party Sonja threw at famed New York eatery Cipriani to thank all her staff, including her "interns" and her pet psychic, for their work during the year. The whole cast was there. Including Aviva Drescher, who was on the outs with everyone after skipping the group trip to Montana, having claimed the dust was bad for her asthma. After drinks and hors d'oeuvres, the seven women sat down around a rectangular table.

"This has nothing to do with asthma. This has to be about more than asthma. I've done nothing but try to be your friend this whole time," Kristen says.

"You've actually been a horrific person to me, just so you know," Aviva replies. Kristen looks shocked and looks to Heather Thomson for validation.

She then tells the women that the doctor lied to her about the severity of her asthma. "This is not my chest," she says facetiously as she pulls out x-rays of her lungs.

Kristen seems to be looking at Aviva with real concern when Heather says to her, "She is making fun of you. She is making fun of you."

Sonja takes the x-rays and makes a show of examining them. "Those are her lungs or her boob job?"

Carole Radziwill expresses her doubts about Aviva's claims. Reviving the rumor she spread earlier in the season that Carole used a ghostwriter on her first book, Aviva says, "The only reason you're trying to brand me as a liar, Carole, is because I know things about your writing."

At this point, Carole, Heather, and Luann (wearing a giant jade necklace that isn't a statement, it's a whole damn speech) get up and walk away from the table, saying they're done.

When they finally sit back down, Aviva says, "If you don't believe me, here, take these home," dumping her passel of x-rays and files into Heather's lap.

Heather is ready for her close-up. "You say that you have never lied to us and that you have been hurt by everyone at this table. I find that laughable," she says, putting so much venom in that last word it could kill all the kangaroos in Australia.

"Let me tell you something, Heather," Aviva says. "The only thing that is artificial or fake about me is this!" She slams her artificial leg on the table. The crowd of facialists, beauticians, and gays who just want to gawk lets out a giant collective gasp. Almost everyone flees the table, but Aviva is not done. She throws her leg into the middle of the room, letting it float there on the carpet like a plank of wood circling the *Titanic*.

"That was one of those moments," Kristen says, years later, "where you're like, 'Who signs up for something like this, and why on earth would you do that to yourself?' End scene. I just kept thinking, there's a leg on the floor, and I feel like I'm in a horror movie. What is happening?

"I think I was never going to be a career Housewife. I think I kind of had a decent little run . . . I was like, 'I think I'm done. Life is good, I'm all good.'" She said that she chose not to return the next season.

Bethenny Frankel would disagree. In response to Carole Radzi-will's hint that she was the reason that she "left" *RHONY,* Bethenny responded on Twitter, "Bravo has reasons for not asking [Housewives] to return. It's based on research and focus groups and YOU. Aside from 3 years I left, no RHONY cast member has ever quit. One saying they chose to depart and attributing it to me is fiction. It's healthier to be truthful about a hard situation."

Whether or not you take Bethenny's tweets as gospel truth, she's not wrong—few give up the Housewife life willingly.

◻ ◻ ◻

If you don't have Andy Cohen on speed dial, you may need Bravo's research department to stay a Housewife. A holdover from the Zalaz-nick days, the network polls fans throughout each season, asking their thoughts on "the cast, story line, location of cast of the trips, all of that," someone familiar with the reports told me. "That definitely goes into the decisions getting made." There is also something called *personality research,* which looks at how fans feel about certain characters on the show. RHOA Kandi Burruss always ranks the highest here—maybe it's her down-to-earth demeanor, unstoppable hustle, or her willingness to throw down in a fight if it comes to that. But the network isn't just looking for people that fans love. Someone like Kandi's castmate Kenya Moore is very divisive, with about 50 percent favorable ratings and 50 percent unfavorable ratings. That's just as desirable. The one thing the network hates is when the fans simply don't care about a woman. That might be her kiss of death.

It's not all a data game. With people like Aviva Drescher, who was both unpopular and difficult for production to deal with, and *RHOA*'s Phaedra Parks, who got caught making false rape allegations (that Kandi tried to drug Porsha Williams in order to have sex with her), Bravo dropped the ax without waiting to hear what fans had to say.

Apparently, Shari Levine, the current head of production at Bravo, is increasingly skeptical of the research department. This may be why positive research also isn't enough to get a Real Housewife promoted. Marlo Hampton, who has been a fan favorite as a "friend of" the Housewives for many years, can't seem to be made into a full-time cast member no matter what she does. A former Bravo employee told me that an executive said, point-blank, that Marlo will never get a peach because of the rumors of her past employment as a sex worker, rumors she denies. (He used a much more colorful term than "sex worker.")

While the research department relies on detailed surveys, the network also looks at "social sentiment reports" from their digital teams. These chart how well the shows and the women are trending on social media, particularly when the shows are airing. I wish I could tell everyone that their tweets about how much they hate Kelly Dodd and her Republican views don't really matter and to save their breath, but that would clearly be a lie. If there is enough unanimity around the sentiment, it might just be enough to get changes made.

The final decisions about who is going to be on a show's next season are usually made a few weeks after the reunion films—because, let's be honest, who is going to show up to the torture of an eighteen-hour reunion if she knows she's not going to be asked back? But one producer told me that the final casting decision is really made right before a season goes to air. He points to examples like *RHONY*'s Barbara Kavovit and *RHOBH*'s Sutton Stracke, who were supposed to be full-time Housewives but relegated to "friend of" at the last minute when they weren't deemed exciting enough. Barbara was filmed with an apple for the opening credits and everything.

Usually two weeks after the reunion airs—almost a full year since filming started on that season—letters go out to offer a position to the returning cast members and to any recurring friends of, like *RHOA*'s

Marlo. That is often how they find out whether or not they are getting re-upped.

Cindy Barshop, of vajazzling fame, got fired in the great bloodletting at the end of *RHONY*'s fourth season, when more than half of the cast was let go. She's the only Housewife I talked to, on or off the record, who got a call from Andy Cohen. She says she knew her number was up because she didn't jell with any of the women. When she saw Andy's number pop up on her phone, she answered and said, "Andy, I don't fail!" He told her she didn't fail, but she wasn't the right fit.

Jill Zarin was fired at the same time. Darren Bettencourt, her former manager, says that after the reunion, she was questioning what she wanted to do. "I think that she started to miss the life before, where she could kind of be happy and not worry about all these things you have to worry about when you're a Housewife, on one hand," he says. It must be nice, after all that attention, to be anonymous again, to not have to worry about being seen in public in a bad outfit, posing for selfies with fans, generally going about life obliviously. "On the other hand, it becomes so much a part of her identity, as it does with anyone that is on the show, that it was hard for her. So she was going back and forth, considering leaving the show."

He says she emailed the producers and resigned, but then immediately regretted it and emailed them back saying she would still like to be considered. But by then, the die was cast, and they told her she would not be asked back.

"I mean, she was devastated," Bettencourt says. "I think you're in a very difficult position. You can understand and you're cognizant of the pain the show can cause you, or your experience can be more difficult than you thought it would be. And sort of all the other, like the negativity from the fans and things like that affect you. And then on the other hand, you're like, 'Oh my God. What am I going to do now?' . . . It's hard to explain, but it leaves them in a state of disarray or a state of confusion, in a way."

Cary Deuber says she got a text from a castmate asking if she had gotten her letter and she hadn't. She then had to text a member of production to see if she could plan a trip when the show is usually film-ing. They told her she was free to go enjoy a vacation, confirming what she already knew but never officially telling her she was fired.

She took the news personally. "I was really upset," she says. "Not be-cause of the fame and the glory but just because it's something I had worked really hard for, and I felt like my family and I had gone through more than anyone on that show. The gravity of it, to me, was huge. That rejection to me was like an overall rejection for women, and working women in general. I think I took that really hard. Because I thought, 'Why wouldn't you want me? Why wouldn't you want someone who's like me? Why wouldn't you want to show America and people who real people are? Because I'm the realest.'"

Lynda Erkiletian says she can't remember how she found out *RHODC* was canceled and she was thereby fired. "I think it was seeing a statement on Twitter from Andy. Andy did not call," she says.

At least she got the decency of a statement. *Real Housewives of Mi-ami* still hasn't been officially canceled; it's just never been picked up, like a dress you can no longer fit into left to linger, indefinitely, at the dry cleaner. Ana Quincoces did say that she and some of the other women involved in the show recently got a call asking if they would be interested in returning. (In 2021, NBC's streaming service Peacock announced it was reviving the franchise for a fourth season.)

"People ask, 'Would you ever do it again?' Absolutely not. Am I glad I did it? Absolutely," she says. That ambivalent attitude is one of the few other unanimous things I heard from every former Housewife I talked to. But that might be because many of the people I talked to are short-termers or those who were on canceled series. I know several former Real Housewives declined to talk to me because they were hoping that one day they might get back on the show.

For those who wade deeper into Bravo territory, getting out can be even more emotionally complicated. "I was really grateful that I had had the opportunity, and I was grateful that I had my life back and that there was some normality," says Erkiletian, adding that losing the show was still hard. "It was like a death . . . I miss it when some really fun, fun things are happening, and it can't be televised. It's like, 'Wow, if the cameras were here now, this would be so Bravo. This would be something our audience would love.'"

This is how someone who spent one season on a canceled show feels after ten years. Imagine what it must be like for Vicki Gunvalson, who was demoted to "friend of" after thirteen seasons and fired in 2019 after fourteen. It might have been because the show wants to focus on younger women, or it might have been, as I was told, some people didn't like looking at her anymore. It might have been the research. It might be that at around $1 million for her last few seasons, her price was too high. It might have been all of those things or none of those things. But imagine what it must feel like for her to face the unblinking abyss of a life unbroadcast after all these years.

One former Housewife described the fame and attention being "like heroin" and that trying to get away from it was like trying to kick a habit cold turkey. Even Bethenny, who did leave of her own accord, has said that leaving the show was like getting a drug out of her system, and she kept feeling the urge to go back.

"For a lot of the women, the worst thing in their lives is being on the show, but the only thing that is worse than that is not being on the show," producer Doug Ross told the *Reality Life* podcast. "While the women are on the show, they are out in the real world being bombarded by people who love them . . . and it sort of screws with your perception of life. When that doesn't happen anymore, when you are not on the show, that has to be something you have to struggle with."

This is why so many of the women sign up season after season no matter how much havoc it wreaks on their personal life. Tamra Judge is estranged from one of her daughters because she doesn't want to be talked about on the show; while Tamra cried about it on camera, she was unwilling to leave to get her daughter back.

"The fact of the matter is none of these women are ever going to walk away," one producer says. I believe him, because aside from Bethenny, NeNe (the first time), *RHOBH*'s Lisa Vanderpump, and a couple of others, I believe no one has done it. "They do this because they love to be on TV. They love the attention of it all. And even when shit goes bad or something goes wrong or they look bad, they're always going to come back. They're always going to try and clear their name."

All the women who have been on the show I talked to said that it changed them, mostly in good ways. "I definitely have become more of a hard-ass after that show, in a good way," Taekman says. "I definitely don't have a problem telling people, speaking my mind a little bit more, in general." She did tell me that the cut she got in her mouth when Ramona threw a glass at her has healed perfectly.

Deuber also says the show hardened her in a good way, but it also made her reevaluate her relationship with her castmates. "I think they're fucked up in their head. I do. I mean, clinically. I did a psych rotation," she says, offering her professional opinion as a registered nurse. "I think they want to be really famous and that this is really important to them, this is very important to them, more important than they let on, more important than they would want anyone to know."

She says it was especially hard for her to lose one of her castmates as a friend, someone she wouldn't name. She thought they were real friends, even before the show, and would talk every morning after dropping their kids off at school and be honest about everything, including what was happening on the show. When the show ended, she realized not only that this friend dropped her but that she was probably being manipulated the entire time. "For me, that was hard," she says. "But also a learning experience."

Quincoces has a similarly negative idea about some of her former mojito graspers. (Yes, that is what the Miami crew held in the opening, since oranges were taken.) "They all want to pretend that they're doing it for the platform or to build the business," she says. "But quite frankly, they're doing it for people to tell them their dress is pretty. And I never gave a shit for anybody to tell me my dress is pretty. It just didn't matter. And that doesn't make me better [than they are]. Yes, I used the system, but everybody uses it for their own purposes.

"And I didn't hate it."

※ ※ ※

In the *Housewife* life cycle, Bravo gets to keep its hands pretty clean. Watch the socials, evaluate the data, maybe take a particularly nightmarish personality into account—and then, like pretty-boy Joaquin Phoenix in *Gladiator,* go thumbs-up or thumbs-down on giving each woman another season. Maybe Andy Cohen will call you, but probably you'll find out in a tweet or something.

Every now and then, though, we are gifted with drama so gloriously messy that the cast members, the network, and even Andy himself need to fight about it.

Allow me to take you back to the season 10 *RHONY* trip to Colombia in 2018, a trip that would become infamous for the Boat Ride from Hell. The day starts off innocently enough, with everyone splashing in the sea off a private island, making fun of Sonja for having the tags still attached to her bathing suit. (It's so she can get a better deal when she sells them at the consignment store, she told us.)

Luann and Sonja are about to perform their rendition of Luann's classic club banger "Money Can't Buy You Class" for her upcoming cabaret debut, when the women are informed that the sea is getting choppy and they have to leave immediately. They board the boat, a midsize white cruiser with an interior cabin the women had complained looked unsafe on their trip to the island, and Sonja starts frantically blaming Tinsley Mortimer. "You've been to Colombia ten times before! Why would you take us on this boat if you knew this would happen?" she screams, clearly worse off from all the wine they had at lunch.

"This is normal!" Tinsley shouts back. "You go like this," she says, waving her arm up and down to indicate the chop of the water. She clutches a drink in her other hand.

Sonja retaliates by peeing in her bathing suit. "Is this yours?" she asks Tinsley, throwing at her a black cover-up she had been sitting on. "Because I just peed on it."

"No, that's mine!" Ramona says in consternation.

The rest of the women are in the open part in the back of the boat. As Luann tries to walk to them, a wave hits the boat, and she's knocked flat on her ass. (Not knocked on her flat ass, because she looks damn good in a bikini.)

It keeps getting worse. Carole sits on the floor puking into a bucket while Bethenny sits behind her, stroking her back and keeping her head-scarf out of the vomit. The furniture on the deck flies around Bethenny and Carole. Ramona tells everyone she can't swim while Dorinda looks for life vests. "We're taking on water!" Dorinda shouts. "We're taking on water!"

A siren sounds, something everyone knows is a bad sign. Sonja clings to Ramona while screaming herself red in the face. "It smells like smoke," Dorinda says as the women slide across the deck and Luann is once again knocked on her ass.

For viewers, the screen then faded to black. "Due to the rough waters, all production crew had to stop filming for the safety of everyone aboard," it read during the episode. In real life, it continued to get worse. The siren was for either the anchor or the engine. At some point during the trip, the anchor came loose and dropped. The boat's engine then had to work overtime to compensate for both the dragging anchor and the rough seas, and either started smoking or caught on fire.

In this situation, a boat becomes liable to capsize. Luckily, a crew-member cut the anchor, which freed the vessel enough to get the women back to the shore.

"It was that bizarre silence after the storm where people just wanted to get off. No one wanted to talk to each other," Dorinda later said about exiting the boat. "We're all just physically like, 'What? Did that just happen?' You know that feeling where you walk off, you're kind of light-footed, light-headed?"

The whole night after that never aired. According to someone who was there, producers kept filming but instructed the women not to talk at all about the trauma they had just lived through. Somehow, they suffered through a dinner without discussing it.

To make the trip even worse, many of the women developed digestive issues, which led to Luann de Lesseps shitting the bed, Ramona Singer pooping on the floor, and Sonja Morgan wearing diapers to the airport (clearly visible in an unfortunate paparazzi photo).

Back in New York, there was a call to end all calls. A call between the women, their publicists/managers, Bravo, network execs, and producers, including Andy.

According to reports in Page Six at the time, the women were contemplating a lawsuit because of the dangerous work conditions, including the boat that they clearly thought was unsafe from the outset. (A source told *People* that the women didn't want to board the boat to return home but producers forced them to because they knew it would make for good TV.) I heard from a source familiar with the call that the women were looking for extra compensation, but the most they were offered was a free spa trip on Bravo's dime.

Darren Bettencourt, who was then Tinsley Mortimer's publicist as well as Jill Zarin's former manager, says that he was busy that day and couldn't join the conversation. Instead, he set it up for Tinsley, got her on the phone, and then departed to go about his other business. He didn't think anything of it at the time.

A few weeks later, he got a call from Jennifer Geisser, the executive vice president for communications and talent relations at Bravo, a.k.a. the head of their PR arm.

"Why did you do it?" Bettencourt says she asked him.

"Why did I do what?" he replied.

"Why did you record the conference call? Why would you record the call?"

Bettencourt says he didn't record the call and told Geisser so. Spooked by the accusation, though, he says he then called Tinsley and ended their professional relationship. "I didn't want to be involved in it because, to me, it felt like another dramatic story line, another *Housewives* thing."

Things started getting weird when he emailed Bravo about other clients of his, David Parnes and James Harris of *Million Dollar Listing Los Angeles*. He would usually confab with Bravo before a new season to get on the same page about the Realtors' promotional efforts, but he wasn't hearing anything back from anyone at Bravo. His emails weren't answered, and his calls weren't returned.

The next call he got wasn't from Bravo; it was from his client Harris.

"You know, the network told us that they're not working with you anymore," Bettencourt says Harris told him.

"Really? Wow. That's surprising," he says.

"They didn't give me a reason. They just said that we're not working with Darren any longer." The pair had to cut ties with Bettencourt.

He still wasn't sure what was going on, if he was banned for life or what. "Then it was affirmed a couple weeks later by Jill, who had lunch with Andy about the upcoming season [of *RHONY*]," Bettencourt told me. "They had a conversation, and Andy told her, 'You know, we'd love to have you back as long as you don't work with Darren anymore.'"

"Andy's never liked me," he goes on. "He used to call me Darren Zarin. He's always been very snarky and kind of rude to me for some reason, and I don't know why." Bettencourt says Bravo likes to manage their talent exclusively. The network wants them doing only the interviews they approve of, keeping the women on message, and making sure the shows get all the publicity, not the individual women themselves.

Another publicist, who still works with some Bravolebs, said it's less like doing his job and more like being "an assistant to answer press inquiries." This trend toward total control, Bettencourt assumes, was the real reason for his firing, more than Andy's dislike or the supposed call recording.

"I think it was about trying to find a way to get me out of there."

␡ ␡ ␡

"Mickey built Disney, but Disney built Mickey," a former Bravo exec says. "The difference is, Mickey is fiction and Bravolebs are real people. They have desires and ambitions and the network has their desires and ambitions, and they don't always stack up. There is a constant conflict there where the network built these people up only to be beholden to them. Then the personalities get so big, but it's like, how far can you go?"

Of course, the Housewives aren't some unruly monolith, and the above probably refers more to some than to others.

This person says that one of Bravo's greatest fears is that some of the stars it created will go to other platforms. This came true with Bethenny Frankel, arguably the most recognizable Real Housewife, who quit just days before season twelve of *RHONY* started filming without a word to either the producers, Bravo staff, or her friend Andy. Now the former *Apprentice* contestant is slated to host her own *Apprentice*-esque show with reality TV titan Mark Burnett, the producer of Bethenny's first foray into reality before *The Housewives*. And why shouldn't she? She can either continue to play in someone else's sandbox by their rules and make as much money as they'll give her or she can play in her own yard, make all the decisions on her own, and make as much money as she can get for herself.

With NeNe Leakes, perhaps the second-most recognizable Housewife, leaving *RHOA* in 2020, what happens if she ends up on her own show on a rival network or, even worse, a streaming service? What if that ends up taking away *Housewives* viewers? That seems to be the network's nightmare scenario, which might explain why it keeps such an iron fist on its talent now.

Bettencourt has no idea what happened on the conference call that Bravo was so upset about. He says he talked to Tinsley after it, and she said it was mostly standard stuff, but he's unsure based on how swiftly the network cut ties with him because of it. "I mean, it must be something pretty serious for them to think that I somehow maliciously recorded it, and they want to make sure that I don't release it or something," he says.

In my research, this call came up a few times with a few different, unrelated sources. Apparently, a recording does exist, and according to a source who heard the recording, the main attraction is Andy Cohen yelling at the women and calling them names, and that might be why Bravo wants to keep it buried. But Bravo being Bravo, they're not keeping it quiet to protect Andy—they're keeping it quiet to protect the brand.

No one has more power than the network, and it will let the Housewives go only so far before exerting that power. Likewise, Andy's just the mascot. The minute he starts damaging the brand, he'll find himself cast off like so many Housewives he never called to say goodbye.

HOW TO WRITE YOUR OWN TAGLINE

Each season, about halfway through filming, the show's executive producers get together and write about a dozen taglines for each woman, while she also brainstorms her own. Several taglines are filmed at the opening credits shoot, but it's up to Bravo which one makes the final cut.

If you want to make your own tagline, just follow these easy steps.

1. **Bring Up the Past:** Is there something from your history you want to convey to people, particularly something about your profession? Examples: "I was a child star, and now my most important role is being a mother."—Kim Richards; "I'm not a bitch, but I've played one on TV."—Eileen Davidson

2. **Tell Us Your Thing:** Are you known for a certain expression? Do you have a catchphrase? Is there a certain behavior that people always associate with you? Well, then just say something related to that. Examples: "Get the Pinot ready, because it's Turtle Time."—Ramona Singer; "My love tank is full, and I'm driving into my future."—Vicki Gunvalson

3. **Be Humble:** Yes, you're going to be on a show about rich women behaving badly, but you don't want people to actually think that about you, do you? Examples: "Planes and yachts are nice, but my happiness starts at home."—Kyle Richards; "Money doesn't give you class. It just gives you money."—Brandi Glanville

4. **Give It a Twist:** This is the most important part. Take what you want to say and then subvert it or make a pun on the first statement. If it's not clever, it's not working. "I won Miss U.S.A.,

not Miss Congeniality."—Kenya Moore; "I'm passionate about dogs, just not crazy about bitches."—Lisa Vanderpump

5. **End with a Bang:** Just go out shouting a random exclamation. "I love my family, I love my work, I love my life. Whoo-hoo!"—Vicki Gunvalson; "A true New Yorker never backs down, and I'm no exception. Holla!"—Heather Thomson

4

I'M NOT A BITCH,
BUT I'VE PLAYED ONE ON TV

THE HOUSEWIVES' TV PARENTS

Recall for a moment, if you will, the confrontation between Denise Richards and Lisa Rinna in the tenth-season finale of *Real Housewives of Beverly Hills*.

Denise goes over to Lisa's house, which is huge and tastefully decorated in a very bland way. They sit on a couch set up with two cameras, one for each of their reactions, and staged to perfection with oversize pillows bearing precise fortune cookie dents.

Denise wears a highlighter-yellow V-neck sweater, and Lisa rocks a tan turtleneck that looks like it's right out of her QVC line. They settle into talking about Dorit's party the night before, which was supposed to be the finale party with the whole cast until Denise found out that Brandi Glanville, with whom the cast believes Denise had an affair, would be in attendance.

"Did you know that Brandi was going to be there?" Denise asks.

"I did not," Lisa says breathily, like she's rehearsed this. "Did *you* know Brandi was going to be at that party?"

"Yes, that's why I didn't show up. I did not want to go there and have her create some Jerry fucking Springer moment."

"So there was no family emergency?"

"No, there was not," Denise says with the cadence of a villain not afraid to lie.

"What's going on here is none of my business," Lisa says.

"There is nothing going on here. Why don't you believe me?"

"I don't know what I believe, to be perfectly honest."

"Lisa," Denise says with a flavor in which shock, bewilderment, and condescension are all struggling to be the top note.

Lisa reveals that she thinks Denise's relationship with Brandi Glanville is deeper than Denise has let on, after Brandi showed Lisa and the other women a long string of text messages the two shared.

"I've met Brandi Glanville maybe four times," Denise says. "She was an acquaintance."

"I don't buy that," Lisa rejoins. "We don't understand why you wouldn't pick up the phone and say, 'What the fuck are you doing?'" With her thumb and pinkie, Lisa mimes what is surely a prop Princess phone Joan Collins would have dialed on *Dynasty*.

"Why would I engage in that?"

"Do you just not engage with that? Is that how it goes away?"

"No, there are things that I dealt with, I don't want to say how it was dealt with, but it is being dealt with."

"So you sent a cease and desist?"

Denise is slow to react, staring stonily at Lisa, her left arm propped on the impossibly plumped pillow. After seconds, she makes a shrugging motion and twists up her face, seeming to say both, "I don't know," and, "Ah-doy. Yeah. I did."

"You wanted the footage taken out," Lisa says.

Denise looks back at her, smiling tightly. "Who told you that?"

Lisa shakes her iconic hair as she stammers that she won't say or she doesn't know and just figured it out.

"Who told you that?" Denise asks. She is visibly pissed now, staring through Lisa's head like she is trying to saw off the top of her cranium with laser beams shooting out of her eyes.

"Oooof." Lisa lets out a long exhale. "You're so angry."

Denise purses her lips in anger and then says, "You're playing dirty." The dramatic music swells with the tension. And then we cut to a commercial break.

Yes, this is *Real Housewives,* but it is shot and played out exactly like a scene from a soap opera. It's two women rehashing the events of a party that brought all the characters together in one of their lush houses. It has high emotional stakes, but also only an incremental furthering of the story line. We learn that Denise has sent a cease and desist to get the footage about her and Brandi's alleged (but, you know, probable) affair taken off the air, but other than that, it's a standard domestic confrontation scene between two friends who are having a falling-out. Both women, I might add, are either current or past soap opera actresses.

There is one key distinction in this scene, though, and it's when Lisa asks, "You wanted the footage taken out?" As produced, edited, and massaged as *Housewives* is, we are reminded that it is the casts' lives, too. It puts them in soap opera contexts to get at their real emotions. Lisa Rinna and Denise Richards have known each other for twenty years, and now one is accusing the other on camera of an affair she has taken legal action to hide from the show; you can't tell me there isn't real tension there. *Housewives* is both a soap and reality show, giving us the best—and some of the worst—of each. While others attempted before it, as the scene above shows, no one has captured the amalgamation between the two as well as *The Real Housewives.*

This specific reality phenomenon might have been started by Scott Dunlop and honed by some creative types at Bravo, but really the phenomenon is a distillation not only of what was happening on television at the time of its release but what had been happening on television since it started popping up in every American home. It is less a moment in television history than a product of it.

※ ※ ※

"If you did the 23andMe of the *Real Housewives* franchise, you would find that its mom is the soap opera and its dad is reality TV," says television historian Robert J. Thompson, who is also the director of the Bleier Center for Television and Popular Culture at Syracuse University.

The *Real Housewives*' mom is quite old, older than Momma Dee and Momma Joyce combined. The first American soap opera, *Painted Dreams*, aired not on television but on Chicago radio in 1930; a nationally syndicated radio soap, *Clara, Lu, 'n' Em*, followed the next year. (No, the Lu of the title is not the Countess.) As many know, the shows got their name from the products that sponsored them—mainly detergents and household goods, aimed at housewives passing the time over chores while the mister was at work gathering up all that bacon.

Two things immediately differentiated these shows from other offerings at the time: serialized stories that never wrapped and could carry on ad infinitum, and a focus on women's stories. *Painted Dreams* followed the lives of Mother Moynihan, an Irish American immigrant, and her unmarried daughter. Unlike then trendy adventure shows like *Tarzan, The Lone Ranger*, and *The Shadow* (which were serialized but would eventually conclude before moving on to the next story line), it focused on the domestic, the interpersonal, and the romantic.

Here's a bit of dialogue from an episode of *Painted Dreams*. "I tell you, Sue, it won't work. I've never worn that shade of orchid in all my life," a character named Irene says. "I'd look like a perfect washout. Besides, that's your very best special occasion dress. I wouldn't think of taking it."

Sue responds, "Gee, with gold slippers and a gold turban hat, you'd be a wow! Wouldn't she, Mrs. Moynihan?" The language is a little different, but doesn't this sound exactly like a conversation that Erika Jayne would be having with her stylist, Mikey, in one of the customary scenes where they're going over her wardrobe before she leaves on a vacation? I also think that a gold turban and gold slippers are things that might theoretically be worn by Erika Jayne. (Who was, actually, named after soap icon Erica Kane.)

More radio soaps followed, like *The Guiding Light,* a serial about a priest and his flock, which kicked off in 1937 before moving to television in 1952. When it was eventually canceled in 2009, *Guiding Light* was the longest-running drama in American history and also the longest-running soap opera.

The television soap pioneer was *These Are My Children* (1949), not to be confused with Andy Cohen's favorite soap, *All My Children,* which didn't debut until 1970. Early TV offerings lacked the amnesia or abductions modern fans have come to expect, and the episodes were aired in black-and-white (duh) and only thirty minutes long. Otherwise, a lot of soap hallmarks are the same as they were on the radio and would be through to modern day. "I think of soap opera proper as daily daytime dramas that not only tell a continuing story but that have women characters at the center of it that are concerned with issues and ideas that are often associated with women in our society: Things about family relationships, romantic relationships, those kinds of things," says Elana Levine, author of *Her Stories: Daytime Soap Opera & U.S. Television History.*

These are all, of course, hallmarks of *Real Housewives* as well: ongoing stories that focus on the lives of women in society, their family relationships, and their romances. Would we even have a season if we couldn't see Ramona Singer try to date after her divorce, Melissa Gorga consider whether or not she should have another child after forty, or Kyle Richards cope with her daughters leaving the house? *Housewives* may not air daily as soaps do, but there are plenty of us fans out there who might wish it to be so.

We also see the visual language of soap opera in *Real Housewives.* A popular strategy on soaps is to show two sets of characters talking about the same thing and shifting between their conversations. On *All My Children,* Erica Kane and her husband, Travis Montgomery, each might be talking to a friend about their marital troubles, while on *Housewives*

Kyle Richards and Lisa Vanderpump argue their sides in a fight between them to separate confidantes.

Then there are the reaction shots. "Reaction shots have a really important function in all of these stories, all of this storytelling," Levine says. We all know the shot on soap operas, the kind of thing Roy Lichtenstein painted in his comic style, where a woman receives bad news on the phone and we see her about to cry before we know who's calling. We see the same thing on *Housewives* when someone says something upsetting or controversial; the frame focuses not on the speaker but on the women hearing the news, so we can know how to feel about it.

"It's important for the viewer studying people's faces, reading emotion, noticing nuances that they recognize because they've studied these faces for a long time and they know how and why they're reacting the way they're reacting, and reading a lot into it," Levine says, both of soaps and their reality counterparts.

There's also the way the plots of both soap operas and *Housewives* come together. "Most of daytime is quite boring," Levine says. "It's just people sitting around having conversations." Same goes for our favorite reality stars, though they are more often doing it after a workout at some new fad gym or sitting around a half-empty restaurant in the middle of the day. But the storytelling rhythms of both are the same. On a soap, all the characters, in different configurations, will talk about some big event, let's say a masquerade ball—or in the case of Denise and Lisa, Dorit's housewarming-party-cum-launch for her brand of alcohol-free champagne. All the story lines converge at the ball for several episodes, and something major happens. Then the next several episodes are just people in smaller groups, talking about what happened at the party.

For the Housewives, a cast trip or Roaring Twenties–themed party will go on for several episodes, leading up to some great confrontation. Then there is the dissection of that event for just as long.

Take, for instance, the season 4 lunch where Luann de Lesseps and Alex McCord sit down for lunch at (entirely empty) Meatpacking District eatery La Gazzetta. Alex is wearing a fur-lined red minicape, and Luann is much more understated in a black turtleneck. They get in a confrontation about a recent fight on the group trip to Marrakech; Alex accuses Luann of being "haughty, condescending, and vile" to her, and Luann tells Alex to mind her own business when it comes to her relationship with Ramona.

"You came after me in the house, I was sitting there having a loving moment with the ladies, and you came in in your Herman Munster shoes," Luann says with a chuckle.

"They're Louis Vuitton shoes," Alex corrects her.

"Well, even Louis Vuitton makes mistakes."

Between the trip, and the reliving and adjudication of it, we get two conflicts for the price of one.

A soap tactic *The Real Housewives* uses more sparingly is the cliff-hanger. Every cut to a commercial break on a soap opera is a chance for intrigue. They can be simple, like a woman picking up a phone and saying, "I didn't think I'd hear from *you* again," as an organ grinds and we all hold tight to find out just who is on the other end. Or they could be more complex, particularly on Friday afternoons when fans can spend the whole weekend thinking whether or not Ashley Abbott (Eileen Davidson's character on *The Young and the Restless*) is about to run off with her ex-husband's cousin's twin, who is a serial killer suffering from amnesia. (I made that particular story line up, but the fact that you even thought it might be real sort of proves the point.)

Bravo saves its cliff-hangers for the end of an episode where there is about to be a fight. We all know that if there is a kerfuffle in the previews, that the throwdown is going to happen right in the show's final moments. Just as NeNe Leakes stands up and comes for Kenya Moore on a patio in Greece, we see those three dreaded words flash across the screen: "To Be Continued . . ." Like any soap opera, we know *The Housewives* will continue, but this signals to fans that the heart of the conflict is coming next week.

While Bravo shows have many similarities with daytime dramas, it usually likens *Real Housewives* to prime-time soaps with a bit more prestige. The network singled out *Peyton Place* as a reference in the show's initial press release. Based on a bestselling 1956 novel by Grace

Metalious and 1957 movie of the same title, *Peyton Place* debuted twice a week on ABC in 1964. Tracing the intersecting lives of families in a small Massachusetts town, it was an attempt to import an English-style soap opera like *Coronation Street,* which airs every day in the evening.

Though the network wanted to distance it from the "soap opera" label, *Peyton Place* had all the hallmarks of what we would consider one: stories about alcoholism, domestic violence, teen romance, teen pregnancy, infidelity, murder trials, wrongful imprisonment, hit-and-run accidents, and the like. It nixed a story line from the novel about incest, but most else was fair game.

The show was an immediate success. It started airing three nights a week instead of two and made instant sensations of stars Mia Farrow, then married to Frank Sinatra, and Ryan O'Neal. When Farrow left the show after two seasons, the ratings never recovered, and *Peyton Place* was scaled back to two nights a week and then canceled entirely after five seasons. As quick as the craze had begun, prime time was scared away from soap operas.

As the '70s peaked, daytime soaps suffered from audience erosion as their typical demographic, real housewives (without the capital R, capital H), left the home to enter the workforce. The mothers of the baby boom generation were now dealing with older children or empty nests and weren't necessarily folding nappies in front of their "stories" anymore. To make matters worse, the first talk show boom was being ushered in by the likes of Phil Donahue and others, making hour-long shows that were nearly as popular at a fraction of the cost.

With adults at work, what other audience has the luxury to sit at home all day and watch soap operas? Young people! From 1966 until 1971, ABC aired *Dark Shadows,* a gothic soap opera that inadvertently attracted a young crowd when it started incorporating supernatural story lines about witchcraft and werewolves into the plot. When it introduced vampire Barnabas Collins, it created an iconic character, later played by Johnny Depp in a 2012 movie remake. Other soaps followed suit with outlandish plotlines involving supernatural or spy elements. In 1981, Elizabeth Taylor was a guest star on her favorite soap, *General*

Hospital, as a villain who was trying to freeze the entire world with a mysterious gem.

In 1976, a cover story in *Time* magazine quoted the number of weekly soap followers at twenty million Americans (including Andy Cohen), including ten million daily viewers for *As the World Turns.* Soap opera's second boom reached its height on November 17, 1981, when the young characters Luke and Laura got married on *General Hospital* (despite the fact that Luke had raped her two years prior). The wedding attracted thirty million viewers, which still makes it the highest-rated daytime soap opera episode in the U.S. of all time. (For comparison, Oprah Winfrey's final broadcast in 2011 only brought sixteen million viewers.)

Andy Cohen got hooked during this period, as a kid on the cusp of high school in the early '80s. He was a devotee of the ABC soaps, including *All My Children, One Life to Live,* and *General Hospital.*

In his memoir, he bemoans that when he's on a trip with his aunt and uncle, she is going to make him watch her favorite show, *Days of Our Lives.* "For the life of me, I didn't understand the appeal of *Days.* It was all fantasy and improbable plotlines. I hated NBC soaps. And *Days* looked especially weird to me, like the tape was old or gauzy or something. (You do NOT want to get me started on CBS soaps—so dark!) ABC soaps, in case you care, were bright and urban and smart—at least that's what I preached."

All the soaps of the era had the aesthetic of a Glamour Shots portrait come to life, and that's an archetype that really stuck. "Daytime is kind of connected to that fantasy era," says Levine. "I think many people think of that as like, 'Oh, that's what a soap opera is.' It's these elaborate weddings, big hair, and crazy adventures. That's really a particular period in the history of soap opera that burns really bright and gets lots of people really excited and engaged, and makes a lot of money for the industry."

The networks tried reintroducing the soap opera into prime time starting with *Dallas* in 1978, about the machinations of a wealthy Texas oil family, and then *Dynasty* in 1981, about the machinations of a wealthy Colorado oil family. These two shows would not only define our idea of the '80s "me decade," with women with huge hair and bigger shoulder pads living in giant and ornate McMansions but also embody the fantasy of conspicuous consumption to which *The Real Housewives* would later aspire.

Dynasty in particular is well remembered, especially among camp-obsessed gay viewers, for the catfights and insults between Linda Evans's Krystle and Joan Collins's Alexis. The best one features Alexis, wearing a dramatic black-and-white hat, going a bit far with the name-calling while standing next to a lily pond in Krystle's backyard. "You bitch!" Krystle shouts, tackling Alexis and launching them both into the pond, where Alexis wallops her with her now water-logged hat. Just as Alexis is about to crawl out, Krystle grabs her by the leg and says, "Oh no you don't," dragging her back and popping her right in the jaw. No one can check Shereé, boo, but she could never.

That show ended in 1989 and *Dallas* two years later, but the cyclical nature of television means that Marc Cherry's *Desperate Housewives* was only so far behind. The ladies of Wisteria Lane carried on the outrageous, murderous tropes of their '80s forebears, but this time back on a Peyton Place–esque suburban cul-de-sac (albeit one that would eventually be hit by a tornado).

꘎ ꘎ ꘎

Just as soap operas hit their low ebb in the '70s, PBS aired a sociological experiment that would end up changing the television landscape as we know it. Filmmaker Craig Gilbert had pitched the idea of going into an average American household and presenting what he found to the public. He chose as subjects the Louds, an upper-middle-class family in Santa Barbara, California. The show was called *An American Family*.

With the help of married couple Alan and Susan Raymond, who ran camera and sound for the production, Gilbert shot three hundred hours of footage on 16 mm film. That was whittled down into twelve hour-long episodes that aired on PBS, of all places, early in 1973. Gilbert captured a lot more drama than he originally anticipated. Bill and Pat Loud, the mother and father of the family, ended up separating on camera and eventually getting divorced. Lance, the couple's oldest son, who lived in New York while the series was filmed, is perhaps the first openly gay person on American television.

An average of ten million viewers tuned in each week to watch what happened. *Newsweek* featured the Louds on the cover with the headline "The Broken Family," and the members went on to become celebrities in their own right, with Lance saying to *Time* magazine that the show fulfilled "the middle-class dream that you can become famous for being just who you are."

The show did not arrive without controversy, and not all of it because of the divorce and Lance's sexual orientation. On the eve of the 2011 release of *Cinema Verite,* an HBO movie dramatizing the making of the show, Dennis Lim wrote about the original program for *The New York Times.* "For the viewing public, the controversy surrounding *An American Family* doubled as a crash course in media literacy," he writes. "The Louds, in claiming that the material had been edited to emphasize the negative, called attention to how nonfiction narratives are fashioned. Some critics argued that the camera's presence encouraged the subjects to perform. Some even said it invalidated the project. That line of reasoning, as Mr. Gilbert has pointed out, would invalidate all documentaries. It also discounts the role of performance in everyday life, and the potential function of the camera as a catalyst, not simply an observer."

It turns out that the first reality stars to complain about their edit were the first reality stars. Rumors swirled that Gilbert, working as a producer, tried to amp up the drama to make a juicier project. People asked just how real this thing could possibly be.

Regardless, some took the experiment incredibly seriously, including the famous sociologist Margaret Mead. She wrote in *TV Guide* (kids, that was a magazine that told you what was on television) that the show is "as new and significant as the invention of drama or the novel—a new way in which people can learn to look at life, by seeing the real life of others interpreted by the camera."

She was right in that *An American Family* presaged the reality television age (as did the classic 1976 movie *Network*), but some scholars stop short of calling it the "first reality show." The style is all wrong, to modern eyes: there's no music, few reaction shots, and the pace is slower than a snail on its lunch break. It looks more like an experimental art-house movie than it does an episode of *Real Housewives.* "We don't need to call that reality TV because we already had a name for what that was," says TV historian Thompson. "It was called a *documentary.* Verité documentarians had been following actual people around since the silent film era. *Nanook of the North,* which everybody watches in film 101 class, was about Robert Flaherty who followed around an Inuit family."

Flaherty also "faked some stuff," Thompson says. Are we sure we're not talking about reality TV here?

In any case, there's a big gap between '70s PBS and *Survivor.* So if *An American Family* isn't responsible for launching the genre, what is? Thompson says, "The big, big breakthrough, the most original thing to happen to storytelling since the novel was invented, is *The Real World.*"

There is no doubt that the 1992 MTV show was groundbreaking in how it showed the real lives of real American youth, but it actually owes as much to soap operas as it does *An American Family.* MTV had been looking for a soap about the lives of its target demographic, eighteen- to twenty-four-year-olds, and approached Mary-Ellis Bunim and Jonathan Murray to create one. Murray had worked in documentaries, and Bunim had cut her teeth working for decades on daytime shows like *Search for Tomorrow, As the World Turns, Santa Barbara,* and *Loving.*

At the time, they were working together on a show called *American Families*—a direct rip-off of *An American Family* for Fox. Instead of following one family for a long time, it focused on short transition points in different families' lives. Fox had been on the air for only a few years at that point and the show struggled to find an audience. The teen soap *Tribes* was also floundering, as Bunim pointed out in her meeting with MTV. And all those sets, actors, and scripts were going to be way too expensive for basic cable in the early '90s.

Bunim pitched another idea: a soap with a reality-based approach. MTV loved it, and pretty soon, they were kitting out an enormous SoHo loft in New York with cameras, sound equipment, and crew, and moving in seven strangers who would stop being polite and start being real. They filmed fifty to eighty hours a week to make each thirty-minute episode, which cost, at the time, $110,000, making it MTV's most expensive show but still much cheaper than any scripted fare. The cast were each paid a paltry $2,600 for their participation, along with the free rent and the exposure of being on an MTV show. (Modern casts on the show don't do much better, netting only a reported $5,000.)

Both filmmakers and executives were delighted with what happened once the cameras started rolling. "It can reliably be reported . . . that the loftmates have generated considerably more bickering and dissension than the producers had expected, that forcing seven people to share a single phone caused such problems that model Eric Nies had to install his own line to keep track of bookings (after which everyone else began using his phone, too), and that the household's weekly food allowance had to be raised from $350 a week to $400," *The Washington Post* reported before the show premiered.

Critics weren't so enthralled. Matt Roush, then the TV critic for *USA Today,* said the show "fails as documentary (too phony) and as entertainment (too dull)." From the start, it seemed like all anyone wanted to focus on about reality television was its artifice and how it was going to ruin the very fabric of civilization.

Spoiler alert: it has not.

Still, watch the original seasons now—before the show devolved into hot tub shenanigans like every other reality show—and one is struck by how genuinely interested the show seems in the sociology of it all. While there is some drama, like a party at the house when housemate Heather B. gets in a fight and the cops show up, the most memorable arguments were between housemates Nies and Kevin Powell, mostly about race. Just like soaps in the '60s, the first few seasons of *The Real World* would take on all sorts of political issues, like a cast member being sexually harassed by another housemate in season 2, and Pedro Zamora's fight with AIDS and death shortly before the premiere of season 3.

During the filming of the first season, after listening to the three women in the house complain about how hard it was to meet men in the city, Bunim had an idea. She called up the Jamaican tourism board and got them to foot the bill to fly the women down to the island for a weekend of casual encounters with guys. *The Real Housewives* have a lot to thank *The Real World* for, but the cast trip is a big one.

What most separated *The Real World* from *An American Family,* and has come to define reality television ever since, is the first-person interview. "Once a week, we'd sit them down in an interview situation," Bunim told *Newsday* in 1992. These interviews offered insight, "not just on what happened but how they were feeling when it happened. That's meant to be the most intimate part, to be able to focus really on how somebody is thinking."

This transformed not just the filmmaking but the viewer experience. "We aren't just viewing this 'real world' from an objective point of view watching people behave but participating in a fresh way," Diane Werts writes in the same *Newsday* article. "Sorting through all those first-hand viewpoints, we're coming to understand where these diverse people are coming from and why they act the way they do. Just as we're developing opinions—and revising them—they, too, are undergoing a process of change and adaptation more subtle than that seen by most soap characters. Their daily conflicts are exceedingly accessible: being annoyed by others' personal habits, feeling prejudged, becoming attracted to colleagues, taking tentative steps toward friendship (or away from it)."

The show was an undisputed ratings and cultural success, though many critics still focused on how unreal *The Real World* was. It might be because of that negative perception that network television, still the dominant force in the TV landscape in the '90s, allowed reality to exist entirely on cable aside from true-crime-based shows like *Cops* and *Dateline.* But since reality proved it could gain an audience with a lot less money than scripted fare, its takeover was inevitable.

"It's like rock and roll," says Thompson. "It started in the U.S., it popped over to England for some cultural interpretation, and it came back to us in the form of the British invasion stuff." The British invasion he's citing are actually two European formats—*Big Brother,* which started in the Netherlands by John de Mol, and *Survivor,* the American take on a Swedish show called *Expedition Robinson* created by English producer Charlie Parsons. Both debuted stateside in the summer of 2000, and both shows had a similar idea: groups of strangers stuck in a situation from which the cast would vote to remove one player each week. The final remaining contestant wins a cash prize.

Back in that naive summer, the idea that a television program could follow sixteen people voting each other off a desert island was absolutely revolutionary, a shock even to the jaded American audience who had endured Fox's reality spectacle *Who Wants to Marry a Multi-Millionaire?* mere months earlier. Fifty-one million people watched Richard Hatch, a gay corporate trainer from Rhode Island who spent a majority of his stay on the island naked, win the big prize. With an audience that big and with the cost of each episode microscopic compared to scripted dramas, the reality explosion was all but assured.

꿈 꿈 꿈

Things happened quickly. The first reality wave brought other competition shows like *The Mole,* followed by courtship and relationship shows like *The Bachelor* and forgotten classic *Paradise Hotel.* There were a few years of wild experiments. Please never forget *The Swan,* a show that took average American women, gave them total-body makeovers and heaps of plastic surgery, and then had them compete in a beauty pageant. It also kept them away from all mirrors so that they could film when the women first see their new faces.

Also for the archives is *Joe Millionaire,* a show that took a hunky construction worker, plopped him in a mansion, covered him in nice clothes, and then had a group of women compete to marry him. But would his bride stay when she found out he was poor? If she did, the couple would win $1 million; if not, they both left with nothing. She stayed, they got the check, and broke up shortly thereafter. Equally cringe was *Mr. Personality,* a show where a woman had to choose a husband from a pool of men who kept their faces covered by elaborate masks until after she made her choice and literally married the winner. Yes, it presaged the Netflix hit *Love Is Blind,* but the real kicker is that it was hosted by . . . Monica Lewinsky.

With the boom in money and viewers in the reality category, celebrities got in on the action. If people wanted to watch regular people go about their lives, wouldn't they prefer to watch famous people? This gave us two important precursors to *The Real Housewives: The Osbournes* in 2002, which charted rocker Ozzy Osbourne and his family in their daily lives, and *Newlyweds: Nick and Jessica* in 2003, about Nick Lachey and Jessica Simpson not knowing that Chicken of the Sea was actually tuna.

Audiences knew that these shows were, if not scripted, then at least heavily produced. The stars on the show, while saying and doing things their own way, were clearly being led in a certain direction by the producers. While some might cry foul, viewers didn't care, and they both proved to be huge hits for MTV.

A 2004 MTV show would prove even more formative. *Laguna Beach* is a direct antecedent to *Real Housewives* because it had the sheen of a scripted drama imprinted onto a reality show—though *Laguna Beach* and its spin-off, *The Hills,* would cop to being a lot more scripted than *Real Housewives* has ever been. Liz Gateley, a former corporate attorney, developed the show based on her life growing up in Orange County. At the time, Fox had the hit teen serialized drama *The O.C.*, about hard-partying rich kids living in affluent communities just south of Los Angeles. *Laguna Beach: The Real Orange County* wanted to be the reality version of that, just as *The Real Housewives of Orange County* would share both a geographic location and a desire to cash in on the success of a popular scripted television show.

The plan was to follow Lauren Conrad and her group of friends on campus as they finished their senior year in high school. However, after Janet Jackson's infamous "wardrobe malfunction" at the Super Bowl in a halftime special produced by MTV, the parents of Laguna Beach High School freaked out and convinced the school board to void MTV's contract, keeping the action off campus.

What resulted, instead, was a show about the kids' extracurricular lives. Gateley's intention all along was to take the footage, shot more like a scripted show than a reality show, and cut it together into narrative arcs like a soap opera. She did away with the confessional interviews that had initially differentiated *The Real World* from documentary endeavors of the past. This meant, particularly for *The Hills,* that occasionally scenes would need to be refilmed or that the subjects would have to describe to each other something that happened off camera.

While many scholars call both *An American Family* and *The Real World* docusoaps, the genre isn't really complete until *Laguna Beach.* It coupled the techniques of documentary filmmaking—or reality TV filmmaking as it evolved—with the serialized focus on relationships and domestic settings typical of soap operas. Its goal is not to show objective real life but to entertain using the stories and struggles of everyday people, distilled and heightened for maximum drama.

◊ ◊ ◊

"Something like *Real Housewives* has this kind of perpetual quality to it. The story lines just kind of continue and there is this play between the extraordinary and ordinary," says Susan Murray, author of *Reality TV: Remaking American Culture.*

Though that was true of early seasons of *Housewives*—like seeing Alexis Bellino running after her kids the next moment and then being thrown out of a dinner party by Tamra Judge after the commercial break—there is something different about later *Real Housewives.*

Housewives and *Keeping Up with the Kardashians* both debuted in 2006, and together, they have changed the way that Americans view and look at reality stars. Yes, they're meant to be just like us with their domestic dramas, but those very domestic dramas and interpersonal fights are underscored by an extenuating circumstance: fame.

Lucas Mann, the author of *Captive Audience: On Love and Reality TV,* put it a bit more simply to me. "A docusoap [is] a show that has eliminated anything other than the central drama of them being on TV."

Yes, the Housewives are filmed in their hometowns and their kitchens, but the multi-limbed monster of notoriety is sitting right outside their front doors. These women are not friends but coworkers, and the conflicts that they have, these days, are more about the show itself and how it's filmed or about the rewards of that fame and how they're meted out. By the virtue of its own success, *Housewives* has snuffed out the original impulses of *The Real World* and created something entirely new. What's left is instead a documentary about the biggest driver in the Instagram age: attention and its benefits.

Because docusoaps have become so popular, many equate their rise with the downfall of the scripted soap opera. "People used to be fascinated by soaps and reality took its place because it provided real-life situations people could get involved in," Lisa Vanderpump told the London *Observer* in 2014.

Andy Cohen said the same thing on *CBS This Morning*. "I think the Housewives have replaced the modern-day soap opera in a weird way for a lot of people. Soap operas—scripted soap operas—there's only a couple on the air right now, and truth is stranger than fiction."

He is only partially correct. There is a correlation in the trends, in that the rise of reality programming coincided with the decline in daytime soap viewing, but that doesn't prove causation. It's not like fans of *Days of Our Lives* turned off their soaps because they decided they would rather watch the real-life Lisa Rinna tell people to "own it!" over on Bravo.

The descent of soaps from their '80s pinnacle started before *The Real World* premiered. In 1990, soap opera ratings were already down 22 percent, with fewer housewives or nonworking people at home to watch, and the youth bump waning. A greater blow came in 1995 when the O. J. Simpson trial and all its media saturation preempted many soap operas during the daytime hours, sometimes giving the networks better ratings for the trial than the soap operas themselves. (While it doesn't seem entirely connected, the O. J. trial would augur our reality television future and be our first introduction to figures like Kyle Richards's bestie, Faye Resnick, future Real Housewife of Beverly Hills Kathryn Edwards, and the entire Kardashian clan.)

By the early 2000s, when *Survivor* opened the reality floodgates, audiences were down another 24 percent from the '90s. By the 2010s, the soaps were getting canceled left and right, leaving only four left on daytime television. Bravo chose to air *The Real Housewives* in prime time, when their target affluent, educated, slightly older audience would be home from a corporate job and could unwind with a glass of wine in front of the TV. *The Housewives* is a treat rather than something to pass the time while ironing. (Although in this streaming age, they're definitely also something to pass the time while ironing.)

Soap operas are also a victim of their own success. Before groundbreaking shows like *Hill Street Blues* in the '80s, most prime-time shows were episodic. Now almost every show is an ongoing story that doesn't seem to end. Every time a drama has a serialized story line, a prestige television show gets its wings. "Television throughout the 1980s begins to acquire a memory," Thompson says. "It starts to accept serialization. The thrill of an ongoing story, the thrill of serialization that you used be able to get only in soap operas, now you could get it anywhere." It's not just prime-time soaps like *Dallas* or *Desperate Housewives* filling this niche. Now everything from the tits-and-dragons epic *Game of Thrones* to the multigenerational family storytelling of *This Is Us* is borrowing a page from how soap operas tell their stories.

There's one person who disagrees with all of this, and that's Andy Cohen's once-and-forever icon Susan Lucci. "I don't think [*Real Housewives*] are the modern-day soaps," she told Page Six in 2020. "There's no storytelling. There's a lot of editing. It's, like, they cut to the chase all the time, and I think it's different." Yes, they are different, but they are often scratching the same itch for people who otherwise might have been drawn to *All My Children*.

It is, in a way, a sort of ironic revenge. While the Real Housewives may not be the cause of soap's decline, the vanishing idea of the definition of a housewife did. Instead, what we're left with are women proudly taking on the mantle of their often-repressed 1950s counterparts and ripping it to shreds one business venture, divorce, and prime-time catfight at a time.

THE ONLY THING ARTIFICIAL
ABOUT ME . . . IS THIS

PRODUCING THE HOUSEWIVES

T he $100,000 question is, is it scripted?" says Ana Quincoces
from *Real Housewives of Miami*. "I don't think it's scripted,
but things are planned. If these women and I would normally
not hang out together, like seriously, you could not pay me
enough money to hang out with them." She says she was put
into some situations she wouldn't have been in otherwise, like when costar Lea Black got a lap dance from a little person or hoisted herself on a
stripper pole in a party bus.

Not to contradict Ana, but the real $100,000 question isn't whether
or not the shows are real. There is a level of documentary that can't
be made up—marriages, divorces, rehab, lawsuits, ill-advised music
careers. However they play out, these are real events happening in the
lives of real women. I think the $100,000 question is: How produced
are these shows? When lives get turned into story lines, how much of it
is reality, how much is for the camera, and how much is it manipulated
in post?

To answer this, we need to go to the troops on the ground: the producers, field crew, sound technicians, camera operators, story producers, editors, production assistants, and various other freelancers who make any *Real Housewives* show happen. The network (and Andy Cohen) gets a lot of credit for the franchise, but none of it would be possible without the hard work and sacrifices the producers and other crew undergo—of their time, their social lives, and mostly of their sanity. They are the unsung heroes, and while their tactics may be shadier than the bottom of the Grand Canyon at sunset, they're doing it to give us what we want.

Each show is made by a different production company, though some companies handle more than one. To work for any of them, one must have "previous Bravo experience," but this is a catch-22; how, exactly, does one get Bravo experience in the first place? "Not everybody was born into the Bravo family. Somebody had to take a chance on you," says one producer who started on *Real Housewives* but has now worked on just about every Bravo franchise. They said to get their first gig, they saw an opening and had to call in every single favor just to get an interview. (I'm using gender-neutral pronouns to protect their identities.) "If a show is desperate enough, that's when you can get your foot in the door because they will make an exception. They'll hire you if you don't have Bravo experience as long as you come with somebody who can really vouch for you."

Getting that foot in the door has its perks, and more than just the excellent craft services at Evolution Media's headquarters in LA. According to industry pros, Bravo always has plenty of work to go around, and it pays better than most networks. *Real Housewives* shows (and spin-offs like *Vanderpump Rules*) make around twenty-five episodes a season, so they can be a good chunk of a freelancer's yearly income. On top of that, reality shows produced for other networks will often say, "Bravo credits preferred." Even other channels regard Bravo as the top tier and want pros who can deliver that same quality.

Of the currently airing shows, Evolution Media makes both *Real Housewives of Orange County* and *Real Housewives of Beverly Hills,* as well as spin-offs *Vanderpump Rules* and *Botched.* Shed Media makes *Real*

Housewives of New York City and now *Real Housewives of Salt Lake City.* Truly Original makes *Real Housewives of Atlanta* and *Real Housewives of Potomac* (as well as Kim Zolciak's family day care sitcom *Don't Be Tardy*). Sirens Media makes *Real Housewives of New Jersey,* and Goodbye Pictures makes *Real Housewives of Dallas.*

Each show has a host of executive producers listed in the credits, from Scott Dunlop to Andy Cohen and other Bravo staff, to the heads of the individual production companies. There is usually one or, more likely these days, two showrunners. These are the people doing the day-to-day work; if there are two, one is usually in charge of running the field operations of filming and production while the other is in charge of postproduction.

Field crew, particularly higher-level producers, stay on location for the duration of each show's shoot, which is generally four to six months. Most of the postproduction crew is centered in Los Angeles, where the majority of the production companies have their headquarters. While most of these shoots have many of the same crew, individual styles vary among the companies, as employees who have worked across the spectrum will say.

So, what do they all do?

⧫ ⧫ ⧫

Every season of *The Real Housewives* starts with the executive producers sitting down with all the women who have been contracted for that season and asking them what they have going on in their lives. They're looking for any special events—weddings, monumental birthdays, baby showers—and general developments, like if they're launching a new business, getting a new job, or otherwise changing their lives.

This is so that producers can find the "story line" each woman is going to have over the course of the season. Some arcs emerge from real life whether the Housewife wants them to or not, like Luann de Lesseps's arrest in Florida for assaulting a police officer and subsequent probation and court-ordered sobriety, or *RHOP*'s Karen Huger dealing with the IRS coming after her husband for $5 million in unpaid back taxes.

Other story lines are essentially emotional, like preparing for a child to go off to college or trying to broker peace between a Trump-loving son and his liberal-leaning half brother. (We see you, Tamra.) Then there are the story lines that are entirely created, like when *RHONJ*'s Melissa Gorga tried to find her long-lost sister (who never materialized) or tried to have a fourth baby (which also didn't materialize).

Others are a combination of the two. *RHOD*'s Cary Deuber says that before the show's third season, she and her husband, Mark, a plastic surgeon, hired a laser technician and decided to open a laser clinic to do cosmetic procedures. "Mark said to me, 'Why don't you run the laser center?'" Cary, a registered nurse, says. "I said, 'Well, why don't I . . . I could do that for my story line.'" But unlike a twinkle in the eye that doesn't turn into a baby, Cary actually did (and still does) run the laser center.

In this sense, there is a difference between the producers producing the women and the women producing themselves. Many of the cast members, like meddler in chief Lisa Vanderpump, learned how their shows worked over the years and who they wanted to be on-screen. Some, like Bethenny Frankel and Eva Marcille, had been on reality television before *Real Housewives* and knew how the game was played before even showing up. Couple that with the motivation for wanting to stay on this cash cow, and that's a pretty healthy incentive to make sure that your story line is fresh and the drama is flowing.

In their initial cast meetings, producers also delve into group dynamics among the women. They want to know who each woman is speaking to, who she might be mad at, and who she might have been hanging out with during the off-season. They're trying to get a sense of where filming is going to go over the next couple of months, which is up to the executive producers (or EPs) and the showrunners to compile.

After about a month of chatting with the women and charting out the season, the showrunners have to provide their first document to Bravo. "You turn in something that's called a show bible," says a high-level producer who has worked on a number of Bravo projects. This is "an actual fifty-page document that literally outlines every woman, every story they have, and the direction we think they're going to go." The details even specify the scene work required to shoot everything.

As you might expect, "it never follows that." While the showrunner might lay out in the bible how two women are the best of friends, that could all change with the smallest slight at a party. Likewise, a Housewife on the outs with the group might find herself forgiven and reembraced contrary to what the bible might have planned out. "It's kind of dumb," the producer says. "I don't know why they still have us do it. But it's a requirement." The showrunner stays in charge of the bible throughout the season.

Filming begins with each woman's personal story, so whatever we're going to be following that season has nothing to do with the rest of the women, like Erika Jayne preparing for her role in *Chicago* on Broadway. These stories often involve filming in the women's homes, which is easiest, as crews are familiar with (and allowed in) the space. For personal footage or, say, a lunch between two of the women where one is maybe or maybe not going to apologize, one of the season's three film crews is sent.

A crew consists of two camera operators, a sound technician, and a camera assistant. While their talents seem mostly technical, the best camera operators and sound technicians have a sixth sense for what producers are going to want. If someone is wearing an outfit that's sure to provoke comment, they know to get full coverage. They're also poised to capture not just the action but the reaction shots that will be useful when the episode is assembled. I hope that whichever camera operator thought to shoot a man clutching both the sweater wrapped around his neck and a martini glass while the *RHONY* women bickered at a Newport restaurant got him- or herself a raise.

Crews need to be hypervigilant, even while off the clock. During the *RHONY* season 5 trip to St. Barts, when the camera and sound techs were on a break, Luann de Lesseps chose to phone her friends about hooking up the night before with a pirate who looked exactly like Johnny Depp. She spoke French in hopes that no one in the crew would pick up on the conversation—but coincidentally, one of the sound technicians was French and kept his headphones on during his break. He immediately flagged the cameramen and the producers to capture the call, much to the Countess's dismay and our endless entertainment.

The women get no say in what makes it on the air. Just ask Denise Richards, who sent those cease and desist letters to keep the rumors of her affair with Brandi Glanville out of the season. Or Vicki Gunvalson, who requested that production remove the footage of her collapsing in tears when she learned, on camera, of her mother's death. Or Teresa Giudice, who tried desperately to ax a scene in which her husband, Joe, is on the phone talking to another woman and saying, "Here comes my bitch wife. She's such a cunt." All three women were ignored.

Producers love to exploit a hot-mic moment. Think back to season 9 of *RHONY* when Carole Radziwill has a conversation with Luann's friend Barbara Kavovit (who would eventually be cast as "a friend of," but at the time was a mere civilian). They are at a charity event and Barbara admits to Carole, when there isn't even a camera trained on them, that she thinks Luann's marriage to Tom D'Agostino is a big mistake.

Turns out she was right, but it was plenty embarrassing at the time.

Along with camera and sound, each of the three production crews on a season comprises about ten people. The leader is a field producer who juggles both ends of the shoot—what is being said and how it's being shot. She makes sure everything that will be needed in post is shot on the day, including restaurant interiors and exteriors and B-roll around the area. Between them, the three crews can capture multiple events in a day: Kyle Richards and Teddi Mellencamp going to a workout class at the same time as Lisa Rinna meets with her daughter's modeling agent, say, while Lisa Vanderpump shills high-end dog toys at Vanderpump Dogs.

Producers sometimes use "beat sheets" to break down things to be addressed in a scene. This isn't a script but an outline of topics; for instance, if it's a scene between Sonja Morgan and her mysterious backers in her fashion line, the beat sheet might include things like, "Talk about whether or not the fashion show is successful," or "Plan for the upcoming meeting with Century 21." Everything Sonja says around those topics are words from her own mouth, though, and on-screen, there's little way to tell which were the prescribed topics to discuss and when Sonja was just shooting the shit.

Could you even imagine trying to keep Sonja on script? In season 12, Luann tries to get Sonja to rehearse with her for an appearance in her cabaret show. "I'm not excited about rehearsing with you," Sonja tells her. "I'm impromptu, okay? I don't need to do a rehearsal with your team."

"But this isn't impromptu," Luann counters. "It's a rehearsed show. Look, there's a script." Sonja does not care and never shows up for rehearsal.

Everyone I talked with denies that the shows, unlike Luann's cabaret, are in any way scripted, so much so that I have to believe them. One producer who worked across a number of shows for more than a decade says, "I have never worked on a Bravo show where anything is scripted like that, where we tell people what to say and what to do." This is, of course, not the case for productions like *The Hills* or *Selling Sunset,* where scenes are so blatantly created you almost admire the balls they have for calling it reality.

◻ ◻ ◻

"Every single episode you're planning for at least one 'tent-pole event,'" says a former field producer. These are the events where the cast comes together. Several crews converge to film store launches, backyard barbecues, and charity dinners. If none of the women are throwing a suitable event over the episode's time frame, production may organize a group outing to an escape room or some other gathering for all the women to attend.

These are the events most planned in advance, but they're also the least predictable.

Who could have foretold that Erika Jayne wouldn't wear panties under her dress to a party and that Dorit Kemsley and her husband would notice, sparking an entire season's story line? Something tells me that season's bible didn't include "Pantygate," as fans call the event and the resulting aftermath.

Beat sheets for tent-pole events are much looser, as producers let the conversation take its natural path. The rules for mandatory attendance are also loosening a bit. "If a certain cast member wouldn't naturally be there because they're not talking to somebody, then they don't have to come," one producer says. "Why force them all to be together if they're not really in that place?" For some events, this makes sense, but mostly I feel like the women are best when they're all together. (Also, isn't it kind of their job to have to hang out with each other?)

There's still a cost to saying no, whatever the rules. Ana Quincoces says, "There were times when the producers would call me and say, 'Hey, we're going to go to [castmate] Joanna [Krupa's] bachelorette party in Vegas and the girls are going to get in the hot tub and they're probably going to take their tops off.' And I said, 'How about no. Does no work for you? Because I'm going to go with no.' And I didn't go, and they hated me. Those producers hated me."

How, exactly, do the producers get what they want out of a scene? Well, it's a little bit like being the animated devil on the shoulder of a cartoon character, driving them to do what they want to do but maybe don't have the guts to do otherwise. It's sort of like being a chaos agent, but instead of making anarchy, they're making a story line.

"If I was out to dinner, sometimes the conversation could be about potty training for two hours," Kristen Taekman, former Real Housewife of New York, says. "The only time production ever came in to intervene with me, they would say, 'Kristen, listen. No more potty-training talk. I just wanted to remind you, remember last night when this and this happened.'"

Lisa Vanderpump used another example in a 2014 article in *The Observer*. "Imagine a friend is always late and you don't say anything. [The producers] say, 'OK, don't just say what you're thinking to us, say it to your friend.' And then that becomes something that ignites a situation."

One producer explains it like this: "When I'm in the field producing a scene, I'm thinking about what the audience is going to think. For instance, they might think, 'Okay, so Lisa Vanderpump is obviously lying to these women. It's just obvious the way her body language or her story is not adding up.' The audience might think that and wonder why nobody is calling her out on it." They say it's the producer's job to get in there and ask the women why don't they say something if Lisa is, hypothetically, lying. (And we all know Lisa does more than hypothetically lie.) "It's just encouraging the women to think larger than just in that moment, what is really happening."

The production companies have different levels of comfort with just how involved producers should get in a scene. Producers who have worked for more than one company told me that the Evolution shows (*RHOC* and *RHOBH*) are relatively hands-off, letting the action unfold as it would naturally. In the Truly Original shows (like *RHOA* and *RHOP*), by contrast, producers intervene in the middle of scenes. They might go as far as pulling aside a woman in the middle of a group dinner to suggest that she push someone harder or make her point of view clearer. They're still not telling the Housewife what to say or how to feel, but they do goad her to think and process outside of the action. This might explain why *RHOA* and *RHOP* tend to be more explosive and careen from drama to drama, where *RHOBH* can spend an entire season fighting over whether a rescue dog was returned properly.

The anomaly is *RHONY,* where producers are reportedly very hands-off, maybe even more than on the Evolution shows—but they can afford to be. The cast is professional and always brings it. When you can have an entire scene of Sonja Morgan narrating what she is going to pack for a weekend trip and have it be funnier than most *Saturday Night Live* sketches, why would you tamper with genius?

That's not to say that producers don't have their tricks, even when they stay out of the action. Shane Keough says they always staggered people's arrival times to parties so that someone would show up at 6:00 p.m., others at 6:30, and others at 7:00. "At first I thought they just wanted to make sure they get everyone entering. But then as it went along I discovered, 'Oh, they want this person there first because they're the most mad about something.'

"Then they're going to talk to the next person that shows up. By the time the person who's the fuel for the first person's anger gets there, everyone's heated up and ready to go. That's what happened with that moment when my mom got the wine in the face."

He, of course, is referencing the famous *RHOC* season 6 finale party in Vicki Gunvalson's backyard where Tamra Judge threw a glass of wine in Jeana's face. Vicki lived next door to Jeana at the time, but producers made her wait while everyone else arrived. Jeana later told BravoTV.com that when she arrived, Tamra was already fired up and had a bigger glass of wine than anyone else. Whether she got that glass from a cater waiter or a producer, we'll never know.

❦ ❦ ❦

A former producer said to me one of the wisest things I've ever heard about the Real Housewives. The key, they say, is to figure out why each woman is on the show. Is she on to launch a business, for love, to get out from under a controlling husband, to find her independence, or the good old garden-variety quest for fame? That motivation is what will drive her story.

If this sounds more like life coaching than TV production, it's because *Real Housewives* is different from many reality shows in one key way: these women have to come back year after year. It's one thing for a producer to manipulate someone on a competition show who doesn't know the ropes and will be gone after one season. Producers on *The Bachelor* are known to interview the women in the house when they're on their period so that they'll be more emotional. They also keep the contestants in interviews for a long time, asking the same question repeatedly until the person caves and just gives the producers the sound bite they want.

Those bridges can be burned, with emotional fallout right out of an episode of the reality TV drama *UnREAL*. As for the Housewives, they're going to stick around (hopefully) so producers not only can't betray them but have to forge bonds with them.

While a season films, each field producer is usually assigned to develop a rapport with one or two women. "I would describe it as like when you talk to your best girlfriend," *RHOD*'s Cary Deuber says of her relationship with producers. "They are just sitting there, and they're like, 'Hey, what do you think of Tiffany over there? What do you think of her? I don't know. I just think her and her boyfriend, they're kind of shady, and I don't really think that they're on the up-and-up. I don't know, I'm just saying, I don't know what you think.' Then that's in your head, right?

"Then you go into a scene and you think, 'Oh yeah, they are kind of shady,' and then you say that. So it's just more like you feel like you're talking to one of your buddies, and then it just taints your whole view of everything."

"I think opening up about your life really helps them kind of do the same," says Pete Garcia, a producer who worked on both *RHOC* and *RHONY*. "You do have to put in a little effort and hang out with them off the clock and just befriend them . . . [so] they realize or feel like there is a human on the other side listening."

Darren Ward, who has worked across the franchise, particularly *RHONY*, told the crowd at BravoCon, "The lines do get a little blurred, and we do become a little bit like therapists because it's our job to be there and help them sort of navigate through this journey, which is what it is . . . I talk to Dorinda every single morning between 7:00 and 8:00 a.m. I call it my 'morning Medley.' We talk about nothing to do with the show, what she watched on television, where she's going for the day."

Now that Dorinda is off the show, I doubt those phone calls are happening. This occurs with most such bonds, because the producer moves on to a new show and has to form those relationships with a totally different cast. There are some exceptions, of course. I've heard, for instance, that Kyle Richards is especially close with some of the longtime producers on *RHOBH*, even during the off-season.

When field producers run afoul of the talent, on the other hand, it does not go well. "There was one producer who got fired in the middle of a trip," says Greg Bennett, who was a featured player on several early *RHONJ* seasons. It was during *RHONJ* season 4 when all the cast went on an RV trip in Napa Valley. "She was rougher, like a real LA reality TV

UNITED

Premier Access

E3E8VW 3C

UA4465 SMFTASS09

CARDENAS/STELLAANNETTE

Washington-Dulles to Richmond

UA4465	GATE	BOARDING BEGINS	SEAT	BOARDING GROUP
IAD - RIC D32		**5:35**PM	**3C**	**1**

THU 08 JUL 2021   Gate May Change

Boarding Ends: 5:45 PM
Flight Departs: 6:00 PM
Flight Arrives: 6:55 PM

Aisle
United First

Operated by Gojet Airlines dba United Express

producer. She didn't want to be our friend, and she was always trying to catch us doing something we weren't supposed to be doing.

"[On the trip] she left a beat sheet out, and it literally said, 'The boys are going surfing but Lauren [Manzo, Caroline's daughter] looks like a big fat whale in a wet suit and won't put it on.' Caroline was not happy and complained to the producers. We never saw her again. I think she was relegated to sitting in a helicopter doing aerial shots for the rest of the trip." Her sin wasn't in showing the beat sheet but in that she was trying to humiliate Lauren by getting her to do something she didn't want to do.

That is the only really malicious story I've heard about producer intervention. Skeptical fans often point to the excruciating scenes when women who are arguing then have to sit down to lunch together—as if ordered to crisis mediation by their bosses. But "it's not so much about forcing them into things that they don't want to do or uncomfortable scenes," one field producer says. "It's just that [the women] know the whole thing about these shows is conflict and then conflict resolution. So if you fall out with somebody, you're going to have to make up at some point, or you are going to have to try and figure it out, because that's just the nature of the beast."

One editor I talked with did say that scenes or phone calls are sometimes thrown together after an episode is in post so that the story will make sense to the viewer. "If two people get in a fight, and then all of a sudden they're getting along again, that happens in real life all the time, and it's fine," they say. "But what [producers] started doing is saying, 'We have to have a scene of them making up.' . . . They don't tell them what to say, it really is them being them, but they know what they're going in there to do."

Another editor likened these scenes to me as "a very expensive improv class."

"If anybody's conspiring to push a story line forward, it's the women themselves," one producer says. "Even on shows that I know are super heavy-handed in terms of the producers talking to the women a lot more and helping them with their story, never do I see them pushing them in a certain direction."

"I don't know that production necessarily goes too far," *RHOD*'s Cary Deuber agrees. "I think a lot of the cast goes too far in that maybe somebody wants to be well known or recognized or famous." One can't help but draw parallels between this and her bête noire and show villain LeeAnne Locken. "Production gets a bad rap, but if it wasn't for production, I mean, what would you do? Just sit there and watch girls eat nachos? You can't do it without production."

Regardless of how close producers get to the Housewives, some of the women are nicer to them than others. Several people spoke the praises of Cynthia Bailey, who is always sweet, professional, and forthcoming about trying to get things to run smoothly. Kenya Moore, on the other hand, is seen as difficult to work with and very demanding. The same is said about Dorinda Medley, one of the fan favorites. Ramona Singer never remembers any of "the help's" names, even if they've been working with her for the show's entire run.

LeeAnne Locken and Tinsley Mortimer are both reportedly extremely professional and ready to deliver no matter what their scenes entail. Same goes for Emily Simpson and Gizelle Bryant. Carole Radziwill had a bit of a prickly reputation. And Tamra Judge is so amenable that the crew called her "Camera Tamra": whenever the camera is on, she delivers.

◼ ◼ ◼

Cooperative or not, all the Housewives are under intense scrutiny over the course of the shoot. Both production execs and the suits at Bravo pay close attention to the story lines as they develop over the season, like a person with a sweet tooth waiting for the "They're Hot" sign to come on in a Krispy Kreme window.

After each scene, there is a text thread between everyone in production about what just happened. (Imagine how long and emoji-filled that chain must have been when Candiace Dillard threatened Ashley Darby with a butter knife at her dinner party on *RHOP*?) Each field producer also files a "hot sheet" for scenes she filmed that day, with notes on what and when everything happened, to be distributed among the crew and sent to the network for review.

Each week, there is a call with the production company, the show-runners, the executives at Bravo, and the EPs, including Andy Cohen. The producers recap how things are playing out so far, and Bravo makes suggestions for the rest of the season. If they're sick of every Housewife starting a sure-to-fail business, they can tell production to stop focusing on an entrepreneurial story line. Or they can ask for the tension between two of the women to be explored more. In general, they're letting it be known which direction they think things should take. They don't say, "Make sure that the Tres Amigas hug it out at the reunion because we need them friends for the franchise to survive"; it's more like, "See where this story goes, and we really don't care about this other story."

While filming concludes, postproduction starts to piece the early episodes together, in a much more time-consuming process than one might imagine. It takes somewhere around ten to twelve weeks to whittle more than forty hours of footage into a forty-four-minute episode. (An episode can cover anywhere from a week of filming to just part of a day, for things like trips and mammoth events.) That means there's a little more than one minute of good material in each of the forty hours of footage.

In his memoir, *Most Talkative,* Andy Cohen crunches the numbers a bit differently. "For Season 2 of *Real Housewives of Beverly Hills,* we shot 1,270 hours of footage to make twenty 44-minute episodes—or a ratio of approximately 85 hours of footage for every 1 hour used," he wrote.

Where field production and postproduction overlap is in the confessional interviews. These tend to happen every two weeks and are conducted by one of the co-showrunners, particularly the one who is involved in post. When editors assemble episodes, they start to see where the gaps are, whether it's unclear what a fundraiser is for or how someone felt when they weren't invited to get their nails done with the rest of the girls. The postproduction crew sends their burning questions to the producers to ask on camera.

There are two ways to do this. Some production companies schedule a full day of interviews for each woman, where they have to sit in the chair from 10:00 a.m. until, say, 7:00 p.m. That is a long day of being on, being funny, and being focused for the camera. That also does not include the ever-expanding number of hours it takes them to get into "glam." At this point, hardly any of the women are doing their own makeup for filming scenes, and they're certainly not doing their own for something as important as the sit-down interviews.

The other way requires the women to film a little bit more frequently, but they're done in two- to three-hour chunks so that the cast can stay fresh. It's a little bit less grueling for everyone and seems increasingly preferred. Confessionals were originally filmed in the women's houses, where producers would have to dress the set and send the photo to Bravo for approval before they could start filming, so one long shoot saved time. Now most are filmed in front of a green screen on a soundstage, so repeat sessions are easier. (For a visual, I direct you to the beginning of *RHOBH*'s tenth season, when we saw Denise Richards sit down in front of her green screen with a captivating smirk.)

All the outfits the women wear must be approved both by the producers and the network before they can start shooting in them. Usually the problem is less what the Housewife is wearing and more how long it takes her to get into it, since some of the looks (hello, Erika Jayne) can be quite involved. One former producer told me that Bravo did have some problems with Kim Zolciak-Bierman on her spin-off *Don't Be Tardy* when her lips got, how can I say this, more voluptuous. They wanted her to wear less bright shades of lipstick, maybe something in a nude tone. Kim didn't necessarily take the note.

Each time we see a woman in a new outfit in one of her confessionals, it's likely a new day of filming. "When you see the ladies on the show, and they talk about the same event in different looks, a lot of times, it's when they may have forgotten they had something else to add to it," Kemar Bassaragh, the *RHOP* producer, said. "I'm like, 'Oh, we're still talking about this party girl?' They're like 'Yes. I have a lot to say.'" The women are contractually not allowed to get a dramatic haircut during the season to keep continuity, but luckily, this does not apply to wigs, hairpieces, or the glory of Dorit's floor-length braid.

The women can drive the conversation, but generally, they're following the producers' questions . . . which are sometimes the same question several ways. "They would always say, 'So what do you think about this person? Well, how do you really feel? Do you think blah blah blah,'" Shane Keough says about the process. "They would just keep pushing at it because they were hoping I would get to a point where I said something that they could snap on and use." See, those sneaky *Bachelor* techniques really do work, especially during one long interview.

A good interviewer is less of a *Bachelor*-esque interrogator and more willing to just riff with the women, getting them to a place where they'll say something that will delight the audience. But every woman has her own style. Usually first-season Housewives have it the hardest and need to learn to say their answers in full sentences and keep the energy high.

One editor told me that NeNe Leakes is by far the best in her interviews because she just talks in sound bites. When asked about the environment, she replied, "I don't know about going green, unless it's green money going in the bank." Once when exasperated with the cast, she said, "Please help me not to have to kill someone today." It's a GIF I have sent more than once.

Bethenny Frankel was all business in her interviews, but she shone by coming up with killer lines off the top of her head. My favorite line of hers happened when she was commenting on Ramona insisting on meeting cute guys at a Skinnygirl launch party: "Getting Ramona laid is like the first twenty minutes of *Saving Private Ryan*. It's going to happen or we're all going to die trying."

Ramona Singer always gets caught saying ridiculous things in interviews because, well, that's how Ramona rolls. These are among the women who know what is going to become a quote that will inspire a meme, and while that's not necessarily more coins in her purse, the more recognizable she is, the better it is for her career longevity. Bloop! (That was for NeNe.)

Teresa Giudice, on the other hand, is "fed every fucking interview byte," according to an editor. "She even says, 'How do you want me to say it?'" Another producer told me that sometimes the women ask them how to say something funnier or request a snappy line. When they hit on something good, many will ask for a few chances to deliver it just right.

Filming the confessionals can create a strange sense of alternative reality. One producer says, "During the interviews, we tell the House-wives what happened in the scene. So they remember what we told them by the way that we have constructed the scene, and then we egg them on to talk about it in an interview." In this way, the producer says, "we can change their perception of what really happened." Without liter-ally telling the women what to say—which everyone still insists does not happen—they can shape the result.

They used the illustrative example of *RHONJ*'s Cakegate, where Me-lissa Gorga and Teresa Giudice started a food fight with a birthday cake for which Siggy Flicker supposedly paid $1,000. (The producer wanted me to add that they have never personally worked on *RHONJ*.) "The cake was probably a production idea that production paid for," they say. "Siggy didn't pay for the cake. Siggy didn't make the cake. Siggy didn't have anything to do with the cake. She's on TV talking about how she spent so much time designing the cake to make it look like Melissa's wall-paper and all this shit, because a producer kept reminding her of that and asking her about that in her interviews. So they see and remember what we tell them to."

If this particular example were true, that would mean production straight up gaslit her into misremembering how much she had to do with the cake. (Or she's playing along for dramatic effect.) When Siggy goes to talk about this cake on *Watch What Happens Live* or write about it in her blog, she remembers the version of reality that is on the show rather than the version that really happened. In her mind, it seems she now believes that she spent $1,000 on the cake, and Melissa and Teresa ruined all her hard work.

Most of the finessing here happens in the postproduction process, as editors work in tandem with story producers. In general, the story producer is given all the rough footage for their "scene" and has to edit it down to about ten to twelve minutes of footage for the editor to turn into the scene. This shortened version is called a *string*. The editors then cut the string all together and add the music cues, graphics, and other bells and whistles to make the completed scene. It's like layers and layers of sifting to get down to the few gold nuggets that the audience at home enjoys.

"It's like sculpting, actually, because sculpting, you have a slab and you just pull stuff away to make art," says one story producer. "I'm watching for the meat of the scene. To move a story forward . . . we really do try to not just rehash, rehash, rehash. We try and push the story forward as much as we can per scene."

Anyone who has watched *The Real Housewives* knows just how Bravo likes a scene, or even a sequence of scenes, to be structured. For a party, we see the women getting ready individually at home, then we see pairs of women sharing black cars as though they're so poor they can only afford Uber Pool. Then we see them at the party and occasionally on the car ride home. Depending on how explosive it was, there will be lunches and phone calls the next day to talk about the party. It's the story producer's job to get all these strings in order for the editors.

Bigger party scenes can be more complicated because a story producer has to watch footage from all the different camera crews to piece the story together. Sometimes they go character by character, listening to the audio and watching the video so that they can piece together what happened like Carrie from *Homeland* pasting scraps of paper on the wall.

A restaurant scene may not take as long, but has a similar flow. You need to see the restaurant, you need to see the women arriving, you need to see them ordering food (which is, strangely, one of Andy Cohen's favorite things about the Housewives, because he thinks it makes them real). There is a flow to these things, and the story editor needs to make sure they're not only including the story beats but everything an editor will need in the process.

"If you notice, the waitresses are always interrupting them and stuff," someone who has worked on Bravo shows for years says. "So they like the scenes to breathe with reality, which a lot of shows don't. They just get to the point." She says the network likes to humanize the women whenever possible. She remembers a scene in which a Housewife was eating takeout, but in the original cut it was already set on plates. The Bravo suits wanted to see her putting the takeout on the plate. Real Housewives, they're just like us—except I would eat it straight out of the carton.

Rummaging through the trashed footage for those food containers isn't necessarily as tedious as it might seem. One story editor likens it to being an FBI agent on a stakeout, wading through the boring stuff to find the best part. "One of the reasons I love Bravo so much is because I can sit there with my mouth hanging open, watching footage that people really say these things," they say. "I think that's the fun part, and I think that's why they're still popular. People sense that they are real. We're not faking anything, because who can make that up?"

Story producers work closely with the editors who are on the same episode or scene as they are, but they also stay in touch with all the other editors and story producers, because the episodes aren't self-contained. They need to know which things are occurring in which episodes, to be able to swap story beats around or to request any missing beats from the field producers.

When the editors have all the strings, they fine-tune and add everything that is going to make the scene sing. This is where the famous Bravo wink comes into play. For every beat of a Housewife saying, "I didn't say that," paired with a clip in sepia tones of her saying the exact thing with the chyron "14 minutes ago" at the bottom of the screen, you have an editor to thank for that. Also, whenever an editor puts "8:49 p.m." or some other time at the bottom of the screen, you know you are in for something good. Either the women will be wasted in an hour, someone is going to be more than two hours late, or something is about to go on far longer than it should.

For all that, editors say that the editing on *Real Housewives* is less intrusive than it can be on similar shows. "We try as much as possible to stay away from using cymbal crashes and stuff on reaction shots unless something really needs a little bit of help to make it funny," one veteran editor says.

They do use some of the well-known tricks of the trade, like Frankenbites, the gruesome name given to a process where an editor splices words someone has said from different sources to make up a sentence the person didn't say at all. "It's usually if we need to change the tense they're talking in or something just to make things clear," says an editor who has worked on multiple seasons across the shows. "But I can't think of any cases on *Housewives* where we've put words in somebody's mouth or completely faked something. I mean, definitely that goes on in reality TV, but I think *Real Housewives* is pretty straightforward."

There's also a trick called a *round-robin.* Let's say all the women are at lunch and the newly sober Countess Luann orders a Diet Coke. The editor can then pause the action and show every woman's face, as if that order were a moment of extreme consequence rather than just another passing second in the scene. One editor also says that *Housewives* will use reaction shots from other moments in the scene to make it look like the cast is having a stronger reaction to something than they really did.

Flashbacks have also always been a part of *Real Housewives,* but now that the shows have more than a decade of fights, drunken shenanigans, and other altercations to pull from, they seem to crop up more often, almost as if the past is always playing along with the present.

Several editors told me that the ideas for the flashbacks often come from producers or showrunners, since they've seen all the footage of the season in progress. Many of the EPs have been with the show for seasons and seasons. One editor told me they worked with an EP who had an almost encyclopedic knowledge of the footage and could pinpoint down to the episode, act, and scene number of a clip to be brought up from the depths.

A *Housewives* storytelling innovation is the "side flash." It's when a scene is given a different coloration, like a flashback, but it's to a scene that we never saw. Vicki will be at lunch with Tamra and say, "Emily told me when we went shopping," and you'll see Emily impart some information, but that's the only clip we'll get from what must have been an otherwise boring shopping excursion. "That is, in my opinion, the greatest invention for docusoaps," one story producer told me. "Then you're not weighing your episode down with a scene that's meh just to get to this one piece of information."

There's also the way that social media and "the blogs" play into the action of the show, especially when something one of the women is saying on these amorphous platforms is infuriating another.

"In the beginning when social wasn't so huge, we tried to cut around social and pretend like these characters lived in a bubble that didn't include the real world, and now you can't," says an editor with a long history with the Housewives. "Now, you will have them having conversations about, 'Did you see their Instagram?' It's like part of the culture, it's their life." Of course, producers and editors make sure to get screen caps of the offending post to show the audience. Just like trying to return a blouse to Target, if you don't bring a receipt, don't even bother.

The biggest questions from fans about the editing has to do with what is colloquially called the *bitch edit* or the *villain edit,* where it seems like the producers want a certain woman to look bad and are using editing to show her in an unfavorable light.

I knew that Denise Richards was in for it from the premiere of *RHOBH*'s tenth season when she and several other ladies were sitting at an outdoor bar in New York City. She ordered what she always does, a Casamigos *reposado.* When her drink arrived, she said, oozing condescension, "That's not the *reposado,* that is a *blanco.* Can I please get the *reposado*?"

"That is the *reposado,*" the waiter patiently explained.

"No, it's not, it's a *blanco,*" she said, dismissing him. "I know my tequila." She tried to cover it up with a laugh, but the damage was done. Yes, it might have been a bitchy moment, but adding in something so extraneous just to make her look bad is the kind of thing that creates the impression that she's a lot meaner than she lets on.

In 2020, Bri Dellinger, an editor who worked for Evolution on the *RHOBH* spin-off *Vanderpump Rules,* said on the *Twisted Plot* podcast that she went out of her way to find embarrassing things that cast member Scheana Marie did and made sure to include all of them in episodes she worked on. (She was subsequently dismissed for talking out of school.)

All the story producers and editors I talked to say that they're never told who to edit well or poorly. They're just following the story, and if that makes a person look bad, that's probably because a person was behaving badly. "What we do has to be true to story," one producer says. "And if the story really is that the cast is down on a character, they have to show that, because what else is your story?" Fair enough, but if the story for the season is "Lisa Vanderpump's fall from grace," they're going to have to make her look bad to make the story line make sense.

"I've never been told, 'Okay, we've got to make this person look bad,'" another editor says. "In fact, the opposite. Notes coming from Bravo most of the time are, 'We can't do this, it makes him look bad or unlikable.' They want these people to be likable, obviously. They want there to be conflict, but nobody is trying to make anybody look bad. So, yeah, whenever somebody says they got a bad edit, I think they're covering the fact that they were an asshole."

One editor told me that when someone is behaving badly, they might actually soften the blow in post. They say, "Sometimes we try and protect the cast from themselves, meaning we just want to show their best face possible. Do they really need to say, 'You're a bitch,' twice when once will do? No."

Bill Fritz, who worked on *RHOC* and *RHOBH* for many years, told the crowd at BravoCon that so-called bad edits are bad for the health of the shows. "If you start to give people a certain kind of edit . . . they will stop trusting you, and they will shut down. We will say, 'You need to open up.' And they'll say, 'Screw you. You know what you did to me last season.' Then you've lost the show."

It's like it's the editor's job to pull the women to and from the brink of unlikability. They'll humiliate someone with a Bravo wink, showing her saying one thing and doing the opposite, but then they'll make her relatable by showing how she can't cook—if she's *RHOBH*'s Adrienne Maloof, by showing her wash a raw turkey with dish soap. Or wait, maybe that's just more humiliation? It's a constant dance of making fun of the women, but also making sure that we like them enough and aspire to be them enough that we keep tuning in week after week. And that the women feel good enough about how they are portrayed.

In my opinion, blaming the edit is the reality TV equivalent of calling in sick to work because you're hungover. It's trying to hide bad behavior behind something innocuous, but also, everyone does it.

Speaking of bad behavior, the Bravo notes process usually starts after about five or six weeks of editing the episode. The editing team shows it to the supervising producers and execs at the production company for fine-tuning before sending what is called a *rough cut* to Bravo. Each episode goes from a *rough cut* to a *fine cut* to a *picture lock,* which is what will be shown on TV. Each of those stages can have multiple iterations as notes are received and enacted, so there can be a rough cut 2 or even a rough cut 5 before the episode moves to the next stage.

Everyone who has worked on a Bravo show commented that the network's notes are harsher than they get from anywhere else. That's really why the job is "previous Bravo experience required," says someone who has worked on multiple *Housewives* seasons. "I think that's kind of what they're looking for when they say Bravo experience, is people who can deal with their bullshit and keep it together and finish the show."

I talked to one editor who worked on an all-time classic episode of *Real Housewives* that I can't name because it would give away their identity and probably ruin their career (and the only career I'm in the habit of ruining is my own). They said the notes on this episode, which viewers love, were especially harsh. "Bravo is the most brutal noting network that there is," they say. "The notes were, 'Was the editor asleep at his desk?' Then, after I addressed the notes, the next week was, 'Did a monkey edit this?'

"My producer was getting so upset because this is the best reality show we've ever seen. Like this episode is fucking amazing! What are they, fucking crazy?"

Another story producer I talked to said that the co-EP they worked for would actually rewrite the notes before delivering them to his staff so they wouldn't see how harsh the Bravo version was. A former Bravo exec said that they would also sometimes rewrite other executives' notes to soften the blow.

The notes start with the production vice president, who is in charge of the day-to-day operation on any show, including *The Real Housewives.*

They will watch the rough cut and send the notes to the production company. Then the senior vice president and the vice president will watch the fine cut and give their notes. Once those are addressed, Shari Levine, the head of the network, will watch fine cut 2. That is where the trouble usually starts. "She usually has a lot of notes, and they can often be different from what the notes were before," a former Bravo exec says. This is especially frustrating for editors and story producers who have to reverse corrections they've already made.

"Shari has famously harsh notes," a Bravo exec says. "She also writes them in shorthand, which contributes to the tone that's just very blunt and clipped. She's not mincing words."

Ryan Flynn and Kathleen French, the SVPs for current production who oversee the various *Housewives* franchises, aren't as terse. "They're not as harsh as Shari's notes. They can be harsh, but the volume of them is a little disheartening," a producer says.

The one person who everyone agrees gives delightful notes is Andy Cohen. "I remember Andy Cohen, his notes were always like, 'Oh my God, isn't so-and-so an asshole?' Like he was just funny and cute and like he was one of the viewers," says a producer who got notes from Cohen back in the early days of *Real Housewives*.

The change started in 2013 when he went from being a Bravo executive to now, where his main duty is appearing on *WWHL* and serving as the host of the various and sundry reunion specials across the networks. He still serves as an EP, and producers say he's paying attention in the weekly production meetings, but when it comes to individual episodes, he's only making some small notes on the picture lock versions. A Bravo exec familiar with his notes described them as "fine-tuning."

"He still plays a big part in *Real Housewives* in New York because that's his baby," says a producer. "But other than that, he's mainly just talent."

One editor says they understand why the notes become so crazy. "It's a billion-dollar franchise, so there's a lot of pressure, and I just think that everybody needs to piss on the cut to make it look like their own," they say. "Shari Levine is the last round of notes, so she has to see everybody has noted it. What I don't understand is, for the interest of saving money and time, why doesn't everybody just watch it together? Because inadvertently, you get notes from the underling and then the person above them, all their notes contradict. And it's really difficult to rip a show apart. It takes days. They blow up every act, and they want stupid shit. They want the most ridiculous things."

Dealing with executive insanity—which multiple people joked to me should be its own reality show—isn't the only downside of working on *The Real Housewives*.

"When I'm working on a *Housewives* show, I am more combative with my husband, and it is completely unconscious because you see the fight in the restaurant for thirty seconds, but I watched that fight and I recut that fight for months," an editor says. "I am stuck with that over and over and over again. It just permeates your brain, so I will lash out on my husband. I haven't worked on a *Housewife* show in a few years, and he always says, 'Thank God.'"

It's even harder for those in the field. "It is all-consuming when we're doing it," Darren Ward, the *RHONY* producer, said. "*Housewives* for me is about twenty-two weeks of my life. I get up, stop going to the gym, I'm just taking care of Housewives, answering Dorinda's phone call every morning, show up to scenes, go to the office, do it all over again. I love doing it. It does take a toll on our personal life for sure."

Kemar Bassaragh said that he once had a date walk out on him because he didn't understand why he had to pick up the phone when *RHOP*'s Robyn Dixon called him. The date did not accept "But Robyn never calls, I have to find out what she wants" as an acceptable excuse.

"You don't see your family. A lot of people have kids, they don't see their kids," says one producer. "A lot of the times, you have showrunners and producers that are based in LA, or based in New York, and are literally picking up their entire life and moving to Dallas, or Atlanta, or wherever to shoot a show away from their families, friends, and normal lives."

But that same producer sees there is a trade-off. Not only is it the steady work and healthy pay at Bravo, it's about being part of a certain universe. "These women are so fun. Normally, everybody's very excited to play ball, and participate, and it's fun to shoot these scenes and tell good stories," he says. "Whether the women are good or bad or making you laugh or cry, as storytellers, that's what we thrive on. Getting to work on these specific shows and franchises like this, they're so fulfilling because it's so much fun."

Being up close and personal with *The Real Housewives* is the ultimate Bravo experience, previous or otherwise.

THESE HOUSEWIVES FOUGHT THE LAW,
AND THE LAW WON

Kelly Bensimon:

> In 2009, she had to do two days of community service after pleading guilty to misdemeanor assault when she punched her then boyfriend in the face. And we thought her biggest crime was jogging in traffic.

Luann de Lesseps:

> On Christmas Eve 2017, she got so wasted that she let herself into someone else's hotel room in Palm Beach, Florida, and then refused to leave. When the cops showed up, she said she was going to kill the officer and kicked him. She spent two years on probation and mandatory alcohol counseling.

Kelly Dodd:

> The future *RHOC* star was arrested in 2014 for domestic abuse after a fight with her then husband. After therapy and mandatory AA meetings, the charges were dropped.

Teresa Giudice:

> The only Real Housewife to actually go to jail, Teresa and her husband, Joe, pleaded guilty to forty-one counts of mail, wire, and bankruptcy fraud in 2014. She spent a year in prison, and then Joe spent almost four years behind bars before being deported to his native Italy. Between a special about life without Teresa, all the episodes focusing on her legal battle, and the

book she wrote about life in jail, Teresa and Bravo have been profiting off her crimes ever since.

Brandi Glanville:

A 2010 DUI stop on LA's Sunset Boulevard led the future *RHOBH* provocateur to pay a $390 fine and go for alcohol treatment.

Karen Huger:

RHOP's grande dame wasn't so grand when she got probation for a DUI arrest in 2006.

Gina Kirschenheiter:

She was arrested for a DUI in 2019 in Orange County and got three years of probation and community service, but then almost went to prison when she didn't show up for a court date, as was captured on the show. Also seen on the show, she has to Uber everywhere.

Jacqueline Laurita:

She is in the staggeringly popular pipeline of women who assaulted a boyfriend and then ended up on reality TV. Her charge was in 1996 in Las Vegas.

NeNe Leakes:

Back in 1992, the RHOA was convicted of stealing $2,650 of service from her phone company and got two years of probation. Now she sells a T-shirt with her mug shot on it at Swagg Boutique. That's the way to turn it around.

Sonja Morgan:

In 2010, she blew a stop sign in the Hamptons and was arrested for DUI. Maybe that's why she still insists on taking the jitney out east?

Tinsley Mortimer:

She showed up on the front lawn of an ex-boyfriend's house screaming at him and insisting her purse was inside. She was arrested for trespassing in 2016, but it was her mug shot that got her cast on *RHONY.*

Marysol Patton:

Both the *RHOM* star and her mother, Elsa, who was featured on the show, were arrested in 2010 for DUI within months of each other. Marysol pleaded down her case and paid a $1,000 fine.

Kim Richards:

In 2015, she was detained for walking off with a shopping cart full of $600 worth of merchandise from a Beverly Hills–adjacent Target. (Okay, fine. It was in the Valley.) There was not a blue bunny among her haul.

Danielle Staub:

If you want to read all about her 1986 arrest for extortion and cocaine possession, by all means, check out *Cop Without a Badge.*

Jules Wainstein:

During her acrimonious divorce, the former *RHONY* star apparently licked her ex's car window and then bashed it in with a baseball bat before punching him in the face. She was arrested in 2020 following the incident. The couple is still not divorced.

Dana Wilkey:

The *RHOBH* "friend of" surrendered to the FBI in 2014 when it was suspected that she defrauded an insurance company of over $300,000. She later pleaded guilty to one count of "misprision of a felony" (which is knowing a crime was committed but not telling authorities) and served no jail time. She could have used those $25,000 sunglasses for bail.

Porsha Williams:

Has been arrested twice, once in 2014 for beating up RHOA castmate Kenya Moore at the reunion taping and the second time in 2020 for protesting for justice for Breonna Taylor. We're going to forgive her for that second one.

6

DON'T CALL IT A COMEBACK, CALL IT A TAKEOVER

HOW TO BUILD AN EMPIRE

Jen O'Connell had a problem. It was 2007, and she had just started as an executive at the production company Ricochet. Now she had to call the Real Housewives of New York City and tell them, well, that they were going to be Real Housewives of New York City.

"I was told that some of the Housewives we had cast before I joined were like, 'We don't want to be like *Real Housewives of Orange County*,'" she says. "The executives there were like, 'No, never, we would never. You're classier than that.' Then I had to call and be like, 'Great news, we're going to be Real Housewives.'"

The brilliance of the *Real Housewives* franchise isn't just in its blending of soap opera storytelling and reality television tactics but in the way it manages to re-create itself in different iterations all across the country (and eventually the globe). At first blush, every city seems the same, with identical graphics, intros, and rhythms, but they're all crucially a little bit different. It's like the trick of telling twins apart.

RHONY is more urban than *RHOC;* all the women, especially in the later stages of the show, have been single; and they drink a lot more than everyone else. Atlanta, of course, was the first ensemble mostly made up of women of color, but they're also the funniest city of the bunch and the ones who make up the easiest after a dispute. New Jersey has not only been as Italian flavored as an Olive Garden but it has also always revolved around families, first the Manzos and then the Giudices. Beverly Hills is the richest, with the best houses, but also the most laid-back. The LA ladies are slow to anger, but when they get something stuck in their craw, look forward to a whole season about one topic. Dallas has that deep Southern twang, and the Potomac gang has stayed pretty consistent in terms of casting, giving deep-seated feelings to their electric arguments.

Just as the cities have their different flavors, the ways they got developed are distinct as well. But of course, they all added up to become *The Real Housewives*.

Ricochet, where Jen O'Connell worked, was a British company whose biggest success in the UK and the US at the time was the show *Supernanny*, which saw professional nanny Jo Frost going into people's homes and teaching their children how to behave in sixty minutes (forty-two without commercials). They were developing a show called *Manhattan Moms* about rich New York ladies struggling with getting their children into private schools. So far, they had cast two women, Jill Zarin, a pushy Upper East Sider married to a fabric mogul, and Alex McCord, a former *One Life to Live* bit player who lived in (gasp!) Brooklyn.

McCord was iffy on the idea of being back on TV. "[It was] not a decision that we took lightly, and it did require almost a year and a half of persuasion by the production company, with constant calls and meetings," she later told *Newsday*. "At the end, I think that my family and I just kind of said, 'Oh, what the hell.'"

Zarin roped in some friends of hers to join the cast: Ramona Singer, who ran a successful company that bought overstock clothing and sold it to discount stores, and the Countess LuAnn de Lesseps, who was married to a Swiss count and still had an uppercase A in her name. They started filming some things when the second season of *RHOC* premiered to fantastic ratings. O'Connell says she got a call from Bravo chief Lauren Zalaznick saying they wanted to start a franchise and change the name from *Manhattan Moms* to *RHONY*.

"We had a better chance to be part of a franchise that was picking up steam, and so in the end, it was good news," she says. "But at first, there was a little suspicion about what it meant."

There was still a problem, though: there weren't enough Housewives. Christian Barcellos, then head of production at Bravo, called O'Connell up and said they might not green-light the show if they couldn't find another addition to the cast. "It was one of those friendly threats. Really what we were missing was the younger housewife," she says.

Jill delved deep into her Rolodex to recruit more friends, but they all kept dropping out because of work or family objections. Sonja Morgan apparently wanted to join the cast in season 1, but there were complications from her divorce. (To paraphrase her, she didn't divorce the banker, she divorced the bank.) The public would have to wait until the tumultuous season 3 to meet the self-styled straw that stirs the drink.

What happened next is something like the *Real Housewives* version of the legend of Lana Turner being discovered at the counter of Schwab's drugstore, except it actually happened. Jill Zarin took some producers with her to an annual event in the Hamptons called Super Saturday. First, there is an enormous sample sale of designer goods sold to raise money for breast cancer research. Since women with houses in the Hamptons can afford full-price designer duds, the sale brings out a lot of people not in the East End full-time who take the Hamptons Jitney (a fancy name for a bus) back to the city, laden down with enormous shopping bags. Then, for those with the real money, there's a polo match that draws the best and brightest of Hamptons society.

It was in the VIP section of the polo tent, where Jill and a casting producer ran into Bethenny Frankel, who was then fresh off a second-place finish in Martha Stewart's low-rated version of *The Apprentice*. Bethenny was billing herself, at the time, as a celebrity chef—or maybe a chef to celebrities?—and was hoping that getting her picture taken at a fancy event would give her some cred.

"Jill's husband, Bobby, brought over the producer. Bethenny shut down," Andy Cohen wrote. "She had nothing to say. But then her boyfriend . . . went into action. He opened up to the producer about his kids and his life with Bethenny. He was selling it; he was selling her."

Bethenny was apparently concerned with doing reality television again, especially after losing the first time around. Cohen was nervous about casting her for the same reason. Back then, having been on another reality show was like wearing a scarlet letter. Now, as people jump from *Big Brother* to *The Challenge* to *Marriage Boot Camp: Celebrity Edition,* it's almost inconceivable. Bethenny agreed to go on tape to audition for the show, and the brass at Bravo couldn't resist her brass. Her caustic humor shone through, and though she didn't fit the brief of the show or its title, she was the final member of the ensemble.

"[Jill] was asking me to meet the people from the show and literally begging me to be on the show," Bethenny later told the New York *Daily News.* "I was like, 'I'm not a mom. Nor am I a wife. Nor do I live in a house.' . . . but I just had a weird gut [feeling] that I should do it."

There has been a long-standing feud between Vicki Gunvalson and Ramona Singer, because Ramona says that *RHONY* is the show that really got the franchise rolling, whereas Vicki Gunvalson sticks to the facts and says *RHOC* was really the first one. I hate to say it, but I agree with Ramona. *RHOC,* though popular, was still seen as something of an anomaly, a show that had latched onto some trends and landed at just the right time. The only paper that covered the development of *RHOC* was *The Orange County Register. RHONY,* on the other hand, was happening right in the national media's backyard, and they were going to have huge opinions about it.

Also, *RHOC* was just a show. When *RHONY* came along, it all became a franchise.

"It means a totally different thing to be a housewife in New York than it does in Orange County," Andy Cohen told *USA Today.* "These women are as iconic to New York City as the other ones are to Orange County. It's dealing with a different universe, but they are still all seeking familial and economic nirvana."

That difference is something Bethenny Frankel discussed in her first interview about the show around two months before the show premiered. "I would not want to be portrayed as the women on *The Real Housewives of Orange County,* to be perfectly honest," she told the New York *Daily News.* "So that was a little scary. But who knows, maybe people in Orange County are saying that about me."

The first seven-episode season was filmed in a tight twenty-eight days. In a city like New York with location shoots happening every day, hardly anyone noticed.

Once word of the show was announced, though, the press pounced. *The New York Times* followed the women to a luxury lingerie party that was being filmed. Jill Zarin started popping up in trend stories about conspicuous consumption, including ones about people who were flying private jets from New York to Miami for the Super Bowl and about the Manhattan mothers who were hiring personal chauffeurs to pick up their children at school. (Jill, reportedly, did both.)

The opinions were flooding in, too. The cheeky, pre–Jared Kushner *New York Observer* followed a few of the women around before the premiere, and interviewed reality producer Michael Hirschorn about the show's brilliance. "I think [Bravo] found a seam of these upper-middle-class women who were highly vulnerable," he told the paper. "You had that sense that at any point they could fall through to the lower classes. There was a certain sense of grasping and striving and very human quality of holding onto the ledge of affluence. That made the drama quite compelling. Also, they're sort of unencumbered by taste." Devastating.

The vitriol from others, like *New York Post* TV critic Linda Stasi, was palpable. "Andy Warhol was so wrong," she wrote.

In the future everyone will not be famous for 15 minutes. Some people will be famous for one minute only which is about 59 seconds too long, in some cases.

Take the women who are about to—for reasons totally inexplicable to anyone with a sense of, er, reality—become reality TV participants on Bravo's upcoming cringemaker, *The Real Housewives of New York City*.

There must be a missing gene in some people that makes them unable to be content with a happy, healthy family, lots of money, and seemingly everything they (emphasis on they) want. These missing-gene types crave fame to go with their fortunes.

Um, *Keeping Up with the Kardashians* debuted the year before, and she reserved this hatred for the Housewives? This was all before the show had even premiered.

When the official reviews came out, they weren't any nicer. The *New York Post* gave the show zero stars. "While the five 'housewives' of this new Bravo series (one of whom is not actually a wife) surely represent a certain kind of woman who lives here, they in no way represent the vast majority of women married or single whom most of us know." This is the laziest and weakest of all criticisms. Like the cast of *The Real World* is supposed to represent all of America? No.

The New York *Daily News* at least gave the show one star. "Just a few more programs like *The Real Housewives of New York City,* and television will be able to start a whole new 24/7 channel. We'll call it 'Ridicule the Rich.' Only thing is, it would be nice if future programs in the genre would be a little better than this one, which is as shallow as its subjects." I don't know, I thought we already had *Ridicule the Rich* except it's named MSNBC.

The cruelest review belongs to Canada's *Globe and Mail*. "A show more frightening than *Taxi Driver*," Simon Houpt wrote, referencing the 1976 Martin Scorsese movie where Robert De Niro plays a lunatic who goes on an armed rampage. "Can a city sue for slander? Tomorrow night comes *The Real Housewives of New York City,* which may be the first on-screen portrayal of this town to achieve what even *Taxi Driver* could not: scaring people into staying away." Oh, come on. I've been to the Times Square Red Lobster. There is no scaring people away from the city.

Most reviews came from old men who were skeptical of reality television as an enterprise and resented having to pay attention now that it had stuck a thumb smack-dab in the middle of their borough. (Well, technically in the northeastern corner, but you catch my drift.)

Alessandra Stanley, then TV critic at *The New York Times,* was one of the few critics to understand the show. She didn't love it, but she got it. "The Housewives are hungry for attention, and even a bit desperate, and their entwined vanity and vulnerability distinguishes these kinds of arriviste reality series from competitions like *Project Runway* or *Top Chef,*" she wrote. "On those, viewers judge the contestants' ability to make clothes or prepare a meal. On *Real Housewives* they measure the gap between the image the heroines hope to project and what they actually look like through the lens of a reality television camera."

That's it, that's the Bravo wink that we've heard so much about. It was that irony that would capture an audience in New York and beyond.

The Wall Street Journal was also right about one thing. "The bloggers are going to have a field day . . . and as the cast of *The Real Housewives of Orange County* has already discovered, the bloggers can be cruel indeed." And they were. Both *New York* magazine and *Gawker,* at the time publications made by and for New York media, recapped every episode. Somewhere along the way, they started to fall in love with it, even when it was to relish in the fact that, thank God, not all women in New York were like that.

The premiere on March 4, 2008, scored 824,000 viewers, which may seem small but was impressive by Bravo standards. The audience would climb week after week, with the show averaging 926,000 viewers by the end of the month. That March, thanks in part to the success of *RHONY,* would be the network's best quarter to date. By the April 15 finale, Bravo had already renewed the show for a second season, and the finale drew 1.4 million viewers, 1.1 million of them in the eighteen-to-forty-nine-year-old demographic that makes advertisers hornier than Sonja Morgan looking at a "Men of the FDNY" calendar.

Those numbers were good enough to warrant a reunion special. The shoot, at the iconic Russian Tea Room, lasted seven hours and featured one very memorable moment. O'Connell, who was an executive producer on the first four seasons of *RHONY,* remembers the day fondly. Before filming even started, Alex's old nude photos leaked to the press and became something of a scandal. As they prepared the special, Ramona told producers, "That is against my morals and I refuse to talk about it and if you bring it up I am walking off the set."

"[The nude pictures] was the kind of thing we couldn't ignore. We had to address it because it was in the press," O'Connell says. "We thought, 'She can't walk off,' but then we thought, 'If she walks off, isn't that great?' So we told Ramona, 'We can't make any promises. If we do bring it up, we have to deal with whatever you do.'"

Of course, when the topic did come up, Ramona was true to her word and headed for the wings. This was the first *Real Housewives* walk off, something that would become a staple of the reunion for years to come. Also, isn't it quaint that Ramona, someone who has pooped on the floor twice to our knowledge, once got this indignant about a cast-mate's nude photo spread?

0 0 0

As Bravo looked to expand their empire, they chose an unexpected next city: Atlanta. More precisely, *Hotlanta.* That was the reality show pitched to the network by True Entertainment, renamed Truly Original in 2017. "Bravo was interested in expanding the series, and so the question became, without repeating what they had done, what would be new and different," one of True Entertainment's founders, Steve Weinstock, told *Atlanta* magazine. True apparently translated *different* as meaning different demographically, and started looking for a mostly Black cast. "So where are you going to find a high concentration of affluent African Americans? Atlanta comes up really quickly in the thinking. So we went to Atlanta and began to cast for a group of women who could work in the context of the franchise. One of the first people we talked to was NeNe Leakes."

NeNe recruited Shereé Whitfield, who she had known for years, as proven in a 2003 picture of the two of them in their most fabulous attire at an Atlanta Falcons game. *The Atlanta Journal-Constitution* ran a story about the trend of attendees putting on their Sunday best not for church but for the NFL, and included a quote from Shereé. "Women are accessorizing more," she told the paper. "In the past, women would be more suited up. Now, it's a nice pair [of] low-rider jeans, a [sleeveless] T-shirt, but the must-have is a nice purse with either boots or 3-inch stilettos."

In the article, Shereé is credited as the owner of Bella Azul boutique, an institution that did not survive until the show aired in 2008 and certainly would never carry SHE by Shereé, a line of joggers—yes, joggers—that is due in spring? Or summer? Spring/summer?

NeNe also asked her friend and fellow Realtor DeShawn Snow, who at the time was married to ex–NBA player Eric Snow, to join the cast. Kim Zolciak, the single white member of the cast, says that she met NeNe at the gym. Kim says she was walking around outside the gym with her trainer, smoking a cigarette, when NeNe approached her and told her that she should come shoot the pilot with her, DeShawn, and Lisa Wu Hartwell, the wife of former NFL linebacker Ed Hartwell (and ex-wife of R&B legend Keith Sweat).

Once the Bravo film crews showed up, rumors about the spin-off and the show's cast started spinning out of control. "There have been rumors galore that camera crews are floating around Atlanta for a possible spin-off of Bravo's Real Housewives reality show," *The Atlanta Journal-Constitution* reported in May, five months before the show's October 2008 premiere. "Bravo's publicists haven't been terribly forthcoming though they say they do test out shows by shooting material that may or may not become an actual show."

The official announcement of the show didn't come from Bravo but from a website called TheYBF.com, which stands for *Young, Black, and Fabulous.* It was an indication of how hotly anticipated a reality show about a group of affluent Black women was for some in the community. "After rumors of this new season have been going around for a while, it's official that Bravo is bringing the show to Atlanta," the site wrote just after the cast wrapped filming the seven-episode season in early June. "And four out of the five Housewives are YBF chicks."

YBF had the names, biographical details, and photos for NeNe, Shereé, Lisa, and DeShawn. As for Zolciak, she was described as merely as, "And another Housewife named Kim." Do you think her eventual enemy NeNe planted this story and told them to print a scorching read like that?

Two weeks later, Bravo officially announced the series. They even gave details about "another Housewife named Kim," describing her as a "single mom" but leaving out her relationship as a quasi–kept woman to a man known only as "Big Poppa" on the show. (He was later revealed in the tabloids to be real estate developer Lee Najjar, whose family was once on MTV's *Teen Cribs* showing off a palatial estate that includes a movie theater, music studio, and an in-home salon . . . for his wife.)

The series was a hit almost out of the gate, especially considering the first episode featured a classic confrontation between NeNe and Shereé, where Shereé threw a huge party and NeNe's name somehow didn't end up on the guest list. The episode scored just below a million viewers, but the show's second installment was up to 1.1 million. By the show's fourth episode, the audience had doubled, and the first-season finale had 2.21 million viewers, then the highest-rated episode in *Real Housewives* history. It was also the highest-rated cable telecast of the night. *RHOA* was Bravo's most-watched freshman series since *Queer Eye*.

"I was surprised at how successful it became and how much of a water-cooler sensation it was," Cohen told *Atlanta*. "It was different than anything else on TV. Even though it fits into the format we've created with the Housewives, I just don't think there are a lot of rich black people on TV, especially reality TV."

Apparently, the first time NeNe ever talked to Andy Cohen was when she called up and asked him if they could have a reunion special. She felt that after filming had wrapped, her former bestie Kim was talking trash about her and she wanted to set the record straight. Cohen naturally agreed—with ratings like that, a reunion special was never in question—and he had a front-row seat to the drama.

Rewatching the first season reunion now is funny. Far from the crystalized gowns that Atlanta would become known for, all the women are wearing clothes from their own closets, and the glam is minimal. Seated on opposite couches in the positions of honor next to Andy are NeNe and Kim. NeNe wears a purple blouse with a slouching cowl neck and her new short wig, a style that would become her signature, while Kim rocks a canary-yellow satin shirt with a black waistcoat. She's also sporting a cheaper wig than usual, her original nose, and lips without the filler that would turn them into balloon animals.

While the looks are subpar, the drama is signature *RHOA*. Ramona's walkout was nothing compared with the scene of NeNe shouting at Kim, "Close your legs to married men!" NeNe gets so upset at Kim that Lisa has to restrain her on the couch. *Housewives* had always been about conflict, but with the addition of *RHOA,* it became about fighting.

▯ ▯ ▯

The Real Housewives of New Jersey would do the Georgia peaches one better. Though it was the fourth show in the franchise to air, it was actually the third one produced and announced. In April 2008, six months before the *RHOA* premiere, Bravo announced the show at its up-front presentation in New York. "We debated a lot whether our next one after New York should be New Jersey because of two states right next to each other," Frances Berwick, then an executive vice president at the network, told the gathering. "But they felt very, very different from the New York Housewives, just in terms of the way they live their lives, their aspirations, their interests."

Berwick also played a short clip of the series, featuring two of the five women cast on the show: Dina Manzo and Danielle Staub. "Partly, it's a suburban life versus a city life," Berwick said of the differences between *RHONJ* and *RHONY.* "I think it is more family-based. There are a lot of close-knit communities."

One exec described it privately to the *New York Post* as "*The Sopranos* without the mafia."

Sirens Media, a two-woman operation founded in 2005, was signed on to produce. Casting started by looking at women in three different New Jersey towns. Where are you going to look for outrageous and outspoken women with hair as big as their taste for drama? Salons, of course. Casting directors struck gold when they wandered into Chateau, the Art of Beauty, the impossibly named salon in the McMansioned hamlet of Franklin Lakes. Producers showed up looking for a salon to film in, and owner Victor Castro thought instead of a "fabulous group of ladies" that were his longtime clients. He introduced them to Dina Manzo.

Dina would lead them to her sister Caroline Manzo, who is also her sister-in-law. Dina and Caroline are sisters who were married to brothers who were also business partners in a catering business and event space. It's all very confusing. Dina also brought in Jacqueline Laurita, who was married to Caroline and Dina's brother Chris, and her longtime friend Teresa Giudice, the only member of the original cast who didn't get her hair done at Chateau (comma) the Art of Beauty. At the salon, Jacqueline met a new friend, Danielle Staub—who, no one realized at the time, was a certified psychopath. These five women, with their complicated familial and personal bonds, would change the *Housewives* game forever.

But they were all a bit wary. "These ladies weren't about to enter into this show lightly or quickly and had many questions about the process and ramifications, questions unlike any we'd heard in the past," Andy Cohen wrote. "For instance: 'Has anyone been audited as a result of this show? Or wiretapped?' From the beginning, Caroline Manzo was their leader; everyone in the room seemed to defer to her. Teresa Giudice, an old friend of the Manzos whom we were eager to cast, dropped out of and then back into the show multiple times before we even started shooting." That doesn't sound like "*The Sopranos* without the mafia." That just sounds like *The Sopranos*.

After all the women signed on and the six-episode season was in the can, it sat on the shelf at Bravo for more than a year. The effects of *RHONJ* and its explosive shoot, though, were already having an effect on the rest of the series.

"The cuts of [*RHONJ*] were coming into Bravo, and you had tables being overturned, and it was like big and loud and fast," says an editor who worked on an early season of *RHOC*, which was in postproduction the same time as *RHONJ*. "[Bravo execs] would watch a cut from *New Jersey* and then a cut of *Orange County* and they would be like, 'No.' All of a sudden, our beautiful slow pacing was out the window. We actually shut down for a week for them to rejigger how we rolled out the story that season.

"We couldn't become New Jersey obviously, but we had to speed up our storytelling, the pace of the story, because that's what they were getting used to. All the franchises took on a faster pace of storytelling."

About a year after the initial announcement, on April 7, 2009, Bravo aired a thirty-minute preview of the series, which was mostly footage taken from the first episode. That preview alone got 1.43 million viewers. This was a hit in the making.

The main takeaways from the preview for viewers were Caroline saying, "My family is thick as thieves," an all-time classic *Housewives* line and an essential GIF for anyone with a tight group of friends, and just how much this whole thing looked like a real-life *Sopranos,* which had gone off the air two years earlier.

The mobster mystique was burnished later in April when both the New York *Daily News* and the *New York Post* ran articles about Albert "Tiny" Manzo, Dina and Caroline's father-in-law. He started the Brownstone, the catering hall run by their husbands. Tiny, who weighed 350 pounds, was murdered in 1983, and his naked body found in the trunk of his car with his arms and legs bound and four bullets in his torso. Apparently, he was killed after getting caught skimming from a Mafia casino on Staten Island.

After this there was the usual outcry from New Jersey residents about stereotyping. "Having lived in Franklin Lakes for 30 years, I have had the pleasure of meeting and working with citizens who place a high value on family, education, personal integrity and volunteerism," Diane Dobrow (no relation to Heather Dubrow) told Passaic County's *Herald News.* "The culture of conspicuous consumption is the exception in this town, not the rule. There is nothing 'real' about [these] Real Housewives."

As annoyed as New Jerseyans were about the show (and they would be even more annoyed about six months later when MTV's *Jersey Shore* created a full-on NJ reality boom), something about it clicked for the critics. Those who were giving *RHONY* zero stars eighteen months earlier finally got the appeal. Maybe they just became accustomed to the Housewives in general by this point, or maybe it was something about the New Jersey ladies themselves. Who knows? But they were on board.

"So I finished watching *Real Housewives of New Jersey,* which is about as real as most of the cleavage on the show, and I was thinking to myself, 'Good Lord, what a piece of trash. That was awful!'" the New York *Daily News* wrote. "Then I put on a Sinatra record and thought about it and realized the problem wasn't the show at all. It was me. I wasn't letting myself smell the roses. What I should have thought was, 'Good Lord, what a piece of trash. That was great!'" Amen, sister. That's what fans were saying all along.

The Washington Post agreed. "The show is supremely entertaining. Smartly edited and cleverly constructed—the George Washington Bridge serving as a visual transition—the series marks another auspicious entry to television's vast stockpile of Guilty Pleasures. It's the Tuesday-night series most likely to be talked about on Wednesday morning, the completion of many a question along the lines of 'Did you see that?'"

Our old friend Alessandra Stanley at the *Times,* who got this franchise from the beginning, couldn't stop her praise. "All those McMansions, swimming pools, boutiques, charity auctions and spa splurges have been merely rehearsals, introductory rounds leading to the apotheosis of the Bravo 'Real Housewives' franchise, *The Real Housewives of New Jersey,*" she wrote.

"The New Jersey housewives are more real and more riveting than their predecessors because, well, they are from New Jersey, and also because they so closely mirror the make-believe characters in *The Sopranos.* The best reality shows look like fiction."

The numbers for *RHONJ* were the best yet for a *Housewives* premiere, with 1.71 million tuning in to the first episode. And what an episode it was. Not only was there a ton of talk of everyone's "bubbies," which is how the ladies of Franklin Lakes say *boobs,* but we also saw Danielle get stood up by a guy she'd had phone sex with. The most memorable event for many was watching Teresa plunk down $120,360 for a room's worth of "French château"–style furniture for her new onyx mansion. She paid in a wad of hundreds pulled from her coat. "I hear the economy's crashing, so that's why I pay cash," she explained to the camera. No one bought it.

The real brilliance of the premiere, however, was that it started with highlights from the season to come, because this included the most iconic *Real Housewives* moment of all time: Teresa nearly upending a table in a blind rage. After showing us that moment from the finale, the episode rewinds months earlier to show us the peaceful women of New Jersey, leaving us to wonder how they got from A to Beatdown.

The highlights-preview tactic worked, because that final episode scored a whopping 3.47 million viewers, the highest for a *Housewives* episode at that time by far. The first part of the reunion scored another 2.89 million.

※ ※ ※

Next up was the franchise's only one-hit wonder, *Real Housewives of D.C.* Bravo had been working on the idea ever since Obama's 2008 election had made D.C. seem like it might actually be cool. (I lived there for ten years, and I can tell you the only thing cool about D.C. is the winter wind whipping off the Potomac.) Reality shows were finally giving our nation's capital a shot—in the case of the D.C. season of *The Real World,* a full twenty years into its run.

For the show, Bravo tapped the two-year-old Half Yard Productions, which was headquartered near the Capitol and had created hits like bridal shopping show *Say Yes to the Dress.* Half Yard was not only working on *RHODC,* but also a show called *Washington Social,* about the party scene in town. They had to fend off rival productions like *Washington Divas, Young Washington, Women of Influence,* and *Blonde Charity Mafia,* all of which were also putting out casting notices at the time.

Not surprising to anyone who has spent time in the 202, most of these never came to light. The problem is that people don't go to D.C. to get famous; they go to D.C. to get powerful. Those in the Beltway were savvy enough to know that the first power reality television gives anyone is the power to humiliate themselves. That's not a good look in anyone's home constituency.

"This is a city of discretion," Emily Miller, a former communications staffer for Senator Tom DeLay and Colin Powell, told *The Washington Post* after the announcement that the show was in development. "No member of Congress's wife is ever going to do this. They're afraid to do Facebook . . . They're not going to let a camera in a room that's going to affect legislation being passed or billions of dollars at stake."

Totally unhip to this, Berwick, general manager of Bravo at the time, announced the development of the show that May. "We're tapping personalities who are among Washington, D.C.'s influential players, cultural connoisseurs, fashion sophisticates and philanthropic leaders—the people who rub elbows with the most prominent people in the country and easily move in the city's diverse political and social circles," she said. The dream was probably to get senators' wives or maybe someone from an elite government agency. Cohen told the press that he would love a Democratic Housewife and a Republican Housewife fighting at a fancy dinner.

Just because no one wanted to be cast doesn't mean that everyone in town wasn't talking about who was going to do it. "Cocktail party chatter in Washington this weekend was all about Supreme Court nominee Sonya Sotamay . . . KIDDING!" blog *Political Machine* wrote. "Cocktail party chatter in D.C. this weekend was really all about who will be and who should be cast in the newest franchise of the Bravo reality show, Real Housewives."

Since D.C. is the only city with a more active media culture than New York, the gossips were spilling ink all over potential cast members. Ana Marie Cox, the political columnist who started the blog *Wonkette*, was rumored to be in the cast, but shot down the rumor quickly. There were also persistent rumors about Abigail Perlman Blunt, wife of Republican Missouri congressman Roy Blunt. It didn't work out, to be . . . straightforward.

Edwina Rogers, a Republican lobbyist who worked in the second Bush White House, got so far as to be followed around by Bravo's cameras. She talked to the Associated Press about the show: "What I find attractive is that it would show people the cute, fun, exciting, tender side of Washingtonians, and our unique culture," she said. Yeah, this lady is not *Housewives* material.

The Post soon reported that she was out, along with Republican fundraiser Lisa Spies, whom Bravo also put on tape. By September, the local gossip columns were spotting model agency owner Lynda Erkiletian, "socialite" Mary Schmidt Amons, and hair and makeup artist Michaele Salahi at events with cameras in tow. The cast would eventually add real estate agent Stacie Scott Turner, the first Black Housewife not on *RHOA,* and Cat Ommanney, a last-minute addition and new D.C. resident. Her husband, Charles Ommanney, was a photographer who covered the White House for *Newsweek* for years, the only direct tie to politics that anyone on the cast had.

The women knew each other, sort of. Mary and Lynda were longtime friends, and Lynda had hired Michaele at one point. She had also sued Michaele and her husband, Tareq, who lived on his mother's winery in Virginia and threw an annual polo tournament in D.C., his big claim to fame.

"I had filed a lawsuit against them three years before we did the show," Lynda says. She says her agency provided models for a polo event, but afterward, Tareq tried to pull a Donald Trump and stiff her with the bill after services were rendered. She did the smart thing and took it to court. "I did get my money," she says. "They brought it to my agency, because they had written two bad checks, and I was like, 'All right, guys. That's enough.' So they came to my office and paid me in person." This wouldn't be the last or biggest story about the Salahis after they crashed a White House state dinner, but we'll get to that in a minute.

❦ ❦ ❦

The women of *The Real Housewives of Beverly Hills* were a lot more familiar with each other, but not because of lawsuits. Alex Baskin, the cohead of *RHOC* production company Evolution Media and a cocreator of *RHOBH,* says that Bravo approached them years before the premiere to see about casting a show in the 90210 zip code that Brandon and Brenda Walsh made famous. Andy Cohen, who has been on the wrong side of so many decisions regarding *The Housewives* (but is big enough to admit it), says he wasn't a fan because it seemed redundant with the Orange County ladies just a forty-five-minute ride (without traffic) down the coast.

As with Half Yard in D.C., Evolution had a tough start with casting. "It was very difficult at first," Baskin told the *Reality Life* podcast. It's probably because everyone in 90210 is either trying to get famous the old-fashioned way or too involved in the entertainment industry to know it could lead to ruin. But unlike in D.C., eventually that icy reception melted. "I couldn't tell you what it was, that hit the tipping point for us, but all of the sudden some people who we were approaching who might have been reluctant to do it reached back out to us, and we had a flood of people who wanted to be on the show."

Andy writes in his memoir, "Soon we had a line of Bentleys outside the production company and a lobby full of fur-wearers with similar faces (I'd later learn they all shared the same surgeons), as five hundred women tried to become Beverly Hills Housewives." Soap star and *Melrose Place* alum Lisa Rinna was interested in joining early on, which prompted Evolution and Bravo to talk about exactly what they wanted from the show. Should it be about the Hollywood elite, or should it be about "regular people" adjacent to fame? They decided on the latter, reasoning that if the show were full of former and current actresses, everyone would think it was fake. This pushed Lisa Rinna out of the running, at least until season 5, when the docusoap would go after her and fellow soap star (and denim jumpsuit devotee) Eileen Davidson.

In January of 2010, Radar Online reported that Lisa Vanderpump, an English restaurateur, was joining the cast. Considering Lisa's alleged allegiance with the tabloid—and the role it would play in season 9's "Puppygate" scandal—one could guess where the leak came from. The tabloid also confirmed former child stars Kyle and Kim Richards, who are also the aunts of Paris Hilton.

At the time of casting, Kyle and Kim were apparently deciding between rival reality projects. On one hand, there was *Housewives* and on the other, a reality project called *3 Sisters,* which would be about Kyle, Kim, and oldest sister, Kathy Hilton, the mother of Paris (and Nicky and Barron). We all know the choice they eventually made.

Around the same time, Brenda Richie, mother of Nicole and ex-wife of Lionel, was rumored to be in the mix. "Richie is rumored to be joining the cast of the Bravo network's *Real Housewives of Beverly Hills*," *The Philadelphia Inquirer* reported. "The marriage between Brenda and Lionel ended violently with Brenda beating up Lionel and his then mistress but soon to be second wife." Um, excuse me? How was this woman not cast? She seems like a natural.

Cedric Martinez, Lisa's longtime employee who lived and filmed with her during the show's first season, describes the casting process differently in his self-published memoir, *The Real Permanent Houseguest of Beverly Hills*. He claims that Lisa and Kyle met at the auditions and soon started texting relentlessly, trying to figure out how to get on the show. (In the book, Cedric does come off as quite disgruntled, so grains of salt.) After Lisa's successful audition, she told the producers about Martinez living in her house, so he needed to be interviewed during her home visit. "Before I got miked," he writes, "Lisa took me to the side and gave me some last-minute advice.

"'Remember you have to make me look good. If you don't it's a one-way ticket back to London for you. Trust me.' She smiled but more than advice this was definitely a threat. A threat I knew she would have executed without thinking twice."

According to Cedric, Lisa was obsessed to distraction with being cast on the show and would have done anything to make it a reality. Lisa, of course, got the gig, but by that time, Cedric had moved out of the house because he wasn't getting along with Lisa or her husband, Ken Todd. Thinking her role was in jeopardy, Lisa convinced Cedric to move back in with them.

Having this grand English lady with a gay former model living with her seems like just the kind of thing Bravo was looking for. Andy later told *The New York Times* what they wanted in the *RHOBH* cast. "To say that we're going to do *The Housewives of Beverly Hills* is a daunting task because it almost seems too obvious," he said. "It's such eye candy. It's dazzling to look in these women's homes. I wanted Beverly Hills to pass what I call the Jackie Collins test. We wanted the city and the Housewives to be aspirational. We wanted other women to look at them and think, I want that."

In March 2010, Bravo announced that the show was happening, and two weeks later the full cast leaked to the press. It included Vanderpump, the sisters Richards, as well as Adrienne Maloof, whose family owned part of the Sacramento Kings NBA team and the Palms Casino Resort in Las Vegas. Maloof lived across the street from Vanderpump in a gated community. She had heard about the show through a friend of her husband's, Paul Nasif, a plastic surgeon. She told BravoTV.com in a video interview that she was reluctant to do the show, but Paul talked her into it because it would be great for her business. It would be great for his business, too, since Evolution Media now makes his reality show, *Botched,* where he and Terry Dubrow, a plastic surgeon married to *RHOC*'s Heather Dubrow, fix plastic surgery mistakes.

Also on the show was Taylor Armstrong, an Oklahoma native whose husband, like so many others on *The Housewives* with inexplicable sources of income, was an "entrepreneur." A late addition to the cast was Camille Grammer, a former *Club MTV* dancer, producer of the TV show *Medium,* and most importantly, the third wife of *Frasier* star Kelsey Grammer.

Camille was friends with Kyle because Kyle's husband, dreamboat Mauricio Umansky, was the Grammers' real estate agent. She was a perfect addition to the show, giving it that Hollywood glow without casting fading starlets. Like Adrienne, she was initially reluctant, but Kelsey talked her into it, even agreeing to appear on camera.

It would soon become clear why she had hesitated. In July, after filming was wrapped, Camille filed for divorce after she got a text from Kelsey that simply said, "I don't want to be married anymore." It came out later that he was having an affair with thirty-year-old flight attendant Kayte Walsh, whom he met when she served him on a plane. They were married fifteen days after his divorce was finalized. It seems like this show and the attendant attention was either Kelsey's way to keep Camille occupied or his parting gift to her on his way out.

Now the show was left with a bit of a problem. How can you look at the cast and think, "I want that," when "that" equals a divorce? (Camille did get a $30 million settlement, so maybe we do want that?)

It also created an interesting dynamic in the show, which critics picked up on. The *Boston Herald* wrote, "'I think it's time for Camille to get a little attention,' [Kelsey] tells the camera. Given how their situation has changed, that could be perceived as a curse. Whatever sympathy Camille might earn with the viewers quickly soars out her McMansion windows. She brags that she had her two children by a surrogate to maintain her figure. She rotates four nannies, two at a time, to care for the kids. 'I'm here all the time for my children,' she assures us. How could they possibly tell?"

Camille, with her porcelain sneers and shoulder shrugs, was a reality TV villain right out of the gate. Not only did she seem like she was above the other women, she also immediately clashed with Kyle. When Camille accused Kyle of saying no one would be interested in Camille without Kelsey, Kyle shot back, in a remark that will live on in GIF infamy, "You're such a fucking liar, Camille."

There was the dramatic tension of knowing that this was a woman who, by the end of the season, would be laid low. Just as she was holding her huge houses, vast wealth, and A-list status over the other women, something was happening to strip her of all of that. It wasn't building someone up to knock them down; it was like sorting through the rubble of your nemesis's house.

This wasn't the only unhappy household on the show, and the dark underbelly of these women's lives is what became fascinating. "What we have in Beverly Hills, of all places, is real: real desperation, real money and real unhappiness," the *New York Post* wrote. "For the first time, I feel like I'm watching real life—albeit with fake faces."

The reviews, of course, were mixed. There were still the (mostly male, mostly middle-aged) critics who hated this enterprise from hair extensions to high heels, and they hated this iteration as much as any others, but it's almost as if their opinion doesn't count. If you had a friend who notoriously hates denim, why would you ask them for an opinion on your jeans?

You're probably wondering right now what genius Alessandra Stanley at *The New York Times* thinks. Well, her review mostly compared *RHOBH* to the still-unfolding *RHODC* White House Party Crasher scandal, but she ended with this prescient line: "Beverly Hills is the nominal setting, but the real milieu is Bravo." She's right. People weren't tuning in because it was set in Beverly Hills; they were tuning in because, by this point, they knew exactly what Bravo was offering and that it would always deliver.

RHOBH definitely delivered. The first episode had 1.53 million viewers, holding on to almost all of *RHODC*'s audience. See! Watch one, you watch them all. Ratings would take a little bit of a dip but would rebound and then grow week over week, particularly because the first season of the show is one of the all-time greats.

☒ ☒ ☒

Things started to sour in 2011 with the premiere of *The Real Housewives of Miami*. In 2009, Bravo aired a show called *Miami Social*, a sort of *The Hills*–esque premise about a group of young male and female friends dating and partying their way through the Latin capital of North America. It bombed.

In 2010, the little-known MC Filmworks would produce a show called *Miami Social Club*. The series was to focus on a group of six women in Miami, each of whom would host the rest for dinner at her house. Hopefully, fights and drama ensue. "As we've said so many times, Bravo is not filming The Real Housewives of Miami," the *Miami Herald* wrote in March 2010. "Finally putting that rumor to rest is the announcement of the voyeuristic network's new series, *Miami Social Club*."

The announcement included the cast: Lea Black, the wife of famed prosecutor Roy Black; PR guru Marysol Patton; gallery owner Adriana de Moura; Cristy Rice, the ex-wife of Miami Heat's Glen Rice; her best friend and fellow NBA wife, Larsa Pippen (wife of the Chicago Bulls' Scottie); and Alexia Echevarria, self-proclaimed "Cuban Barbie" and owner of the local *Venue* magazine. Also hotly rumored to be in the cast (probably of her own devising) was South Beach drag queen Elaine Lancaster, a bosom buddy of Lea's. She would eventually appear in a number of episodes but would never make it full-time.

Of course, Bravo soon decided *Miami Social Club* was too risky and just called the thing *RHOM*. The *Miami Herald* never issued a retraction. The show's promotion to *Housewives* status came at a tumultuous time; though Bravo had already been airing promos for the fourth season of *RHONY* (the first without Bethenny) starting in February 2011, it pulled the show to keep editing the episodes and replaced its original premiere date with *RHOM* instead.

"We decided yesterday that our best bet was to give ourselves a little breathing room," Andy Cohen said in the press release. "I would rather get the show right than rush it to air." Page Six reported that Bravo was rejiggering *RHONY* because the women, including new Housewife Cindy Barshop, were just too boring. Cohen, of course, denied this.

No one could really get excited for Miami, though. "Has Bravo run out of fun cities?" the *Boston Herald* asked in its review. "[*RHOM*]—the seventh installment in the cable network's unnervingly popular unscripted franchise—plops down in 'The Magic City' for the most yawn-inducing series. The ladies are so desperate to be noticed, they recycle bits from other shows: One hits a shooting range to learn how to fire a gun. Another hosts a dinner party in which the guests shuffle through a cooking lesson."

The *Miami Herald,* being the hometown paper, had the classic worries about representation of their fair burg (though they did it with a pile of self-deprecation as big as the piles of coke in *Scarface*). "But best of all may be that *The Real Housewives Of Miami* will forever erase the unfair image that television has created of Miami as a corrupt hellhole of narco-traffickers, serial killers and transvestite porpoises," the paper wrote. "At last we will get recognition for our unacknowledged but indisputable achievements: Our indolent trashiness. Our incandescent superficiality. Our establishment, beyond the shadow of a scientific doubt, of the inverse ratio of breast silicone content and IQ points."

What did our old girl Alessandra Stanley, the Cassandra of *Real Housewives* criticism, think? She didn't even review this iteration. Sick burn. Her colleague Ginia Bellafante wrote, "The Real Housewives formula is feeling stale. The louche locations all seem to blend into one another, and every kitchen is the same, with acres of space and double-wide Sub-Zero refrigerators that seem to hold enough food for an Olympic swim team."

Only 1.2 million viewers turned up for the premiere, the highest rating of the season, which showed viewers weren't in love, but the numbers did hover around one million per episode. Maybe the problem was burnout, or maybe it was the product itself. The seven-episode first season was oddly laid out, since the dinner parties were still the center of the narrative; compared to all the other shows, then in their primes, it was a bit of a snooze. The breakout star wasn't even one of the Housewives but Elsa Patton, Marysol's plastic surgery–addicted mother who proclaimed herself to be a witch.

Bravo renewed the series and ordered a whopping fifteen episodes, but it completely reshuffled the cast. Cristy and Larsa were out, and Alexia demoted herself to "friend of" status after one of her sons was in a near-fatal accident and she needed to spend time caring for him. They were replaced with Victoria's Secret model Joanna Krupa, lawyer Ana Quincoces, always-smiling dentist Karent Sierra, and plastic surgeon's wife (and frequent patient) Lisa Hochstein.

They also fired MC Filmworks and tapped a new production company, Purveyors of Pop, whose founders were producers on other *Housewives* seasons. The second season was much better, featuring simmering tensions between Karent and Adriana, and Joanna and Adriana. The latter's spat boiled over at a lingerie-themed party at Lisa's house, where Joanna pursued Adriana down a hallway, and Adriana turned around and clocked her in the face. That was the season's most-watched episode, but even that didn't make much of a dent.

Season 3 came around in 2013 and was a poor showing. "They were trying to imitate an *Atlanta* or a *Jersey* or something that had more ratings by doing things that were like just weird," Ana says about the third season, where she was a "friend of." "It looked contrived to me."

The ratings didn't budge, even as Lea and Adriana's friendship unraveled in a less compelling version of the Jill-and-Bethenny drama several years earlier. Bravo never officially canceled the show, but they didn't renew it either, leaving it like an abandoned sandcastle. (In 2021, the streaming service Peacock announced it would revive the franchise, but it's unclear if any of the original cast will return.)

"I think that they were very disappointed, and they were trying desperately to revive it," Quincoces says of the cast after season 3. "They would try to get together and do stuff on social media so that they looked like they were all really still friends." It never worked. (Maybe they needed Elaine Lancaster after all.)

※ ※ ※

Maybe because of the Miami and D.C. disasters, it would take another four years for the network to announce the addition of its two newest cities, Potomac and Dallas, both of which would debut in 2016.

Much like *RHONY, RHOA,* and *RHOM* before it, these shows were initially conceived as something else. *RHOP* was called *Potomac Ensemble* and featured a cast of Black and mixed-race women in the tony town inside of the D.C. Beltway. It was (and still is) produced by True Entertainment, the same production company that makes *RHOA.* Unlike other shows, there were some older, established women like self-appointed grande dame Karen Huger, married to the "black Bill Gates," and Gizelle Bryant, the ex-wife of a Baltimore mega-pastor, alongside up-and-coming society types like restaurateur Ashley Darby and Katie Rost, whose biggest claim to fame was that she used to date hip-hop mogul Russell Simmons. The show was supposed to be about etiquette and what it's like for young people to break into society. That's why the word *etiquette* has more prominence in the first season than the hair extensions that have become synonymous with Housewifery.

"So Bravo came to me and said, 'Is there another African American cast out there that isn't derivative, that doesn't have the same feel?'" *RHOP* EP Steve Weinstock told *The Wrap.* "And we were able to find this incredible group of women in Potomac, Maryland, of all places. I would liken it to the feeling of ['80s prime-time soap] *Falcon Crest.* They're very upwardly mobile, they're the daughters of very old-monied families. The social grace, etiquette, class, these sorts of things are important in the context of their everyday interactions."

Weinstock said that they looked at casts in Philly, Houston, and Baltimore, but everyone else was trying to be "too-Atlanta-y," which they didn't find in Potomac. Shari Levine, VP of current production at Bravo, told *The Baltimore Sun* that they found this cast when looking into Baltimore. They settled on the nucleus of Karen, her friend Gizelle, Gizelle's bestie, Robyn Dixon, and mutual friend Charrisse Jackson Jordan. Both Charrisse and Robyn were wives of former NBA players. Ashley and Katie were added later as outliers.

As for Dallas, there were rumors of a *Housewives* flag being planted in Texas soil as far back as 2010—mostly coming from Heidi Dillon, a TV producer who was connected with some of the figures behind *RHOM* creator MC Filmworks, who claimed interest from Bravo as far back as 2007. In 2011, the rumors kicked up again that "socialite" Gina Ginsburg and Dillion were "interviewing other potential cast members" for a project that was potentially *RHOD*. They might not have been far off, since Andy told *Variety* the same year, "We've tried to mount a Texas [incarnation), but we never hit the nail on the head with casting."

In 2012, the gossip got very intense, and some local blogs shared a purported cast list for the program. Several of the women on the list issued statements that they weren't doing the show.

"I have been apprised of a report including me in the cast of the *Real Housewives of Dallas*," Lisa Troutt, the wife of Dallas-based communications billionaire Kenny Troutt, said in a press release. "While I am familiar with the Bravo series, this information is completely erroneous. I am in no way associated with *Real Housewives of Dallas* or Andy Cohen." It sounds like she's denying she and Andy had an affair!

Tiffany Mullen, wife of Mike Mullen—the CEO of a company that provides infrastructure to oil companies—issued a similar press release. Rhonda Aikman, the ex-wife of Dallas Cowboys great Troy Aikman, did not deny the rumors; when she was arrested for drunk driving that year, several outlets identified her as a cast member on the nonexistent *RHOD*.

Fast-forward a few years, and Bravo finally got its Texas women. Originally called *How to Make It in Dallas*, *RHOD* was created by Goodbye Pictures, a production company whose principals were formerly associated with *Project Runway*. The idea was for the show to compare the haves and have-nots of Dallas society, featuring people like Brandi Redmond, a former Dallas Cowboys cheerleader who has a lot of money and little class, and former carny LeeAnne Locken, who is well connected in charity circles but has shallower pockets.

Along with Brandi and the hotheaded LeeAnne, the cast also included registered nurse and plastic surgeon's wife Cary Deuber; Brandi's bestie, Stephanie Hollman, who is married to a locker magnate (you know, like in schools and gyms); and Tiffany Hendra, an actress who was in several Skinemax erotic movies. Heidi Dillon, despite years trying to get on a reality TV, was not cast and would have to be happy to be background filler in a few scenes. Don't worry, she still lists those appearances on her personal website.

RHOP would be first to debut, and Bravo made the smart decision of airing it after *RHOA*. The season premiere got 2.5 million total viewers, which Bravo, yet again, was touting as the highest-rated franchise premiere. While the first twelve-episode season averaged an excellent two million viewers, things have dwindled from there, even as the show now has the twenty-ish episodes per season that all the other shows have.

The ladies of the least famous city on the roster have become favorites for die-hard fans who tune in for the shocking drama of Karen Huger's tax debts, Ashley's forever cheating husband, and the physical altercation between later additions Monique Samuels and Candiace Dillard that led to them filing assault charges against each other. All this goes on while the women have trenchant debates about race in modern America and on modern American television. Seriously, this thing could power a million American studies thesis papers.

RHOD didn't fare as well as its new sorority sisters in Potomac. The premiere cracked one million viewers, but just barely, and has yet to achieve that number since, despite being renewed for five seasons.

░ ░ ░

By this time, major outlets weren't really reviewing new *Housewives* franchises. *The Washington Post* ignored the *RHOP* iteration despite it being in their backyard. But since Texas is obsessed with itself, a couple of local newspapers waded into the murky waters of reality criticism. The *Fort Worth Star-Telegram*'s assessment is actually quite astute.

"For fans of Bravo's Real Housewives franchise, it's not so much whether any new edition of the series is good ... but whether it lives up, or more accurately down, to what has come before," the paper wrote. "The explosive Atlanta and New Jersey versions—where table-flipping and wig-pulling are the order of the day and at least one Housewife and two spouses have gone to jail for financial flimflams—as well as the original Orange County show are the standards by which all their spawn are measured. Some, like Miami and Washington, D.C., don't make the cut and get canceled. Sadly, judging from the first two episodes, The Real Housewives of Dallas may be joining them."

Though Potomac and Dallas aren't the blockbusters that their older, wiser sisters are (the fact that so many *Housewives* fans are sleeping on *RHOP* is an actual, literal crime), they still are distinct voices—different stars in an ever-growing constellation. And we can't wait to see which star will appear in the heavens next. (Spoiler alert: That celestial body ended up shining on Salt Lake City, of all places.)

REAL HOUSEWIVES INTERNATIONAL EDITIONS, RANKED

———

Bravo's hit franchise hasn't just spread across the country, it's gone around the world.

So far, there have been fourteen international versions, two of which—*The Real Housewives of Bangkok* and *The Real Housewives of Jersey* (the English island, not the state of New Jersey)—hadn't aired in late 2020 when this list was made. Of the remaining twelve, five of them were canceled after only one season, so maybe there's something a little bit American about this phenomenon. Here are the rest of the international franchises ranked from worst to best.

12. **The Real Housewives of Sydney (2019):** This dreck is what happens when you get a group of women pretending to be other Housewives they've seen before and who only want to fight.

11. **Les Vraies Housewives (2013):** The French version of the franchise couldn't find any women actually in France to cast, so they had to hire a bunch of Frenchwomen living in Los Angeles instead. *Mon Dieu!*

10. **The Real Housewives of Athens (2011):** The show came out just as the Greek credit crisis was at its worst. It's not only slightly depressing but also forced the women to hold back on the ostentatious displays of wealth.

9. **The Real Housewives of Toronto (2017):** The second Canadian outcropping committed the cardinal sin of all *Housewives* shows: it was boring. Maybe Canada is a little too nice for this game.

8. **The Real Housewives of Hungary (2017–Present):** Known in its home country as *Feleségek Luxuskivitelben,* the cast features not one but two models. So far, it hasn't made its way into English, but since I speak the international language of "reality TV," I would give it a shot based on the trailers.

7. **The Real Housewives of Auckland (2016):** A ratings smash from the outset, this still only lasted one season, possibly because one castmate used the N-word when referring to a Black costar. While it led to constructive conversations about racism, it was not the kind of attention the network wanted.

6. **Me'usharot (2011–2013):** The title for this Israeli version translates to "Rich Women," but it was a lot realer than others, with women fighting about the problems with Palestine and one woman whose mother was a Holocaust survivor who was experimented on by Dr. Mengele.

5. **The Real Housewives of Vancouver (2011–2013):** Die-hard Housewives fans swear by the first Canadian rip-off, but I could never get past the hollow passive aggression.

4. **The Real Housewives di Napoli (2020):** It has yet to be translated into English, but just looking at the Housewives, a mixture of aristocratic women and new money, shows no one does tacky glamour like southern Italians.

3. **The Real Housewives of Johannesburg (2018–Present):** The only African version (so far) features a diverse cast and some discussion of race and the difficulties of living in South Africa, even if it sometimes misses out on the fun.

2. **The Real Housewives of Cheshire (2015–Present):** This English version has packed in a whopping twelve seasons in only six years and focuses on the WAGs ("wives and girlfriends" of soccer players) in the northern suburb. The production values look a little cheap, but the drama is just as expensive.

1. **The Real Housewives of Melbourne (2014–???):** Spanning five seasons of delightful fights Down Under, this series introduced

us to lawyer Gina Liano, and the only thing bigger than her ego is her hair. The only installment in the *Real Housewives* diaspora to hold a candle to its American sisters, it has not been officially canceled, so we keep hoping, in vain, that new seasons are to come.

PROSTITUTION WHORE!
THE GOLDEN AGE OF HOUSEWIVES

On June 16, 2009, Bravo aired an episode of *The Real Housewives of New Jersey* that would go down in pop-culture history.

Sisters Caroline and Dina Manzo, their sister-in-law Jacqueline Laurita, and their longtime friend Teresa Giudice are surrounding a table with their spouses and children. Also at the table was the last member of the cast, Danielle Staub, Jacqueline's friend who had been rubbing everyone else the wrong way for the entire season.

Their large party is alone in the basement of a New Jersey restaurant, the kind where the white tablecloths drape to the floor and the embroidered beige fabric on the chairs fails to look as fancy as it thinks it does. Just as Teresa is finishing up a sex story about her and her overly muscled husband, Joe, Danielle places a hardcover book on the table.

She says nothing, just takes a sip of water and peers coyly through her bangs, waiting for a reaction.

"Look. The book," Teresa says in Italian, rolling her eyes.

"I feel like we're getting ambushed," Jacqueline says.

"I'd like to talk to all of you for a minute," Danielle says. "I brought this book with me, because it seems to be haunting me." She's addressing Caroline and Dina, who are seated across from her; Caroline's adult son, Albie, is next to Danielle and looks like he wants to take off his skin, set it on fire, and then run screaming into the damp New Jersey night.

"There's a lot of lies written about me. There's a lot of lies spread about me. I didn't appreciate that people had to talk about me behind my back. This was written by my first husband. There are two truths in this book. I was arrested, and I did change my name. I was never a prostitute, I was never any of the other things mentioned in here. I would like to say that I feel flattered—"

"Can I stop you right there," Dina says.

"Be good," Caroline warns, patting her on the back.

"No, you can't," Danielle interjects.

"Yeah, she could," Teresa says, wineglass in hand. "You knew we were going to find out about the book eventually, so if you were really our friend, you should have told us."

"Are you done yet?" Danielle says, getting hotter.

"No. Are you done yet?" Teresa, like a playground bully, retorts.

"No, I'm not done. I just begun."

"So I just begun, too," says Teresa, who has never heard of a debate society.

"When I'm done, you can lay into me all you want, but right now, I have the floor," Danielle continues.

"Okay, finish," Teresa says. Dina, wearing a baby-blue sleeveless dress, walks around the table and puts her hands on Teresa's shoulders as she lowers herself down to share half of Teresa's chair.

As Danielle monologues, Teresa says, "Should we get the kids outside?" The camera flashes to her eldest daughter, Gia, no more than seven, fidgeting at the kids' table nearby. Everyone agrees to have the nanny take the kids into the next room.

"We're all adults here, and we'll act accordingly," Caroline says in her best schoolmarm voice. "Say what you need to say."

Danielle accuses Dina of taking the book out in public and telling everyone in town its lies. She says it literally made her sick. "I sat home alone, throwing up with diarrhea for three weeks because of you. For what reason would you do this other than to make yourself feel better?"

"I never had the book in my hands, and that's the god's-honest truth," Dina says.

"When I'm done, I'll tell you I'm done," Danielle says.

"Let her speak," Caroline says. She stretches out one arm to silence Dina at the end of the table. "But do me a favor. Speak to me. Because I'm the one that told them."

Danielle takes a minute to process. "That is not what I heard."

"Well, that's a lie. And let me tell you something," Caroline says, pointing her finger across the table.

"Don't point your finger at me," Danielle says a few times as Caroline rolls.

"You are attacking my sister, and I will not sit here and allow you to attack my sister when it is not true," Caroline says, her temper thinly controlled. "Let me tell you something about my family. We are as thick as thieves, and we protect each other to the end. I am the one who showed the book. If you have something to say, you say it to me."

"It must be very comforting to you to sit there and be a nice, cozy family," Danielle says. "But I will not turn the other cheek. When I'm attacked, I'll attack back."

"Jacqueline, why don't you tell her the truth!" Dina, now back in her chair next to Caroline, shouts down the table.

"The two of you brought it into the salon and were telling everyone, and the same person who told her about it told me," Jacqueline says.

"I did not find out about that book on our own. It was the three of us who found it together," Dina says, pointing to herself, Caroline, and Jacqueline.

"No, you said, 'Come over to the computer, look what I found, look what I found,'" Jacqueline says, clapping gleefully. "I saved your ass and didn't even tell her until this minute. You're a liar, Dina!"

Danielle looks at Jacqueline across the table and mouths the words *Thank you.*

"You are two-faced. You are not her friend. I am so done with this," Dina says to Danielle, taking her purse and walking toward the exit but not able to fully tear herself away. In the frame are several sound technicians, camera operators, and producers, unable to get out of the way as the chaos unfolds around them.

"I didn't want this," Danielle says quietly. (As if.) She shakes her head and looks down at the table.

"You didn't want this? Why'd you bring the book?" Caroline says, voice dripping with incredulity.

"I wanted clarity on this. I wanted to clarify this. And I'm supposed to say I caused this. I didn't look this up and find it," Danielle says.

"We're not talking about the past, we're talking about the present!" Dina shouts, standing back next to Caroline.

"The past is very much in the present, thanks to you."

"But why did your ex-husband write that book?" Teresa says, breaking her silence. "Obviously, something in that book has to be true."

"I told you, Teresa, were you not here?" Danielle is angrier than ever. "There are two things in the book that are true." She holds up two fingers and ticks them off as she speaks. "Name change. I got arrested. Pay attention. Puh-lease." Danielle turns away from Teresa and back toward the sisters Manzo.

"I am paying attention. Obviously, there has to be something else. It's not just name change and arrested," Teresa says. She ticks off two fingers, aping Danielle, her fingers, wrists, and neck dripping with different strands of gold.

"There has to be something else. Were you stripping? You prostitution whore. You were fucking engaged"—Teresa's hands slam down on the tabletop, her eyes bulging, face red—"nineteen times!"

Then it happens. She puts both hands under the table and heaves upward. "You stupid bitch!" she yells. There is a small "Whoa" from one of the husbands seated nearby, who have been silent up until now.

Then she does it again, this time with her palms on the edge of the table, lifting and pushing it into the adjoining table, which had been covered with the same tablecloth for a banquet effect.

A chasm opens between the tables, and it swallows plates, glasses, pitchers, and a bottle of wine that spills first on the tablecloths and then on the brown, patterned wall-to-wall carpeting under everyone's feet.

Teresa bellows incomprehensibly as her husband leads her off into a dark corner, away from the action. Dina is alongside them, trying to touch Teresa's face, which seems, at that moment, like putting her paw too close to a bear trap. "You fucking bitch!" Teresa screams one more time as the screen cuts to black and we're whisked off into a commercial.

We didn't know it at the time, but we were living in the golden age of *Real Housewives.*

The "table flip" scene (though, let's be honest, it was more of a table *shift*) had everything that *The Housewives* promises us. There is at least the veneer of wealth in this fancy though tacky restaurant. There are explosive revelations, ever-shifting interpersonal relationships, and just a little bit of violence. The fans don't know who to believe, who to love, who to hate. We believe all of them and none of them. We love them all and hate them all and we love them all for making us hate them. Above all, like all the best *Real Housewives,* it is unexpected. We had never seen anything like it, and we couldn't have even said that this is what we wanted to see, but once we saw it we would never be able to look away.

This is *Real Housewives* at its creative peak, riding the razor's edge of aspiration and humiliation, feuds and blind hatred, unseen chaos and outright litigation. While there would be many scenes in the next decade that would come close to this, none has ever topped it.

At the end of 2009 and into 2010, *Housewives* would be as good as it would ever be creatively and was riding a ratings and zeitgeist high, all while the delicate balance of all the things that make it great was threatened by a brewing political scandal.

Unlike that New Jersey restaurant's cleaning crew, the Housewives had plenty to celebrate in 2009. Across the river, everything in the machine was running as smoothly as a freshly Botoxed forehead. *RHONY* wrapped its second season—featuring its newest Housewife, Kelly Bensimon, and her infamous jog in Big Apple traffic—in May with an average for season 2 of 1.67 million viewers, up more than 500,000 from the season 1 average. It was like season 2 saying to season 1, "I'm up here and you're down here," just like Kelly said to Bethenny.

In October 2009, the *RHOA* finale, which featured the first SHE by Shereé fashion show (or as NeNe's friend Dwight Eubanks called it, "a fashion show without fashions"), clocked nearly three million viewers.

In November, *RHOC* debuted its fifth season. Jeana Keough left after several episodes and was replaced by Alexis Bellino, leaving Vicki as the only OG left in the roster. This is the season when the 2008 financial crisis really hits the women—when Lynne Curtain finds out on camera that she's been evicted from her home because her husband wasn't paying the rent, and Vicki and Jeana have a falling-out because an investment home they went halfsies on lost a ton of value in the housing crisis. The premiere would score 2.58 million viewers, the highest ever for the series, and the highest ever for a *Housewives* premiere.

But all of this was prelude, in my opinion, to 2010: what might go down as *The Real Housewives'* best year ever.

A big reason for this was the premiere of *The Real Housewives of Beverly Hills,* with an all-time classic debut season. Its first peak was episode 9, "The Dinner Party From Hell," when Camille invites all the women, plus Kyle's friend, "the morally corrupt" Faye Resnick, over for dinner. Also in attendance are Camille's friends Dedra Whitt and Allison DuBois, the real-life psychic who inspired the TV show *Medium,* which Camille produced.

Most of the night was quiet, with the cast sitting in high-backed, maroon fabric chairs (what is it with high-backed fabric chairs and these women?) for two staid hours. Then Allison, who had been inhaling giant-size martinis, starts acting out. She gives clipped answers while pulling on an e-cigarette to Kyle's and Lisa's repeated requests at a reading.

That sets off a spiral of bad behavior around the table, and what happens next is riveting television. Camille calls out Faye, Nicole Brown Simpson's former best friend, for posing for *Playboy* after the O. J. Simpson trial; Allison tells Kyle that her husband "will never emotionally fulfill you"; Taylor gets up from the table shouting, "Enough!" to try to stop the squabbling. It might have been hell, but it clocked 2.12 million viewers, a high for the series. It is also, to this day, the best self-contained episode of *Real Housewives*.

"What I most remember about [the dinner party] is that Allison Dubois had some conversation about the showrunner of [*RHOBH*] season 1 and didn't think she was interesting for TV," Baskin said on *Reality Life*. "Obviously, no one could be more interesting than Allison was. The fun of it for everyone involved—and the women didn't have fun at the time but looking back on it—was that it was nuts. It was completely real, obviously, and really strange. Just a very memorable night."

The season's other blockbuster event was the simmering over of tensions between Kim and Kyle at the finale's rooftop party. Kim showed up drunk, she and Kyle got in a fight, and Kim stormed off. Kyle followed her sister to her limo, and everything that the two had tried to hide from the public for the season's thirteen episodes came out. Kyle called Kim an alcoholic and said that she and her husband wouldn't support her financially anymore. Kim accused Kyle of stealing her house, which didn't make much sense at the time, but, well, Kim was drunk. It is a moment of reality television gold, one that seems almost particular to *The Real Housewives*, when the veneer falls away and we see the sadness in these people's lives.

It was not easy for either Richards, and the day after the finale, Kyle put out a statement via Bravo saying, "This has been difficult for our entire family as we both said and did things that we regret. My sister and I love each other very much. We want to move forward and put this behind us." Maybe the 2.76 million people who tuned in to the episode, the season's highest, would help to comfort her.

RHOBH wasn't the only boon in the *Housewives* universe in 2010. In May, the second season of *RHONJ* launched, with 2.33 million viewers tuning in to watch what would happen now that everyone on the cast was done with Danielle Staub. The real highlight of the season, however, was the season's tenth episode, "Country Clubbed," which saw the annual fashion show hosted by local "designer" boutique Posche turn into amateur-hour *GLOW*. Initially, it seemed like the kind of event not even a suburban mom would enjoy, but after this episode, people would pay top dollar to attend a Posche Fashion Show no matter where or when it was held.

Greg Bennett, a friend of Caroline's son Albie, was at the legendary event as Teresa's "gay date." "When shit really started to go down I was nervous because I was young and had a job and didn't want to be super associated with it," he says, specifically remembering the aftermath of when Jacqueline's daughter, Ashley, pulled out chunks of Danielle's weave in a fight.

"Out of nowhere it was chaos. It was ten times more chaotic than you see on TV," he says. "I remember being outside after Ashley pulled her hair, and she is like, 'Where is Greg? I need Greg,' and I was hiding behind a bush smoking a cigarette, and *no,* I did not go to her. In the moment I was smart enough to know that she was not who I needed to be consoling on national television."

With more than three million viewers, the episode would be the season's peak before the first part of the reunion special, which saw Teresa so worked up that she grabbed Andy Cohen by the shoulders and pushed him back into his seat as he tried to pull her away from Danielle. Oh, those were good times indeed.

In October, the third season of *RHOA* premiered, replacing Lisa Wu Hartwell with Phaedra Parks, attorney for fellow Bravolebrity Bobby Brown, and Cynthia Bailey, a former supermodel. The season finale featured Cynthia's ill-fated marriage to Peter Thomas and had 4.38 million viewers dying as Cynthia's mom and sister tried to prevent the wedding by hiding the pair's marriage certificate. It was the highest-rated *Real Housewives* episode of all time, a record that would stand until season 6's battle royale at NeNe's pajama party. (Episode title: "Peaches Divided.")

Though it wasn't as highly rated, *RHONY*'s third season aired in March and, for my money, is still the best single *Real Housewives* season of all time. It includes such classic moments as Luann recording "Money Can't Buy You Class," Ramona's bug-eyed walk in Brooklyn Fashion Weekend, Alex saying, "While you're in high school, I'm in Brooklyn," and Ramona tearing into Bethenny about how she ruins all her relationships on the world's longest walk across the Brooklyn Bridge.

The dramatic undercurrent of the season, however, was the dissolution of the relationship between Jill and Bethenny. Always the Lucy and Ethel of the group, they were not only the comic relief but also often the audience surrogates, rolling their eyes at the wider cast's ridiculous airs. That all started to crumble as the show was set to film.

The day before Jill's meeting with producers to talk about what was going on in her life in advance of filming, she got a message from Bethenny saying that she should "get a hobby" and that their friendship was over. It was the opening salvo in a fight in which Bethenny accused Jill of wanting too much credit for her success and looking to ride her coattails, while Jill felt Bethenny was ungrateful for everything she'd done for her, which tacitly included Bethenny getting on the show in the first place.

"Jill and Bethenny had worked together in the past to create different scenarios on the show," says Darren Bettencourt, Jill's then manager. "I think when that message came through, Jill saw that as a sign that was the narrative she was supposed to jump off of, because the cameras were going to start rolling." Bettencourt says Jill figured things would blow over quickly. "Maybe it would be a three-episode arc in the story."

Things did not blow over and got only more and more heated as the season went on. "I remember Jill being very surprised," Bettencourt says. "They kept asking her how she feels about it, and it became a topic of conversation amongst her and all of the other girls. Jill, at that point, was cognizant that it was going to be a major story line."

Andy Cohen wrote about the feud in his memoir: "'No!' I thought. 'These women are ruining everything. For us and for themselves!' I had a terrible feeling that the crack in this beloved friendship wouldn't resonate with our audience and that it would spell the end of the show." Once again, Andy was wrong and fans were enthralled.

Things all boiled over at the end of the season when Ramona took Bethenny, Alex, Kelly, and newest addition, Sonja, on a trip to St. John to celebrate before her vow renewal. Jill couldn't make it because she had a prior trip planned with her husband, and Luann stayed behind because, I don't know, she wanted to start her music career or something? The episodes documenting this trip would become a triptych known to fans as "Scary Island," and they will live forever in infamy.

Things started well enough, with Ramona slurring, "Turtle Time!" while doing a swivel-hipped dance to get the party started, as though stirring a cauldron of unripe regret. The day after Ramona's dance, things seemed off with Kelly as she badgered Bethenny about the difference between her being a "chef" and a "cook." By the time they reached their luxury villa, Kelly was on the verge of a full-fledged breakdown.

The dinner that night is still miraculous to behold. Kelly accuses Bethenny of being a vampire and trying to kill her, while eating gummy bears from a bag and talking about "satchels of gold" and "Al Sharpton" until no one can understand what she's saying. Kelly later claimed she wasn't drunk or on drugs, but she sure as hell seemed like it. Bethenny finally shouts at her to "Go to sleep!" repeatedly, to no avail.

Kelly claims that she had an anxiety attack because all the other women teamed up against her and were bullying her, though at least on this trip, all the conflict seemed of her own making. "I was toxic, you couldn't touch me at all," she said on the show's one-hundredth-episode special. "No one wanted to go around me, no one wanted to be near me. Everyone was like, 'What is wrong with Kelly?'"

On the same special, taped four years after the incident, Bethenny offered her own review. "I think she's extremely sensitive and extremely fragile, and I guess she perceives that as bullying," she said. "Kelly was not built for reality television. She couldn't take the heat in the kitchen, so she wants to blame us for ruining her reputation. Not being true to who she is ruined her reputation."

Kelly viewed Bethenny as the chief bully, and it seems she still hasn't forgiven her. In a 2019 interview for the *Out in the Wild* podcast, she accused Bethenny, who was pregnant on Scary Island, of not caring for her unborn child to the point that Kelly was afraid she would miscarry. She also says Bethenny tried to control everything the night of her breakdown. "She would literally scream into the camera, 'This is not what this scene is supposed to be about!' and I was like, 'What is going on here?' You can't do that," Kelly says. "It's not fair. She's trying to be the executive producer or the Kim Kardashian of *Housewives,* fine. But she created such a disconnect between Bravo and us, so there was so much animosity and underlying tension."

On a subsequent appearance on *Watch What Happens Live,* Bethenny said that she heard the podcast and that, just like back on Scary Island, Kelly seemed unhinged.

For the producers, the filming was frightening as well. "I wasn't there [at Scary Island], but I was on the phone with our showrunners every day, hearing everything that was happening," says Jen O'Connell, who was an EP at the time. "I thought it was scary, and we needed to make sure that if at any point if people needed to leave if it was too much for them and we needed to protect it. We were just following the drama. There was nothing else to do but see what happens next. And it got pretty wild, and then Kelly left early, and that was the right decision." For the short remainder of the season, Kelly would be back to her batty self, but fans would never forget.

Darren Ward was the field producer tasked with taking Kelly home early, but she left a note for her castmates letting them know she was gone. "I flew with Kelly on the plane back home," Ward said at Bravo-Con. "She was angry, and she wanted to get back to the city. She wasn't sure if she belonged in the group anymore. That whole experience was very surreal. Something like that stays with you."

That morning, Ward was in for another surprise when he got to the airport. "A plane had just landed. As we were walking down the corridor, Jill and Bobby passed us," he said. "We couldn't talk to them, but they were headed to the house to surprise the ladies." Jill had booked a private plane to bring her and Bobby to St. John so she could pop in on the women for a day and then head off on her originally planned Caribbean vacation. When she got to the villa, though, Ramona turned her away. Jill left in tears.

Ward says producers knew she was going to pull this stunt and book the plane, but they had no hand in it at all. It was Jill's doing, and it ended disastrously. "For Jill to do what she did, as much as I loved her back then, she was very obnoxious," Ward said. "I think she got what she deserved."

At the time, Jill's relationship was fractious with most of the women who were still in the house, particularly Bethenny, and she didn't understand why they wouldn't want her interrupting their spa day. To her credit, she had no clue of the trauma Kelly caused the night before and that no one would be in the mood to deal with Jill's antics that morning.

The season finale, the episode after Jill got sent packing, featured a lunch between Jill and Bethenny, and Ramona's vow renewal. It had 2.64 million viewers, the biggest for the season and still a series high.

As the season wrapped up, Bravo immediately aired the special *Bethenny Getting Married?* which would eventually be called *Bethenny Ever After.* The original ten-episode run focused on her impending marriage to her fiancé, Jason Hoppy, while pregnant. The premiere had more than two million viewers, which Bravo touted in press releases at the time as the highest-rated series premiere in Bravo history. This proved that Bethenny was a bankable solo star, not just a part of the ensemble.

"We waited a long time to [have a spin-off] with Bethenny," Andy told the blog *Crushable.* "I'm really more focused on the ensembles. With Bethenny, we had lightning in a bottle and I never expect lightning to strike twice. I think that was a really unique situation. We really focused on the motherships in each city, as it were. I don't think that there's going to be a wave of Housewives spin-offs coming your way."

Once again, he was wrong, as Caroline Manzo, Kim Zolciak, Kandi Burruss, Tamra Judge, NeNe Leakes, and others would get spin-offs focused on their weddings or lives beyond the show. But Bethenny was special. Her series would run for three seasons, about as long as her marriage. In 2011, she sold an interest in her Skinnygirl Margarita brand to Jim Beam for a reported $120 million, proving that *Housewives* could be a path to serious riches.

The flagship shows would never again capture the magic that was 2010. Likewise, no Housewife would have a payday as big as Bethenny's—yet she's the exception that still drives the whole franchise. Every subsequent Housewife signs her contract thinking that she is going to be the next Bethenny. So far, nearly one hundred women have been wrong.

░ ░ ░

The suits at Bravo were probably coasting toward a nice, quiet holiday season in the fall of 2009, where they could celebrate a banner year with big bonuses and a boozy staff Christmas party. That would all be derailed on November 14, the date of Barack Obama's first state dinner at the White House, which was to be interrupted by Michaele and Tareq Salahi. These future stars of *The Real Housewives of D.C.* would soon be better known as the White House Party Crashers.

This was the drawback of coasting in the gray area between TV-gold drama and real-life disaster, as *Housewives* did at its peak. Sometimes disaster won out.

RHODC's Lynda Erkiletian says that the Salahis had misled producers from the get-go. Because Tareq's mother wouldn't allow filming inside the house on the family's winery, she tells me, the couple broke into a mansion whose owners were on vacation to throw a lavish party for their casting tape. Then never bothered to pay the caterers or bartenders.

Obama's state dinner was honoring the prime minister of India, with whom Tareq claimed influence on camera because his polo match that year was against the Indian national team. The Salahis brought the Bravo cameras in tow for their whole big day, starting with filming Michaele for seven hours at a salon in the city's ritzy Georgetown neighborhood where she got her hair and makeup styled and got into her red-and-gold, sari-inspired gown. She wore $30,000 of borrowed David Yurman diamonds, which allegedly took the designer three tries to get back from her.

After their town car (full of cameras and producers) was turned away at the East Gate of the White House, the Salahis walked up to the first checkpoint, where an official told them they were not on the list. A woman at the gate nevertheless forwarded them on to the next checkpoint, saying, "They can figure it out."

This was as far as the camera was allowed to go; the last we see of the couple on TV is them kissing, Tareq in his tux, Michaele in red, as a light rain falls around them and they walk into a darkness that might as well be infamy. The pair post photos on Facebook of themselves in the dinner and with Obama and Joe Biden.

The cameras were there again the next morning as the Salahis woke up in a hotel room, reviewing the photos of the night before, including a famous one of Michaele with Biden, her hand resting seductively on his chest like they're in a Kay Jewelers ad. "It's just such a wonderful moment that we're going to treasure forever," Tareq says to her.

Even that morning, though, Tareq gets a message on his BlackBerry that interrupts their idyll. *The Washington Post* is reporting that they snuck into the party. On camera, the two wave it off as an insult both to them and the Secret Service, who would never let two people not invited into the party. But they seem to have underestimated how quickly media sleuths work, especially if you help them out by posting the evidence yourself.

This security breach would have been an international incident no matter who perpetrated it, but the news that they were filming a reality show—a *Real Housewives* show, at that—was just the kind of bludgeon the press needed to beat them to death. Politicians got in on the circus, too. The only thing that can unite the red and blue sides of Washington, it turns out, is their disdain for the reality television arts and sciences. Suddenly, months before it was set to premiere, everyone knew about *RHODC* and its scam-artist power couple, and everyone had something to say about their particular American dream.

The Post's gossip column, Reliable Source, named the Salahis their People of the Year for 2009 and wrote, "The Salahis took what could have been an enjoyably seedy little horse-country melodrama and catapulted it into the gossip stratosphere with one fateful night at the White

House that exposed the dark secrets of our decade's major growth industries: national security and reality television."

They were on cable news around the clock, in every paper, and splashed across every tabloid like the proverbial headless body in the proverbial topless bar. A sketch on *Saturday Night Live* mocked the two, and they were grist for late-night talk show monologues for months. *Law & Order* ripped the case from the headlines for its own episode.

When a *Post* reader complained about the blanket coverage in June 2010, just before the season premiered, the paper's ombudsman reported that *The Post* had 110 stories about the couple, with enough content to fill an entire novel. More than thirty reporters and researchers had contributed to one newspaper's coverage of the story.

The deeper the press looked, the more it found about the Salahis. Apparently, the couple had pushed a Defense Department employee for days about securing an invitation and were told explicitly not to come to the dinner, because they were not invited. The UK's *Telegraph* reported that Tareq emailed the producer of a UK reality show, *MTV Blaggers!,* about a group of people who crash high-profile events. "I am wondering what technique you would suggest we use for a formal engagement, black tie event, state event? . . . What has been successful in the past and what should we look out for?" he inquired.

The press also uncovered that the pair crashed a fundraiser thrown by the Congressional Black Caucus in late September—off camera, but when the show was filming—by sneaking in through the kitchen. It is unclear if this was practice for their big game or just meant to burnish their image as up-and-coming socialites. The CBC did a better job than the White House and asked the pair to leave when they discovered there was no invitation. To add to all this, there were the shady business dealings and unpaid bills any petty grifter leaves in his wake.

In all their press appearances, including a December 1, 2009, interview on *Today* (not coincidentally, Bravo is owned by NBC), they maintained their innocence. "We were invited, not crashers," Michaele told Matt Lauer. "And there isn't anyone that would have the audacity or the poor behavior to do that. The White House is the most—it is the house, and no one would do that."

The Secret Service and the FBI each requisitioned Bravo's footage of the day in question. By December 3, the U.S. House of Representatives Committee on Homeland Security requested that the Salahis appear at a hearing into the matter. They refused to attend. The committee then officially subpoenaed the couple to appear before them in January 2010.

Before the hearing, Tareq told his local Virginia newspaper, the *Loudoun Times-Mirror,* "It will truly be a historic moment . . . Not since the 1950s has Congress held hearings of such a historic nature," possibly alluding to the anti-Communist McCarthy hearings. Just like everything with the Salahis, it was a bit of a letdown despite the hype. Tareq and Michaele exercised their Fifth Amendment right not to self-incriminate and didn't answer any questions. No, this is not where Andy Cohen got the idea for his classic *WWHL* game Plead the Fifth.

"This was not a hearing looking for information. This was an opportunity for a public flogging," Stephen Best, the pair's attorney, told, who else, *The Washington Post.* He's not entirely wrong. After further investigations into the security breach and a grand jury convened to look into whether the Salahis broke any laws, no formal charges were filed and no fines were paid. The price these two had to pay for misbehaving while under the influence of reality TV was public humiliation.

A fact many people forget: there was a third person who crashed the party that night. One Carlos Allen did not appear at the hearing and did not have a grand jury opened looking into his behavior. The Salahis might have had a similar fate were it not for their fame-mongering and brazen attempts to deceive the public once they got caught.

It's not like there were *no* consequences. Tim Kaine, then governor of Virginia, asked Tareq to resign from the state's tourism board, and the Department of Agriculture investigated a grant he had received in connection to the vineyard. Sponsors also dropped out of Tareq's signature polo event, though he continued to list many of them as sponsors anyway.

For Bravo, the incident threw production of their show into chaos.

It happened right at the end of filming and suddenly made weeks more work for the cast, who met to talk about the fallout of the Salahis' behavior. Castmate Stacie Scott Turner says, "People assume that because we know them, I'm fearful that they'll think we're like them." Unfortunately for her, the assumption that she was like them—not just the Salahis but every Real Housewife, every aspiring reality star—was made as soon as she put her pen to her contract.

The Salahis continued to be a nightmare while promoting the show's August 2010 debut. Lynda describes a scary incident while the cast and several producers were having dinner at the Hilton Hotel. When producers told Tareq he couldn't attend the show's launch party, he freaked out.

"I saw him push Michaele, because I've always, always felt that he was controlling and abusive with her. Always," she says. "So he came over the table [toward the producers], and when he did, I stood up and said, 'Tareq, you've got to bring it down. What are you doing?' And he threw his wine at me. I had water, and I threw that at him. I never should have thrown anything at him. But it was just unbelievable . . . From then on, they had to sequester him and get bodyguards for us, because we had to be separated."

There was also an incident backstage at *The View*, when the women were interviewed live by hosts Joy Behar and Sherri Shepherd. When things got away from the White House during the interview, Whoopi Goldberg walked out on set, touched Michaele lightly in her arm, and told everyone on the dais to get back to the White House stuff. After the segment, Michaele accused Whoopi of hitting her; Tareq started taking her picture, claiming he had evidence of her assault, which is when Whoopi says she "let him have it." The exchange prompted Whoopi to explain the whole incident in another segment, putting further out of reach what she had been looking for in the first place: answers from the Salahis.

No one would ever get those. Even in the show's reunion, the pair dissembled on every question they were asked, not only about the White House but about things like whether or not Michaele was ever a Redskins cheerleader. The simplest questions led to a Möbius strip of bullshit.

By the time *RHODC* finally aired, everyone knew what the show was going to be about. "This was the first time the public would have any significantly preformed opinion on any Housewives cast members before the show even premiered," Andy wrote in his memoir. "And those preformed opinions were ugly."

The premiere delivered ratings—1.62 million, the highest-rated premiere after *RHONJ*'s. But viewership for the rest of the season's nine episodes flagged, with only the second part of the reunion slightly outperforming the premiere as viewers tuned in to watch Michaele's verbal gymnastics.

The audience for *RHODC* was the oldest for any *Housewives* franchise, which is hard when networks are only after eighteen- to forty-nine-year-olds. All in all, it didn't really connect with Bravo's core audience. "The level of discourse on this show is different," Andy told, yes, *The Washington Post,* on the eve of the show's finale. "For people who expect to see table flipping or wig pulling, that was never going to happen on this show."

It was quickly canceled, the only *Housewives* show to last one season, and Andy later swore it's because the Salahis left a stink that wouldn't wash off. That wasn't all; every couple on the show got divorced after it aired, like some kind of *Poltergeist* curse. The only cast member who didn't get divorced was Lynda, because she wasn't married. She did break up with her boyfriend shortly after.

Charles Ommanney, husband of the show's villain, Cat, had so many regrets that *The New York Times* did a whole profile on them. "In a way, I was naïve and foolish to sign off on doing this," he told the paper. "But, at the end of the day, it was innocent. I wanted happiness for someone I was in love with. I put all my reservations aside and said: 'Go for it. Do it if it makes you happy.' Then I regretted it. I lost touch with everyone, and mix that with my marriage falling apart and the show taking over, it was very sad."

The strangest divorce, naturally, would belong to Tareq and Michaele

Salahi. Just as everyone was starting to forget their names, in September 2011, Tareq called the police because he could not locate his wife. She had told him she was going by her mother's house, but when Tareq called her mother, she said Michaele had never stopped by. Michaele told police she had left Virginia of her own accord and didn't want her husband to know where she was. While Tareq was appearing on the local news talking about plots to kidnap his wife, she had really run off with Neal Schon, the guitarist for rock band Journey, with whom Michaele had a short-lived love affair years before she'd met Tareq.

Tareq should have seen this coming. Shortly before calling the police, he received an email from Schon's account that contained only a close-up photo of his junk. It would be described in court documents as a "very large penis." This was accompanied by a short voice mail message on Tareq's phone that said, "This is Neal. I'm fucking your wife."

Naturally, a lawsuit followed, with Tareq seeking $50 million from Schon for scuttling the business deals he had in the works with Michaele. The suit was later settled for $12,000 and a year's worth of mortgage payments, according to tabloid Radar Online. Michaele and Schon were married in 2013 in a pay-per-view special and remain hitched to this day.

A 2016 profile of Tareq in *Washingtonian* magazine says that, at the time, he was cashing in on his reality fame by renting out his house on the vineyard for $200 a night and was about to launch an affordable wine called Housewinos. It never materialized.

I'M RICH, BITCH

HOW THE HOUSEWIVES CASH IN
(OR DON'T)

hate the question-and-answer period. After a perfectly good event, here comes some yahoo on the microphone to talk about how he once went on a spiritual sojourn through Prague that reminded him so much of whatever it is that the audience just listened to. I curl my toes in disgust when I hear the phrase, "This is more of a comment than a question." No. I'm sorry. Sit your ass down.

That said—at BravoCon in 2019, one of the day's most electrifying exchanges happened when a woman named Erica got up at the Producer's Tea panel, where five veteran *Real Housewives* producers from across the franchise talked about life behind the scenes.

"So, who pays for the trips?" she asked. "It's always someone's trip. Someone gets to decide who picks the rooms, how rooms are decided, they decide the itinerary, supposedly. Can you tell us the details?"

Glenda Cox, who works on *Real Housewives of Atlanta,* was the first to respond. "I have a question for you: Who do you think pays for the trips?"

"Bravo!" Erica exclaimed as fans shifted expectantly in their seats.

"Some of these are really freaking glamorous, so I don't know that all of these ladies are dishing out this kind of money for this kind of plan."

Kemar Bassaragh, who has worked on *RHOA* and *Real Housewives of Potomac,* said, "I don't know. It's whatever you think it is."

"You can't say that!" an incensed Erica said. "I'm asking you."

"Why can't they pay for their trips?" Cox asked. "Look at them, they are friends."

"So the Housewife whose trip it is pays for the whole thing?" Erica, the Woodward and Bernstein of Housewivery, asked. "That's the deal?"

"They can chip in. When I go with my girlfriends, I chip in," Cox replied.

"I chip in. I pay for my own trips," Bassaragh said as well.

And the crowd started to boo.

That's the thing about the Real Housewives. They're supposed to have these glamorous, unattainable lifestyles, and we often see how much money they're spending on shopping trips or we read about how much their houses cost. But Bravo is never transparent about their salaries, who pays for their parties, and what kind of freebies they get for being on the show. The fans know the truth—that there are all sorts of deals going on behind the scenes. Why can't the network just acknowledge it?

To get the crowd to calm down, Darren Ward, a veteran of *Real Housewives of New York City*'s best seasons, said, "The trips are always rooted in something that's really going on in the show. It is based on something that the ladies really want to do. It's places that they really want to go to. It's places they've been to before."

That, obviously is somewhat true, especially when it's a trip to a Housewife's hometown or to her vacation home. Andy Cohen said onstage at the Tribeca TV Festival in 2018 that Ramona has been trying to get the show to go to Aspen for almost a decade, to no avail. (Get it? A VAIL!) At the same panel, when asked who paid for the trips, Cohen said, "It's a combination," and the crowd booed him then, too. "You're booing us?" he said from the stage. "We came out on a Sunday and you're booing us?"

A year later, at BravoCon, the answer was a little different. While

Ward was speaking, we could see a woman on the side of the stage with an earpiece and a clipboard, the universal accoutrements of a "PR maven," getting into a tizzy. She then walked out and whispered something in Cox's ear. When she left the stage, Cox looked at the woman still standing at the microphone in the middle of the aisle.

"What's your name?" she asked.

"Erica," she said, suddenly almost sheepish.

"A little birdie just told me to tell you . . . Bravo pays for the trips," she said with a broad smile.

The room erupted in applause. This is what the fans want: to be told that we're not stupid. We want the acknowledgment that what goes on behind the scenes is really what we think it is. Sure, it's best for the trip to have an organic basis, like when Bethenny took the women to Mexico for a tequila-tasting trip for her Skinnygirl Margarita brand. However, it's not like she got them access to an exclusive factory that wouldn't have had them otherwise. They totally went somewhere that is used to hosting tourist groups.

There have also been plenty of bogus trips, like when Meghan King Edmonds dragged everyone to Ireland to "find her ancestry" and was left wandering around a small Irish town asking if anyone was her nineteenth cousin three times removed. However fake the idea, though, trips are always worth the hassle for the fans. It was that trip to Mexico where Luann fell into a bush, all the women got into the pool naked, and Ramona had to wrap her face to protect a recent chemical peel. Iconic moments happen when the women are out of their natural habitats, whether it's Vicki being wheeled to the hospital in Iceland, Shereé and Marlo getting in a fight in South Africa, or Brandi slapping Lisa Vanderpump in Amsterdam—oh! or Lisa Rinna threatening to choke Kim Richards on the same trip. I don't want to scroll through my friends' trip pics on Instagram, but I will never stop reliving these.

Trips keep the women together and out of their comfort zones—a recipe for tensions boiling over and drama ratcheting up to the next level. There's nowhere to hide; if you get in a fight with someone at dinner, you have to confront them about it the next day at breakfast. It's also a treat for fans at home, watching our girls swan around ridiculously ornate hotel rooms in Dubai with sharks swimming past the beds, for instance. But all of that costs money, and someone has to pay.

Finally, we know it's Bravo. Like Andy said, though, it's also a combination. Not a combination of the women paying and Bravo paying but a combination of Bravo paying and also getting things for free by making more brand deals than an influencer (or affluencer?) with past-due car payments.

Every trip starts with the showrunner coming up with a budget. This has to be done for every trip, not just the glamorous international vacations but also the little jaunts out of town, the invitations to a Housewife's second home, or even a day trip to an apple orchard in upstate New York for Sonja to pee in a corn maze. Along with the budget, the producers have to state the reason they're going on the trip, what stories they hope to pursue while they're there, and which of the women is the purported host.

As many fans have deduced, the host of many trips is fairly nominal—unless, of course, they're staying at Ramona's Hamptons home, in which case, she is in charge of who sleeps in the "lower level."

Kristen Taekman was the host of the *RHONY* season 6 trip to Montana. "I mean, I didn't do much. I did fun welcome bags. They obviously organized it all," she said of her duties. "I helped facilitate, like these are the options of things to do. They pretty much do it all, but somebody's got to host it."

The locations are often chosen by where producers can get the best deal or where they can find a hotel that is going to house the women for free. (Or, as was the case one year when a *RHONY* trip to Buenos Aires had to be scrapped at the last minute, where their cast can't travel given their parole restrictions.) Those swaps of exposure on the show for rooms or other services are called *trade outs*.

"There's a lot of times where Bravo will say, 'You can't go on this trip unless you can get a trade out,'" says one producer who has booked several trips, noting that in recent years, the budgets for trips have gone down, but can still be in the several hundreds of thousands of dollars.

Once a hotel is selected, a representative from the property and someone from Bravo—not the production company—hashes out a contract. A production company can never guarantee airtime to someone, particularly when services are being exchanged for publicity. It's a conflict-of-interest issue. Imagine if Truly Original, who makes *RHOA*, promised Coke that they would be displayed prominently in an episode but Bravo has sold a bunch of ads to Pepsi. There'd be a clash like Porsha and Kenya at a reunion special.

The contracts with a venue stipulate all the things you imagine they would: the number of rooms for both the women and the coterie of producers and crew needed to film the episodes (usually between ten and thirty, depending on the size of the vacation), the number of nights they'll be filming in the location, and the amount of the discount that the production company will get.

There are also negotiations around how many episodes the hotel will be featured in, the number of mentions of the hotel, and the context of those mentions.

Many hotels will agree to these deals only when the property isn't at peak occupancy, so you'll see the women going to visit either in the off-season or midweek. Production companies will also pay for the amenities the Housewives use—room service and the like—and any excursions the hotels book for them, like camel riding through the desert or a trip to a private island beach club. These are often also part of the contract. If the hotel has a spa, they can stipulate that the women visit it, or if they offer in-room tequila tastings, they can risk sending a poor tequila sommelier to a roomful of drunk, horny, middle-aged women who will probably treat him in a manner that would get a #MeToo activist's hackles up. To keep any of these awful details from getting out to the press, everyone involved has to sign a nondisclosure agreement. I'm sure it's especially strong for whichever member of the household staff Ramona decides to boss around on that trip. (JK, Ramona. Love you!)

Some places require that the women sign a code of conduct. Someone who has worked on a number of these deals says that the code usually stipulates that while wine can be thrown, punches certainly can't be.

No word on how venues feel if Teresa Giudice and Melissa Gorga end up on a food fight with a $1,000 cake, but we know that Siggy Flicker hates it. Of course, the hotels know there will be drama, but they want to keep it away from the other guests. Production also usually agrees to a filming curfew—say, midnight—which fans can thank for every time they've been irate that the cameras didn't get the heated, late-night discussions the women always have after boozy dinners.

One thing Bravo will not pay for, which has become more and more common thanks to Erika Jayne, is the women bringing staff members of "glam squads" along with them. Those arrangements are made on the women's own dime.

The other thing that can become an issue is flights. While some of the bigger stars—and even some higher-up producers with good agents—have it in their contracts that they fly business or first class, Bravo will only pay for the women to fly in the back of the plane. If they want to upgrade classes, they have to pay for it themselves. This became a plot point on *Real Housewives of Dallas's* season 3 trip to Copenhagen, where most of the women paid the $1,200 to upgrade themselves to first class but D'Andra Simmons and LeeAnne Locken were with the rest of the rabble back in Middle Seat Land.

Not every trip plays out like this. When the women are staying in a villa or (gasp) Airbnb, the production staff has to be put in a hotel nearby, which doesn't get the exposure of being on the show so probably doesn't give them a discount. The same arrangement applies when the women go to one of their second homes. Dorinda can't have thirty crew members sleeping in cots in the garage of Blue Stone Manor, so they need to retreat to a nearby hotel. In this example, Dorinda doesn't get any money for hosting production, but she will get some special considerations, like production paying for cleaning before and after the women terrorize her Berkshires manse. The over-the-top Halloween decorations, though, that comes right out of her own pocket.

While most production companies do all this legwork on their own, a 2018 profile in the *Philly Voice* looked at the role of Sally Serata, a luxury travel agent who got involved in booking the Housewives' travel after reaching out to Kim Zolciak-Bierman on her Instagram account and coordinating a trip for the Bravoleb for the finale of her spin-off, *Don't Be Tardy*. She has since booked trips for *RHOA, RHOP, RHONY,* and *RHONJ*.

She arranged the *RHOA* trip to San Francisco, where NeNe got so mad at dinner that her bun fell out and Marlo had to fix it on her head while NeNe continued ranting. "We were supposed to start filming at 9," Serata told the *Voice*. "These ladies—these divas did not walk in until way after midnight. 12:30! They're in full glam, they've been glamming for three hours. They get into a fight within the first 15 minutes. Everyone leaves. No one ate anything. All the makeup and hair and those Dior and Gucci ensembles, and that's it!"

Serata, who declined an invitation to speak to me for this book, also worked on *RHOA*'s disastrous trip to Spain, where the women were so unhappy with the Airbnb that Cynthia Bailey booked that they had to disembark for another hotel. She was on-site for that vacation and one day had to figure out how to get the ladies back to their hotel after their driver got too drunk while waiting for them at the spa. It took ninety minutes for her to work out how to get them home. How did we not see them sweating under the hot Spanish sun for more than an hour?

Whether the venue was found by a travel agent or a producer, it's nothing but good news for the places where the women travel, even the ones where Luann literally shits the bed. One person who has worked on multiple *Housewives* trips told me that the publicity is fantastic, though it's impossible to track whether or not a *Housewives* episode led to more rooms being booked. It's not just the episode; it's also the blogs, recaps, and fan accounts that end up writing about the episodes and the women's trips, giving them even more free press.

Janet Scanlon, the senior marketing manager at the Willard Hotel in D.C., arranged for Kyle Richards to stay there while the family dropped daughter Sophia off at nearby George Washington University (my alma mater). Even though the hotel wasn't prominently featured in the episode and Kyle's family mostly filmed in their rooms, Scanlon says the hotel's website saw a major spike in traffic after Kyle posted about her stay on Instagram.

Some Housewives have even returned to favorite destinations and paid their own way, which just gets the businesses more exposure. In an attention economy, even the cringiest tabloid story works if it will get people eyeing your luxury vacation spot.

Hotels aren't the only businesses that can benefit. What about all the restaurants where the women are constantly meeting to air their grievances? Ideally, these are a reflection of places the women go in their real lives. However, what production really needs are places that will allow them to film. Filming at a restaurant isn't just showing up with the women and a couple of cameras; it involves setting up the lighting and location of the table sometimes hours in advance, sometimes setting up a monitor so that producers can watch the scene as it's being taped, and then breaking it all down after someone has stormed out after being confronted by the Cookie Lady who says she got hit on by one of the ladies' boyfriends.

Producers ask the women for recommendations, but they're not always helpful. "My husband, Josh, has a lot of restaurant connections," Taekman says about finding venues. "He'd tell them, 'Kristen's on this show. She wants to come up and do cocktails on your rooftop bar.' And people would literally say to him, 'We can't, because Ramona might show up and misbehave.' That's what literally came out of their mouths."

Yes, plenty of restaurants, particularly in New York and LA, either don't want the bother of production setups or are full enough that they don't need the publicity. Either that or they feel like having Housewives there would be off brand. One location scout told me that when they first started looking for venues for their show, they would just cold-call places near the women's houses. About three in ten of those places were interested in filming. Better tactics turned out to be calling PR firms and asking which of their restaurant clients might be interested, or finding newly opened restaurants and dangling the possibility of attention.

Samantha Wan, the vice president of public relations for Barton G. restaurants, said that she initially reached out to location scouts working for Evolution Media about filming one of their shows in the chain's Los Angeles location. The restaurant's signature cinematic platings—popcorn shrimp brought out in a popcorn machine, a swordfish with a giant samurai sword protruding from it—were perfect for television. The production used the restaurant for a season 12 party for Tamra Judge's husband Eddie's birthday party.

Because the restaurant is smaller and only open for dinner, it opened early for production and held a private party for the Judges. That, however, is usually a no-no. According to several producers, Bravo hates it when the restaurants appear empty or to be catering only to the House-wives. They want them to look full and popular, like the ladies walked in off the street and waited for a table like everyone else.

Barton G. has since been featured on *RHOA* and *RHONY,* both at the Miami location. Wan says that they give the women the menu in advance so they don't waste time during filming—which became evident when Bethenny ordering the lobster Pop-Tarts (which come in a pink retro toaster) for the entire group became a topic of conversation. The highlight of *RHONY*'s visit, of course, was the iconic fight when Bethenny finally yells at Luann, "Life is not a cabaret!"

"It wasn't negative on our brand," Wan says of the drama. "That being such a memorable moment is always mentioned in our restaurant, so I think it's still decent overall to be tied with it." She also confessed that, yes, fans do show up at the Miami location because of the show and she's heard of people reenacting the encounter in the restaurant.

One of the most noticeable things from that scene isn't just Bethenny screaming—and Tinsley snidely saying, "Yes, I'm drinking, Luann"—it's the reactions of the other patrons to their dinner being disturbed by reality TV insanity. Wan says that the restaurant put a sign on the front door alerting guests that filming was going on, and those who ended up on camera were asked to sign a release.

That's not always the case, as my friend Suzanne—who ended up in the background of a *RHONY* episode sneering at Bethenny when she got loud in a Hamptons eatery—will attest. She never signed anything, but thankfully her epic side-eye lived to make it into the episode.

Benny Ramos, the general manager of Añejo in Manhattan's TriBeCa, had a different solution when *RHONY* filmed there in season 11. He not only put a poster on the door about filming, but anyone who didn't want to end up in the background could be seated in the restaurant's basement (ahem, "lower level"). "You never know if someone's bringing their wife or someone else," he joked. "Nobody wants to find out that way, so we offered our other dining area."

Ramos's restaurant has had several TV shows film in the space, and he says he had a positive experience with the Housewives, who have individually dined there both before and after the cameras were there. "I think it was fun," he says. "The staff was having a good time. The mood was very lighthearted . . . But we give them their privacy and we give them their space because they do pay for it. We treat it almost like a private event."

By "pay for it," he doesn't mean charging a location fee, as all the restaurants I talked to said they do not do so. But production pays for the women's food and drinks, so it's not a total freebie. Some restaurants offer a discount given the incoming publicity, which might not be a good idea considering the amount we've seen some of these women drink in one sitting.

Ramos says at least once a month someone comes in to ask if the Housewives filmed there and what they were like, but he never gets people asking if the eatery was on *Blue Bloods,* which it also was.

I always assumed that the random restaurants in an episode without a major incident, like Añejo, wouldn't see much of an impact from the show. Yes, it makes sense people would want to go to Barton G. or the Quiet Woman, which became infamous for a season 12 fight between *RHOC*'s Kelly Dodd and Shannon Beador. But why go check out just another dinner spot? Well, Ramos disabused me of that notion. It turns out *Housewives* fans will notice anywhere that's been on their favorite program. Though, that said, a couple of extra people a month isn't really a boon for a busy Manhattan eatery.

It's even better business for those who show up all the time. Rails Steakhouse, which is near several of the *RHONJ* women's homes, has been on the show more times than Teresa mispronounces a word. Mike Mulligan, the director of operations at Rails, says that once when the restaurant was closed, he arrived at work and saw two women peering into the locked doors.

"They had flown in from California to shop at Melissa's store and come to Rails to have lunch," he says. They might have bought some clothes at Envy, but steak and fries was off the menu. But Mulligan let them in and gave them a tour of the place and some free T-shirts. They were so happy they sent him a handwritten thank-you card.

While that is an extreme example, Mulligan says that fans come to the restaurant all the time, though not as much as during the first few years when Rails was like a seventh cast member.

It's hard to put a dollar amount to the Housewives' impact on a brand, but Felicia Garay-Stanton, the PR and marketing director for Jovani, tried to. Both Luann and Dorinda made the brand iconic when Dorinda got them to lend Luann a few dresses for her cabaret debut. That might have been a little footnote in *Housewives* history, but when Dorinda got mad at Luann for not inviting her boyfriend John to the big premiere, she heckled Luann by shouting, "Jovani! Jovani!" repeatedly at the show.

Garay-Stanton says that, after the cabaret episode aired, the brand's web traffic shot through the roof. She said it would have cost them $2 million to $2.5 million in advertising to see an increase in traffic like that, and they didn't have to spend a dime for it. That famous incident led to Luann recording her track, "Feeling Jovani." She didn't ask permission to record the song, but apparently, it was a hit and played on repeat for a few weeks at Jovani HQ in Manhattan. They even let her film the music video at the brand's LA flagship store, which has become a go-to stop for *Housewives* fans visiting the West Coast.

"It has definitely amped up the name Jovani and helped us go beyond prom," Garay-Stanton says. "A lot of people just think of us as a prom brand. We sell dresses for your bat mitzvah to your granddaughter's wedding." (You're welcome for this PR, too, Jovani.)

There were drawbacks. She said some stylists the brand worked with stopped recommending their dresses to certain celebrity clients because it became a "*Real Housewives* brand."

"I think the ship has sailed a little bit on that," she says. "I know we'd love to make sure the brand is still elevating. We don't want to get stuck in that one-song, one-note-type thing. Sometimes I think with the reality TV shows, you can end up stuck, and you want to make sure you're still dynamic in a lot of ways . . . I hope that we won't be considered a joke later on."

Garay-Stanton also says that, after loaning Dorinda and Luann dresses (they both also pay retail at Jovani), she's heard from other Housewives looking for free things. Several ladies she refused to name had deals with local stores that carry Jovani, so they thought that meant they should be able to come by the showroom and pick out a free gown or two. Garay-Stanton turned them down or told them to talk to the store.

That makes us wonder, just how much free stuff are these women getting? It's hard to tell exactly, but we know they're out there wheeling and dealing to get every freebie they can. Just like production can't promise brands any amount of airtime, neither can the women, but that doesn't stop them from trying.

Greg Bennett, who lived with Albie and Chris Manzo starting in season 3 of *RHONJ*, had a great rental agreement at an apartment tower in Hoboken thanks to the show. "The building was having trouble filling their units, so they struck a deal, not through Bravo. They said we could live there for a very fair amount of money for having the building advertised on the show," he says. "The first season, we didn't pay anything. I'm twenty-two or twenty-three and paying to live in some shoebox in Manhattan and then going to this apartment on the Hudson River with a washer dryer and a terrace. It was amazing. As the years went on, the jig was up little by little. When I moved out, we were each paying eight hundred dollars." But the jig wasn't totally up since an apartment that big could have probably fetched more.

Bobby Berk, the design guru on Netflix's reboot of *Queer Eye,* shared a horror story about working with a Housewife when he was on Jenny McCarthy's SiriusXM radio show.

"I had a New York Housewife come into my store years ago in New York, and [she] was like, 'Oh, I'm buying this new place . . . I want you to come in and design it all. I'm gonna put you on the show,'" he says about the incident. "I wasn't on TV yet. I still kind of liked *The Housewives,* so I was like, 'Oh, okay, but just so you know, I'm not doing it for free. I don't need to do it for free. I don't necessarily know if *The Housewives* is really the exposure I want anyways, so I'll do it for you at cost.' And she's like, 'Okay, okay, that works.'"

Berk says then he got a call from her husband trying to bully him into doing it for free. He decided that he didn't want to do it at all and canceled the verbal agreement. "She came into my store the next week when I wasn't there and told my staff that I had said she could take anything out of the store that she wanted to design her house for the shoot, and here was her credit card, and 'If I don't bring anything back, if I like something, you can just charge the credit card.'"

Months later, he was looking for some inventory and was informed that it was at her house. His staff had been calling and calling to get it back, and she wouldn't return their calls. When they tried the credit card, it was declined. Berk says that when he called the Housewife and demanded she return the items, she said to him, "You know what? Then let's go to court. This'll be good TV. It's easier for us just to have our lawyer deal with it than it would be to actually pay you." He never did get his goods back.

While Berk didn't reveal the person's name on the show, he later acknowledged that it was none other than our favorite unijambiste, Aviva Drescher.

Trading airtime for favors became a part of the story line in *RHONY*'s twelfth season, when Dorinda Medley and Sonja Morgan got mad at Ramona for dragging them all the way to Long Island to meet with a party planner so that she could get a discount on a fancy birthday party with sixty of her closest girlfriends. A source close to production told me that, yes, Ramona did get a discount for flogging this man's services on air.

But wait, you might be thinking, *doesn't Bravo pay for all those lavish parties?* Again, it's a combination, and it usually comes down to motive. If the Housewife is going to throw the party anyway, like Taylor Armstrong's famous $60,000 birthday parties for her young daughter, then all the planning and cost is left to the Housewives. This certainly goes for business launches.

However, if there wasn't going to be a party, and production instead concocts an "all-cast event," then they kick in a lot of the budget. So, for instance, if they see that a Housewife's fiftieth birthday is around the time production wraps but no one's planning anything, production might say, "Can you put together a birthday party? We'll pay for it." Within reason, of course.

The women try to get the most out of production, however. "They're all so cheap," says one producer who has worked on multiple shows. "I mean, they will turn in a receipt for five dollars. It doesn't matter. They're all so cheap, they want to get the most out of what they put in."

That is, if they're even using their own money. This producer says a lot of times the women (or whichever PA they have doing the event planning) will just tell vendors to invoice the production company directly so they're not out of pocket for anything.

Each production company has an events budget for the whole season and needs to keep that in mind when promising to pay for soirées. How much does a typical event cost, and how much do they get? It depends, one producer tells me. "It depends on how good a Housewife is at negotiating," they say. "I know one woman who got her entire wedding paid for."

The same logic goes for the women's shopping trips. If it's something the women planned, then they have to lay down their own credit cards at the till. However, if it's a scene that the producers need for any reason and they decide on a shopping trip, they'll pick up the tab for whatever it is the ladies purchase.

The Housewife could also have a deal going with the store, though that's not always the case. When Dorinda brought Luann to Jovani, Dorinda had already established a relationship with the brand and liked their clothing. She asked if she could film there, they said yes, and Luann got to borrow a few gowns. Everyone wins.

Is it a quest for swag every time the women walk into a boutique? (Even Swagg Boutique?) Probably not, but I heard from several people who said the women are often on the lookout for handouts. Sometimes the trade-off is more altruistic. The Housewives have shops, restaurants, and products run by their friends and want to show them off to help out. They may not even be thinking of the thank-you gift they'll get in return.

❊ ❊ ❊

Aren't these women rich, though? Why do they always have one manicured hand out? Think about how you—yes, you—load up on free samples at Costco and then ask that question again. That's about right.

Also, only some of the women are really rich. Several of the ladies from New York, Beverly Hills, and Dallas have a fair amount of money, but the secret about some of the other franchises is that most of that money comes from the show itself. Tamra might have been swapping mansions in her last few seasons, but remember the town house she and her ex-husband Simon started in. All that cash didn't come from Cut Fitness, it came from *Real Housewives* and the attendant businesses.

The salaries of Real Housewives are much debated across the internet, with Radar Online saying that NeNe made $2.85 million for season 12. I was told by several people familiar with the franchise that Kandi Burruss is the highest-paid Housewife across all franchises and makes slightly over $2 million a season. (And that was even before NeNe "decided to leave" *RHOA* again.) The same Radar Online article that pegged NeNe's salary at $2.85 million also said Kandi made $2.2 million, so maybe they know what they're talking about.

These figures might be a bit misleading, because the contracts went from promising the Housewives one paycheck for each season to paying them per episode, like they're members of the *Friends* cast. While apparently Bravo suits were transitioning the salaries to an episodic basis for a while, Lisa Vanderpump quitting in the middle of filming *RHOBH*'s ninth season is what made them institute it across the board. Now Housewives get paid only for the episodes they appear in.

Most of the main cast, of course, will be in every episode. In previous years, some women who were holding out on their contracts before filming started would later have their "personal stories" cut into the early episodes so that they would get a full season order. NeNe Leakes reportedly did not get that courtesy for season 12, and her absence for several episodes cost her around $120,000 an episode.

Things are different for each franchise and for each woman, obviously. The way it generally works now is that a woman taken from obscurity and cast on the show will make about $60,000 her first season. Someone like Denise Richards, who was a star Bravo wanted to cast and probably had an agent to do her negotiating, could get a lot more. Multiple gossip blogs report she pulled in $1 million for her first season and was guaranteed four years, but we all saw how that worked out, and she left after two.

That $60,000 figure was confirmed by *RHOC*'s Gina Kirschenheiter's divorce filings after her first season of the show, where she claimed $63,000 paid by the production company and $5,450 paid by NBC-Universal.

If a woman stays on the show for a second season, she'll usually double her salary to $120,000. If she's invited back yet again, her salary will be around $300,000 for the third season and then hover between that figure and $500,000 for the length of her stay on the show.

The Atlanta ladies make a bit more, since they have the highest ratings, and the *RHOD* cast make less because they film fewer episodes than the other franchises and are the least watched.

Cary Deuber told me she made barely any money her first season on *RHOD*. "It was less than nothing. Less than a handbag. Less than a Birken," she says, and I will note she was joking about the Birken. She said by season 3, she was making around $200,000 a season.

She was invited back for season 4 as a "friend of the Housewives," which has a totally different pay structure. These women get paid per day of filming, which could be a two-hour lunch or an eight-hour outing. They still get the same rate, and it's not much, relatively speaking. "Oh, it's definitely less than a Birkin," Cary says.

The figures haven't always been as generous. Bethenny Frankel has been on record saying that she made $7,250 for her first season of *RHONY*. When you figure in how much they were filming, that can't possibly be minimum wage. If you'll recall, when I asked *RHOC*'s season 2 addition Tammy Knickerbocker how much she made in her first season, she was too embarrassed to admit the figure.

Cindy Barshop says she made about $50,000 when she filmed season 4 of *RHONY*. Ana Quincoces says she made $40,000 when she started on season 2 of *RHOM* and that the cast had "favored nations" clauses in her contract. (Ana is a lawyer, so she knows this shit.) That means they all got paid the same rate, and their salary only increased 5 percent season by season. That means she made $42,000 for season 3.

Naturally, the franchise has stars that need to be looked after. Bethenny Frankel, according to someone with knowledge of her salary, was pulling in around $1 million when she left the show. Tamra told Jeff Lewis on his SiriusXM show after she was fired from *RHOC* that she made $1.2 million her final season. Radar Online pegs Teresa Giudice at about the $1 million mark and Lisa Vanderpump in the same range for her last season.

Kyle Richards was also making that much money, it seems. I was told Kyle and her sister Kim's contracts stipulated equal salary when they were both full-time cast members, and other clauses stipulated the same parity for Kyle and Lisa Vanderpump.

Just as the stars make more money, there are some "friends of the Housewives" who do all right, like *RHOA*'s forever bridesmaids Tanya Sam and Marlo Hampton. Radar points to them making $150,000 and $300,000, respectively, for *RHOA*'s twelfth season. I know Bravo is against it, but #GiveMarloAPeach.

Let's be honest, most of the Housewives, especially the newbies, are going to take whatever Bravo offers them. They want the fame, they want the platform, they want the possibility of cashing in like Bethenny did. In her memoir, *Pretty Mess*, Erika Jayne says that her ex-husband, attorney Tom Girardi, told her to sign her first contract without even reading it. "You need them more than they need you," he counseled her. Now she has an agent who probably does the bargaining, and the contract reading, for her.

Some of the Housewives now have agents, but most still represent themselves. Andy tells a funny story in his memoir about one season when Ramona decided she was going to negotiate her contract herself but walked out of the meeting halfway through when she got bored.

There are other Housewives who use dirty tricks to hold out for more money. According to someone working on the show at the time, when Siggy Flicker and Dolores Catania returned for *RHONJ*'s eighth season, they negotiated that their salaries would double and they agreed on the deal. They were set to sign their contracts on the first day of shooting.

That day came, and they refused to sign their contracts, saying they wanted more money. Shari Levine, head of production at Bravo, got on the phone with all of the channel's lawyers and everyone from the production company and said, "We have doubled your salary. If you do not want to sign the contracts, you need to let us know now because we have a crew there that we need to release and you can go home. We're not playing this game." They signed on the spot. I picture this happening while they stand outside in the New Jersey winter breathing steam and shivering in their fur coats, but that may just be my imagination.

An agent who works with several reality clients told me that Housewives' contracts are pretty standard in the industry, but there are a few vagaries. There is what is called the *Bethenny clause,* which stipulates that any Housewife who starts a business venture while on the show and that is featured on the show has to give Bravo a 10 percent cut if they sell the business for more than $1 million. I'm sure someone at NBCUniversal headquarters is still waiting for Sonja to get her toaster oven off the ground just for this.

There is also something called the *Kelly clause,* which was instituted after Kelly Dodd was going after some of her *RHOC* castmates on social media while the show was airing. It says that Housewives can be fined for disparaging their coworkers online. If any of you follow Kelly's

Twitter, it seems like she's decided to just pay the fines rather than keep her mouth shut.

RHONJ has a special carve-out in their contracts, too. They're the only cast whose husbands also get paid for appearing on the show, which is why they still film together when the ladies are away on a trip. In the past, all of the cast's children who were over eighteen also got an annual stipend for appearing on the show. I've also heard that some veteran Housewives' children who appear frequently, like Tamra's son Ryan, also get paid for their participation.

There are a few other Housewife bonuses. In recent years, they get a stipend of about $1,200 to buy a reunion dress, which, depending on the dress, might not cover the whole thing. They also get their hair and makeup covered for the reunion and for other official shoots.

There's also a weird new way for them to make money off the show, which is doing *Housewives*-branded commercials and brand integrations. You know, like when you're fast-forwarding between acts and suddenly you see Melissa Gorga, Phaedra Parks, and Sonja Morgan in an ad for the upcoming movie *Alice's Adventures in Wonderland,* narrated by Andy Cohen himself.

Let us not forget the *RHONY* episode when Sonja and Dorinda Medley came out of the movie *The Hustle* talking about how much they loved it and how it related to their friends. Or what about Tinsley Mortimer making a big deal of using Nivea hand cream when getting her makeup done.

Someone told me that the women get about $5,000 to film one of these spots, but that seems low. A company that booked several Housewives for such a commercial wouldn't give exact figures but said the women not only got cash but also equity in the company. That's a pretty good deal. The commercial itself costs as much as a national cable ad would cost in the time slot, plus the cost of production, though it can essentially only be used on Bravo. Sometimes these commercial deals are totally independent, like when Sonja, Porsha, Tamra, Dorinda, and Melissa recorded a fake music video for the brand Fiber One.

Someone close to *RHONY* also told me that when Bethenny returned to the show, the Skinnygirl product placement was actually paid for as brand integrations and that the show had to fulfill certain obligations to show Skinnygirl parties, products, and that unmissable red-and-black logo.

It's a lot easier for the women to be used by Bravo for this kind of stuff than promote partnerships with brands themselves. Just look at Jill Zarin's disastrous party for Kodak on season 3 of *RHONY*. Her former manager, Darren Bettencourt, says she got a "mid–six figure" deal with the photo brand as an ambassador and even threw a Kodak-themed launch party on the show. Then Ramona showed up and trashed Kodak and asked why Jill would want to be associated with such an "antiquated brand." After the episode, Kodak pulled the sponsorship.

A bad turn on the show can cost even normal people a lot of money. Rey Bolic, an ex-boyfriend of Luann's whom Ramona brought to a party hosted by Dorinda and her dry cleaner boyfriend, learned that the hard way. Yes, he was drunk and acted inappropriately to the point of getting thrown out (and calling everyone "trash" on the way), but the self-employed marketing consultant says he lost a $500,000 contract because of the incident, which lasted less than five minutes.

"They told me that they couldn't have someone representing their brand with that kind of persona," Rey says. After his appearance, there were all sorts of rumors about him on the internet—like that he was Luann's cocaine dealer, which he denies—but now when potential clients google him, that's what they find. "Recently, one potential client, just before signing, said that they know about the PR that came along with that and it was kind of a deal breaker," he says.

Being on *Housewives* can also be great for business. Cary Deuber says that the laser center she and her plastic surgeon husband developed while on the show is still flourishing thanks to its *Housewives* exposure. She says 30–40 percent of her business comes from people aware of the practice because they saw it on television.

Cindy Barshop, who was trying to sell a line of intimate hair removal products during her one season on *RHONY*, says she walked right into Target to pitch her product and walked out with a deal. "All the people there watched the show," she says. "That's how I got in."

There are even more obvious examples. Reviews on Tripadvisor say that there can often be a two-hour or longer wait time to get into Kandi's Atlanta restaurant, Old Lady Gang (and that it's totally worth it once you get in). The three restaurants at Lisa Vanderpump's *Real Housewives* EPCOT Center, at the intersection of Santa Monica and N. Robertson Boulevards in Los Angeles—Sur Restaurant Lounge, Pump Restaurant, and TomTom Bar—always feature lines, well, at least they did before the COVID-19 pandemic. A few years ago, when I went to Pump with some friends, it was so busy we couldn't even flag down a waiter to get our bill. After thirty minutes, we left without paying. Sorry, Lisa. You can hit me up for the forty dollars. But we saw Lisa, Ken, one-season Housewife Kathryn Edwards, and, most importantly, Lisa's hairless dog Giggy (RIP), so it was totally worth it. (Well, it was free, so of course it was worth it.)

But so many of the *Housewives* brands come and go (Vicki's Vodka, anyone?) or don't get off the ground at all, like every idea Sonja has ever come up with. Being on *Housewives* is not a promise of business success, it's just a loudspeaker to shout a message into.

Outside of entrepreneurship, being a cast member offers as many opportunities as a Housewife's dignity is flexible. There are the dance singles, podcasts, and YouTube channels. Some went on to be featured on *Dancing with the Stars* or *Celebrity Apprentice,* back when its host wasn't ruining the free world. NeNe, Kandi, and Erika have all appeared on Broadway to a big boost in ticket sales. Luann charges sometimes upward of one hundred dollars for tickets to her cabaret show that tours around the country. Many of the Housewives have books, and some of those are even bestsellers.

Then there are the public appearances, sponsored social media posts, and $150 Cameos so that Ramona can talk about herself for three minutes and then wish your best friend a happy birthday. There are a million different ways to monetize fame, and it seems like the Real Housewives have found just about every single one.

Just, please, whatever you do, don't ask them to pay for their own trips.

THE *REAL HOUSEWIVES* DANCE SINGLES TOP 10

"Tardy for the Party":

The original and still the best, including a chorus by Kandi that is impossible to get out of your head.

"XXpen$ive":

It's expensive to be Erika Jayne, and this killer track and its music video are worth the investment.

"Money Can't Buy You Class":

The single that launched a thousand cabaret shows is still great to hum along to, even if Countess Luann de Lesseps doesn't have the most natural singing voice.

"Fly Above":

This mid-tempo track about perseverance in the face of discouragement is another of Kandi's triumphs, this one featuring her robust voice as well as her songwriting talent.

"On Display":

Just like Melissa Gorga herself, this is an underrated gem. It is also a meta-text on what it's like to live life in the public eye. Deep!

"How Many Fucks":

When Erika Jayne does hip-hop, she does it hard, translating her spiritual ethos into a banger that doesn't care if you love it, even though you will.

"Chic C'est La Vie":

The countess's follow-up isn't nearly as savvy as her first single, and the music video, featuring Jill Zarin and Kelly Bensimon at an Atlantic City casino, isn't one to bet on.

"Google Me":

Kim Zolciak never met an electronic voice effect she didn't like in this dance track about just how damn famous she is.

"The Ring Don't Mean a Thing":

Too bad Kim couldn't figure out how to make this track that Kandi wrote for her a reality. At the bottom of the list because it's a missed opportunity.

"Coffee and Love":

Ashley Darby gets points for performing this at Gay Pride in Virginia, but the lyrics seem written by a teen drunk on Boone's Farm wine coolers.

YOU NEED TO GET A HOBBY
WHEN FANDOM IS A FULL-TIME JOB

Mary Mahoney, a kindergarten teacher in San Francisco, and Courtney Frain, who works in tech in Los Angeles, were Delta Gamma sorority sisters at San Diego State and have been friends ever since. In 2016, they decided to take their love of Bravo and turn it into the podcast *Two Judgey Girls.* It was great fun and more successful than they could have imagined, but they ended up with a strange problem: Facebook.

Things got so contentious in a fan group for the podcast that Frain had to take charge. "It's just trolling [but] that one bad apple ruins the whole bunch," she says. "It got to the point where it was like 'What is going on?' People would be sending me personal messages. I'm at work. I just cut it at the neck." She took administrative control of the group so that she could approve or deny each post. "I can't have people attacking each other . . . People are passionate to a fault. Sometimes you have to calm people down. It's Bravo, it's not that serious."

For plenty of people, though, it is that serious.

It has been said that if you do what you love, you will never work a day in your life. That's kind of a lie. Even if you love waking up before dawn to feed the chickens, you're still going to be the person cleaning up chicken shit. But there are plenty of *Real Housewives* fans out there who have turned their love of the franchise into hobbies, those hobbies into business opportunities, and those business opportunities into full-time jobs, complete with chunks of cash miraculously outside Bravo's control.

"It was an outlet for a job where I wasn't being as fully creative as I wanted to be," Christina Haberkern (Favorite Real Housewife: Porsha Williams) says about her line of cards, Hello Harlot. "I started making them for friends. I just started selling on Etsy, and it turns out there are like-minded people out in the world. People that love Bravo."

At the time, Haberkern, who lives in Los Angeles, was working as a graphic designer in TV and movie production. After the sales of her cards (like one featuring Erika Jayne on the front that says, "This Birthday Card Is XXpen$ive") took off, Haberkern started making *Real Housewives* coloring books, featuring her line drawings of classic scenes—like a fake postcard that depicts the Boat Ride from Hell with the slogan "Visit Cartegena, Where Everything Is Swell but the Ride" or Dorinda shouting, "I made it nice!" in the middle of a floral wreath— that fans could fill in at home or, for the less industrious, give as fun gifts. Trust me, you've never known relaxation like coloring in an illustrated re-creation of Sonja Morgan, Tinsley Mortimer, and Leah McSweeney naked in Ramona Singer's Hamptons pool in between Sonja's famous words: "Seeing double, feeling single."

"We are a fan base of people who send things to each other to make people laugh, and they are in-the-know laughs. People buy the books for friends for Christmas presents, because they can't believe it exists," she says.

Haberkern says she does between twenty and thirty orders a week, often packing and shipping them while sitting at home watching Bravo on repeat. She left her full-time job due to a disability two years ago, so this is now her full-time employment. "It's not like I'm making Lynne Curtain cuff money," she jokes about the former Real Housewife of Orange County and her horrible line of bespoke jewelry. "I'm not making as much as my full-time job, but it's also enough work that I couldn't do it all if I had a full-time job, too," she says.

It seems like *Real Housewives of New York City* merch does especially well for Etsy sellers. Danielle Peterson (Favorite Real Housewife: Bethenny Frankel) says that the bestsellers on her Hollaback Cards line are one with Dorinda Medley shouting "Clip!"; one with Luann de Lesseps in the bushes after her famous Mexican stumble; and one of Ramona Singer saying, "It's your birthday. Are you kidding me? Are you kidding me? Are you kidding me?"

Peterson, who works in Miami as a lawyer, never went to art school or had any formal training, but the designs she makes for her cards are her creative outlet. "I post my new designs first and gauge the reaction to them on social media," she says, adding that her profits now account for about a quarter of her income and she spends between twelve and twenty hours a week on her side hustle. "It's something I do for fun," she says. "I think honestly it's even more fun than when I started. I get to talk to so many people who love the Housewives as much as I do."

Daniel Adomako (Favorite Real Housewife: Luann de Lesseps) and Peterson have a few things in common, including that his *RHONY* cards sell the best both on Etsy and his own website, the Boy Heroine— particularly one of Ramona Singer with googly eyes—and he also got into selling cards after making them for his friends. "My friend Adam initially forced me into watching the Housewives," says Adomako, who lives in London, where the Housewife fandom isn't as intense as it is stateside. "It was his birthday, and I wanted to make him a card. It was classic Ramona, 'Take a Xanax,' and the cheapest way to make it was to have ten made, so I got them all made. I thought I'd chuck them up on Etsy and see if anyone liked them. They sold really quickly."

Adomako now has more than eighty designs, almost all of them *Housewives* related (though British reality icon Gemma Collins has some representation as well). He says he can usually chart how popular a Housewife is based on sales. "NeNe's cards always sold well, because she has so many catchphrases. Recently, she doesn't sell as many cards because I don't think people are enjoying her as much," he says.

Like many of the independent merch hawks, Adomako says most people find his line of goods through organic search, but one of the best ways to find things is through the Housewives themselves. "I remember the day when Sonja Morgan posted about a card I made of her," he says. "I was freaking out in my living room. I was like, 'This is a very important day.' And then I got like twenty orders from her post."

Getting discovered by one's muse isn't always a good thing. Carolann Parran (Favorite Real Housewife: Caroline Manzo) is a full-time Etsy seller under the banner of Pink House Press. She does a fair amount of *Housewives* trade, but also posters, cards, and other objects for the tastefully decorated home. (What tasteful home doesn't want a Stars Fell on Alabama beer koozie?) She designed enamel pins with the faces of Dorinda Medley, NeNe Leakes, and Luann de Lesseps (with her slogan "Don't be all uncool")—but the Vicki Gunvalson pin caused her trouble.

One day, she received a cease and desist notice in the inbox for her Etsy store. The very formal letter told her she had to stop using Vicki's likeness without her permission. "It was a little scary, but I was like, 'Oh my god, Vicki has seen my pin. That is exciting!'" she says. Parran is not the sort of person to let an opportunity like this go to waste. "So I wrote him back and told him I would stop using it and I was like, 'Hey, Mr. Lawyer Guy, if you want the rest, I can send them to you.' So I sent them the rest of my pins, and maybe Vicki has the pins. That would be kind of amazing." Personally, I would have held off on the shipment . . . a parody drawing of the OG of the OC is probably covered under the fair-use doctrine.

While Vicki got some free swag in the mail, the pins weren't free for Carolann. She has to make an up-front investment of $250 for one hundred pins, the smallest batch she can order from her manufacturer. That isn't a lot of money, but it's enough when running on the tight margins of Etsy success. "I thought about making one of Bethenny, but I was scared off by the cease and desist," she says. "Now I'm kind of scared because I don't know who is going to be litigious and who is not."

This is one of only a few stories I heard from secondary sellers about the subjects of their work threatening to sue, which surprised me. To avoid any sort of copyright claims, Liz Ver Hey (Favorite Real House-wife: Sonja Morgan), who operates her Etsy shop under the name GarbageMom, uses artwork that is already in the public record: Real Housewives' mug shots. She sells coasters, magnets, or handmade Christmas ornaments with the images of Luann de Lesseps, Tinsley Mortimer, Sonja Morgan, Teresa Giudice, and Kim Richards when each of them was arrested. She has other Housewives items but says the mug shots are her bestsellers. Even if a Housewife did sue, Ver Hey thinks it might cause them an image problem. "It would look petty if a major Housewife was like, 'You can't use my face,'" she says. "Lady, you're rich. I ate noodles for dinner last night. You're going to come after me?"

Ver Hey didn't get into the Etsy business as a hobby; her reason was purely capitalistic. After her maternity leave, she and her husband were having a hard time making ends meet. He noticed that she was in a popular *Housewives*-related Facebook group. "Look at this group," he told her. "There are twenty thousand people here you could sell trinkets to. There is a market for this."

She made samples of her coasters and ornaments and posted them in the group, and started to get orders that way. She says, even still, the best boost she gets to sales is when someone posts a linked picture of her wares in an affinity group. "I know if I put the time into it, I could reach more people and get more sales. But I am clinically apathetic and bad at self-promotion," she says. "I think my first or second year doing this, someone from *Entertainment Weekly* sent a message saying they wanted to feature my store in an article about the best gifts for Bravo, and I said no. I was working crazy hours and was barely holding it together to finish the orders I had!"

Ver Hay says now she makes about $8,000 a year from her Etsy page, which supplements the $70,000-a-year salary she gets working as an executive assistant in the San Francisco Bay Area. "When we were a single-income household, having an extra hundred dollars a week here or there was huge. It helped buffer things so we weren't living super tight," she says. "I was thinking the other day that if I won the lottery, I would quit my day job, but I don't know that I would quit Etsy. It gives me an excuse to not watch the kids, so I go watch *Housewives* and make my crafts, and it's very therapeutic."

Many of the creators I spoke with were surprised (and glad) that the women don't have their own merch. Bravo, of course, has its Shop by Bravo website, which it opened in 2008 to sell the products of Housewives and others on the network. In the launch press release, it singles out True Faith, Ramona Singer's former line of religious-themed jewelry, and the designs of several contestants from the once and future Bravo hit *Project Runway.*

Now the site sells all sorts of tat, from Turtle Time pillows to socks that say, "I Cooked, I Cleaned, I Made It Nice," inspired by the catchphrases of Ramona Singer and Dorinda Medley, respectively. The network not only owns their images for the purpose of the show, it owns—and commodifies—the intellectual property they make up on the spot. Dorinda should be especially angry. Between the "I survived the fish room" T-shirts inspired by the iconic room at her Berkshires mansion, the "Welcome to Bezerkshires, MA" sweatshirts also inspired by her home, and the mugs that say, "Clip! Clip! Clip!" she's a one-woman merch factory.

Maybe it's the cash-in culture that makes the fan-made art seem so much more appealing to me. It's one thing for Bravo to wring as much dough out of this phenomenon as they can. It's another for an amateur artist who loves the Housewives to make something for others who love them just as much. They're selling cards, but they're also selling a little piece of a community. Bravo is just selling stuff.

◻ ◻ ◻

While hawking pop-culture wares on the internet may be the world's second-oldest profession, another class of professional fans has come along in the last few years: those who create Bravo meme accounts. These are people across social media—but these days mostly on Instagram—who produce images, GIFs, and short videos of our favorite women to express very relatable feelings. A picture of Sonja Morgan and Ramona Singer cowering on the Boat Ride from Hell bears the caption, "If the

Real Housewives of New York can make it through their Cartagena trip, you can make it through the rest of this week."

That particular meme was shared by the account Bravo Betch, which has more than four hundred thousand followers and shares several comedic takes every day. It's the brainchild of Alexa Beridon and Katie MacArthur (Favorite Real Housewife for both: Ramona Singer), lifelong friends and Orange County residents. (Yes, they sometimes run into the ladies around town, but usually don't talk to them.) "We always text each other through the episode while we're watching them," MacArthur says. "Nothing has changed. Now we put it on the internet for everyone. We're sharing our thoughts and love with four hundred thousand people."

The Betches say that Ramona, with her crazy eyes and insane mannerisms, is by far the most meme-able of all the Real Housewives, and posts with her image tend to do better than others. This was echoed by all the other meme creators I spoke to. Otherwise, the success of a post has less to do with a Housewife's popularity than with whether it's a good joke.

For Finnish Instagram star Sebastian (Favorite Real Housewife: Sonja Morgan), who didn't want to give his last name, his first joke is still his best. "When they revealed the Obama portraits of Michelle and Barack, I saw an opportunity of inserting Luann in the bushes," he says, referring to the wall of plants in the president's iconic oil portrait, much like the plants into which a tequila-fueled Luann de Lesseps once fell. "I uploaded to a Facebook group. It was very unrefined as a photoshop, but then people really liked it there and asked if they could share and I created an Instagram account for that, so people could find it there and it would carry my watermark, so to speak." Thus the meme account Realityguy was born.

It really took off thanks to an official endorsement from Bravo. "Someone sent it to Andy [Cohen], and he showed it on *Watch What Happens Live* and that was the first *Housewives* meme I had ever made," he says. "It was the peak and pinnacle of my meme career, and I haven't been able to recapture the magic since then." His account now features mock-ups of Housewives on movie posters, like one dropping Vicki Gunvalson into the poster for *The Greatest Showman* with the title changed to *The Greatest Conwoman*. It made perfect sense after Vicki was accused of aiding and abetting her ex-boyfriend Brooks Ayers faking cancer on national television.

For Sebastian, who has about fifty thousand followers, his account is a great way to join a community of fans, since the Bravo canon is mostly unknown in his home country. "My friends are very supportive, but they are very dumbfounded by it," he says of his account's success, adding that he initially got into the franchise through the popular podcast *Bitch Sesh*. "I might be super excited about something, like, let's say, having Danielle Staub leaving a comment that she's going to send me a cease and desist and involve the authorities. I want to tell them about this, but it would be such a long explanation to tell them that I don't say anything." Meanwhile, nearly everyone reading that sentence knows what a big deal it actually is.

Maggie Kelley (Favorite Real Housewife: Lisa Rinna) runs an Instagram account called Best of Bravo that has about one hundred fifty thousand followers. She says it's about a thirty- to forty-hour time commitment. "Honestly, it really is like a full-time job," says the full-time IT recruiter. "Even when I'm at work, I'm checking Instagram and replying to people. When something crazy happens, like when Bethenny quit, I freaked out and ran away from my desk and I looked up all the articles on my phone. My bosses know about it and are cool, but I don't want to play all these clips at my desk." Kelley did say that her bosses let her leave a meeting early when tickets for BravoCon, Bravo's first fan convention, went on sale.

While many of the meme makers say that they spend close to that amount of time on their accounts, it can be hard to turn their online success into cold hard cash. Brandon Graeter (Favorite Real Housewife: Bethenny Frankel) is the creator of the account Pet Shop Boy, known for its use of Housewives clips and images in hilarious Instagram stories. He's leveraged his thirty-five thousand followers to do partnerships with the gay dating app Chappy and the Trojan condom brand. He also hosts a party at a Manhattan hotel where participants play a version of the kids' board game Guess Who? with the pictures swapped out for Real Housewives, and in 2020 launched *The B List* podcast, where he has interviewed several Housewives.

Lucy O'Connor (Favorite Real Housewife: Lisa Rinna) runs the meme account Lucy on the Ground and started a monthly Housewives trivia night at a local bar in Chicago. "We have friends who own a bar called the Happy Camper, and they said, 'If you can get twenty people, you can do it,'" she says. "The first night, there was a line out the door, and it was at capacity at 330 people."

The night included some possibly regrettable interactions with the crowd's favorite women themselves. "We set a bad precedent for ourselves. We said if you get a Housewife or someone from Bravo to respond on social media, you get free shots," she says. "These Housewives were all responding. [Real Housewife of Dallas] Stephanie Hollman responded to everyone. Everyone was so wasted."

O'Connor's trivia night is still a roaring (and drunken) success, even if some teams can't think up any creative names. "We won't let anyone have the team name Prostitution Whores anymore," she says. "Now people are like Tres Amigas. Go back and get better." Ironically for the Tres Amigas, I feel like someone has definitely said that to Vicki Gunvalson, Tamra Judge, and Shannon Beador before.

Stephen Krugle (Favorite Real Housewife: Kim Richards) is a registered nurse in LA working the night shift but also runs Faces by Bravo. He says he gets requests to partner up and advertise to his hundred thousand followers, but it's usually questionable businesses. "I've gotten a lot of offers to do certain things, but I said from the beginning I'm not going to post things that don't make sense. If it's not Bravo related, it doesn't make sense to promote a real estate company on my page," he says. "I think the weirdest one I've gotten was a credit repair specialist wanting me to post their services. I thought I could make a joke out of how some of the Housewives have really bad credit, but to me it didn't make sense." Teresa Giudice's bankruptcy attorney still hasn't sent Krugle a muffin basket for his discretion.

Podcasters have had better luck capitalizing on their fandom to create a livelihood. Ben Mandelker (Favorite Real Housewife: Luann de Lesseps) and Ronnie Karam (Favorite Real Housewife: Lisa Vanderpump), the cohosts of the popular podcast *Watch What Crappens,* have been enjoying their pet project's success since 2012. "We've just been around a long time, and it just keeps growing and growing," says Karam. Initially an outgrowth of the pair recapping the show for different websites, the podcast now does five weekly episodes and gets about 2.5 million listens a month. The duo says that their income is split pretty evenly between three revenue streams: doing live shows across the country, advertising on the podcast, and fans sponsoring them on Patreon, where they pay a monthly subscription fee and get access to premium episodes of the show.

"With Patreon, I thought, 'Who is going to pay to listen to free shit?' Like, no one," Karam says. "Thank God for Ben, because he's said, 'No, no. Let's just try it.' And so then [with that money], we were able to stop our other jobs. Ben was driving Ubers, and I was waiting tables, and we were slowly able to take less shifts and less shifts. It just grew and grew." Now the show is both of their full-time jobs.

At press time, thirteen former and current Housewives have their own podcasts, including everyone from Bethenny Frankel to Gretchen Rossi and her partner, Slade Smiley. Bravo also has its own *Daily Dish* podcast, which confusingly only comes out once a week. There are dozens and dozens of fan-created podcasts, both large and small, that cover the shows either exclusively or as part of an otherwise healthy reality TV diet.

Danny Pellegrino (Favorite Real Housewife: Ramona Singer) was working as a ghostwriter and supplementing his income with bartending shifts when he started his "little hobby" in 2017. His podcast, *Everything Iconic,* has since expanded to two episodes a week and about one million downloads a month. While it is technically pop culture–focused, Pellegrino (not heir to a bottled water fortune) says it is now about 85 percent *Real Housewives* and Bravo related.

The show grew after booking guests from the Bravo firmament,

Pellegrino says, and in a glamorous feedback loop, this made it easier for him to book guests. "It's really fun to interview them," he says of his Bravolebrity encounters. "I always get them when they're being nice. They know I'm going to interview them and people are going to listen. It's always fun for me when I'm talking to them and they throw some shade. Sometimes it's so subtle and I get so happy and my endorphins are flowing when, say, LeeAnne [Locken] throws D'Andra [Simmons] under the bus."

A perk of his Housewife interviews, which he conducts at his West Hollywood pad, is what happens once his microphones are switched off. "What I love most of all is they come to my house and they stick around; that is when I get the real juice and when they go off on the castmates," he says. "I keep that confidential because I don't want them to stop doing it! I get the biggest kick out of it."

It was at such a session when Pellegrino asked Ariana Madix, one of the stars of the *Housewives* spin-off *Vanderpump Rules,* what was going on with a cocktail book she was supposedly cooking up with her boyfriend and costar, Tom Sandoval. She told him it was dead in the water. He proposed that they pick it back up, batted around some ideas for it, and came up with a book proposal the trio took to Pellegrino's book agent. Now *Fancy AF Cocktails* is decorating Bravo-loving home bars across the country.

That's not the only opportunity Pellegrino has had from the show. Since Bravo fans are legion and installed in the highest echelons of media, a film development executive reached out after chuckling along to one of his episodes to ask if Pellegrino was working on any film projects. Pellegrino gave a polish to a languishing screenplay and sent it along. It has since been optioned to be made into an actual film. See, if you take your love of Bravo public and are good at it, other opportunities will come.

I've had similar experiences to Pellegrino. In the near decade I've been writing *Real Housewives* recaps, I still get paid less for them than for any other articles I write. However, since all the editors at fancy magazines are fans of the Housewives, and thereby liable to come upon my work, I get the more lucrative work I do off the back of the writing they see every week. It's almost like the *Housewives* recaps have become a loss leader.

I often say I owe my entire career to *The Real Housewives,* a joke that Danielle Schneider (Favorite Real Housewife: Porsha Williams) uses, too. She and Casey Wilson (Favorite Real Housewife: Kenya Moore) are the cocreators of the popular podcast *Bitch Sesh: A Real Housewives Breakdown.* Their creative alignment with our franchise goes back much further to a show Wilson, a former cast member on *Saturday Night Live* and the cult favorite sitcom *Happy Endings,* put together something called *The Realest Real Housewives* at the UCB theater in Los Angeles. At the event, she had Schneider and other actor and comedian friends read transcriptions of famous *Real Housewives* scenes, ending with a dramatic two-hander, where Schneider and actor Adam Pally played Camille and Kelsey Grammer in their limo on the way to the Tony Awards, which capped off *The Real Housewives of Beverly Hills'* first season.

"We dressed in all black, and we did it like serious theater," Wilson says of the night. "I'll never forget, we hired Mike Cassidy to play piano. He played a gorgeous classical rendition of 'Don't Be Tardy.' We came out with candles and just read the text like it was a play."

After that show, Schneider was approached by comedian Paul Scheer and producer Jonathan Stern about doing a *Real Housewives* parody. Stern had already made a spoof of *The Bachelor* called *Burning Love* that met with some critical success when it debuted on Yahoo!, back when both Yahoo! and videos on Yahoo! were a thing. Schneider and her writing partner, Dannah Phirman, created *The Hotwives of Orlando,* which aired on Hulu in 2014. The following year, it was followed up by *The Hotwives of Las Vegas.*

Schneider and Wilson starred in both seasons, with other actresses playing archetypes borrowed from the *Housewives* canon. In *Hotwives of Orlando,* Wilson was Tawny St. John, based on Gretchen Rossi and Tamra Barney, and Schneider was Shauna Maducci, based on Teresa Giudice. On *Hotwives of Las Vegas,* Wilson was Jenfer Beudon, a Kim Zolciak wannabe, and Schneider was Denise Funt, a mash-up of Shannon Beador and Taylor Armstrong.

It was a challenge to heighten something already so insane to the level of comedy. "I was just thinking about how psychics always come to the Housewives," Wilson says. "And when we did it, we were getting into fistfights with the ghosts. Just craziness was happening."

Schneider says that, just like all those psychics who show up, their insane antics have been oddly prescient about actual Housewives' goings-on. "It's funny because on the show some things that we thought as heightenings on the show have now come to fruition," Schneider says. "Funerals for dogs and things like that, what we thought we were taking a stab in the dark and making fun of something is now a real thing, which is crazy."

Bitch Sesh, which kicked off at the end of 2015, came about similarly to *The Hotwives.* "Paul Scheer, again, was on a podcast network and said, 'Do you want to do a podcast?'" Wilson says. He arranged a meeting. "We thought, this will be fun and it'll last five episodes and we'll just shout into the void. Truly, it became so popular. I've worked on other projects for years and years, blood, sweat, and tears to no attention. This, sitting in my kitchen, became huge."

Part of the boost for *Bitch Sesh* was an appearance in the main feed of a popular podcast, *How Did This Get Made?,* where Scheer; his wife and Wilson's best friend, June Diane Raphael; and Jason Mantzoukas talk about awful movies from the past. From there, it got recommended by *Entertainment Weekly* and other publications and wound its way through *Housewives* fandom. Now it gets about one million downloads a month, but Wilson and Schneider always joke that they aren't tech savvy enough to really know its impact. "We don't know numbers," Wilson jokes. "It could be ten million people, it could be ten people."

The success of the podcast has led to sold-out live tapings across the country, including one at Broadway's Town Hall theater in early 2020, where Andy Cohen himself dropped in to surprise the women and had the crowd roaring like a pack of lovesick tigers.

While *Bitch Sesh* brings in money, it's the boost to both of their careers that has been the real boon. Wilson says she was cast on the HBO show *Mrs. Fletcher* after a casting director who is a *Housewives* fan heard the show. "To cast me off that podcast, what a courageous woman," she says.

Schneider and Phirman sold a pilot to ABC after an executive at the network called them in for a meeting on the strength of Schneider's *Housewives* commentary. "I think people hear us on the podcast, and I hope they think we're funny and smart and want to hear what more we have to offer," she says.

Since its inception, *Bitch Sesh* has featured fans highlighting their "Boots on the Ground," or real-life interactions with Real Housewives. It could be anything from a waiter who served a cast member at their restaurant to a guest at a live show who is the daughter of a former Real Housewife. These interactions between fans and the women they idolize, and the minute glimpses they give us into their psyches, have become a favorite element of the show. Once, at a live show, a woman approached the mic and said she was from St. Louis, where *RHOC* cast member Meghan King Edmond's husband, Jim Edmonds, was working at the time. She alleged he had been spotted in gay bars around town. They are now divorced. At a live New York recording, one woman alleged that Sonja, Ramona, and Luann once had a, ahem, very good time together with the owner of Hooters. Stick about seven million *allegedly*s in both of those sentences.

A few fans eventually took Boots on the Ground too far in one of the Facebook groups dedicated to *Bitch Sesh* listeners. As the podcast took off, fans established a Facebook affinity group to talk about it, the shows that inspired it, and to share their own Boots on the Ground—or Bs on the G, as members used to say. The group was called the Whispering Alenes, named after Whispering Angel rosé, initially a favorite brand of Wilson and Schneider, and Kyle Richards's Beverly Hills store Kyle by Alene Too. Members vied to see who could get the best B on the G, which led to some uncomfortable moments for Heather Dubrow.

One Whispering Alene posted that her sister was going to be babysitting for Dubrow shortly and would share pictures of her house with the group. The story has calcified into legend among members and former members as someone getting this job expressly for the purpose of sharing the pictures with the Facebook group and that the pictures were posted. I was unable to find proof that it actually happened. When Wilson and Schneider found out about the plan, they distanced themselves from the group, and it was shut down.

"Ninety-nine-point-nine percent of the fans are truly so lovely and sweet," Schneider says about the incident. "We want to have fun, but when you invade someone's privacy in that way, it just feels like, guys, what are we doing here?"

There was another Facebook group called the Nook, named after the place in Wilson's kitchen where she and Schneider usually recorded the podcast. A member of this group posted, "So my friend just delivered a Postmates order to Chateau Dubrow!!! Facts: she ordered kabobs." The user then went on to describe how many gates it took to enter Heather's house, details about the inside of the house, which of her children answered the door, and other very specific details of Dubrow's abode (which fans had watched her build in its entirety on *The Real Housewives of Orange County*). The user also revealed they had pressed the friend for the gate codes to gain access to Dubrow's house, but the request was denied.

A Twitter user shared a screenshot of this post with Dubrow, who responded on the social media platform that she felt this was "beyond" a violation of privacy.

While the Whispering Alenes numbered in the thousands (a resurrected version of the private Facebook group has about twenty-seven thousand members), a fringe offshoot that called themselves Thunderdome was more intimidating. Thunderdome, named after the free-for-all arena in one of the *Mad Max* movies, started out with seven hundred members who were drawn to a forum with few rules and didn't have, as they saw it, any of the mewling by members or bans by moderators that happened in the main group.

They eventually whittled their number below 250, the maximum number a Facebook group can have where each member can still tell who has "seen" a particular post. They did this through a method called "#BullyDontBoot," because one of the few rules of Thunderdome was that they didn't throw out members. The Thunderdome's expansive seventeen-page glossary—with terms of art, descriptions of members, and an actual list of enemies, like they were part of Nixon's White House—defines the policy as, "since we do not boot Domers . . . we had to bully people out with draggings, GIFS, photoshops and such."

(Here are some other entries in the glossary. **Save it for your bullet journal:** Whenever people overshare their feelings or get too basic, "Save it for your bullet journal" is a go-to suggestion. **RIPIP:** Chelsea once said many moons ago "RIPIP" as a joke, and it has stuck since then. Stands for "Rest in Peace in Peace" for when someone leaves the Dome or actually dies. **Receipts:** If you're gonna throw out an accusation, you'd better have evidence to back it up. If you're gonna troll a group, get receipts. Receipts are screenshots of a post or PM. Don't be an idiot. If you see something you want to use against a TD enemy (see list below), add it to the Receipts album.)

Instead of getting rid of members who didn't participate enough, the more active members took it upon themselves to call those members out and force them to participate more. If they didn't, they would bully them with name-calling ("draggings") or photoshopping their image in unflattering ways. "The Dome," as its members called it, was not for the faint of heart.

At one point, the group took it upon themselves to send Wilson and Schneider an Edible Arrangement backstage before a live recording, signed simply "Thunderdome." Former members of the group say this only happened once, but Wilson and Schneider say it happened regularly for a while. "Weirdly enough, I would just call Edible Arrangements and get the name and number of the person who did it. I never called them up, but I know the name of the person who did it," Schneider says. They didn't really want anything, it seems, except to be noticed. As the TikTok kids say, they did it all for the clout.

"While we're making the record clear, I want to note that the Edible Arrangements sent to Casey were allegedly the good kind, with chocolate covered strawberries and pineapple, and not the all-melon garbage kind," a former member emailed me.

Thunderdome's biggest "accomplishment," however, was attacking

Kelly Dodd on *Watch What Happens Live* in 2016. Someone in the group had gotten their hands on texts Kelly apparently sent to her then husband admitting that she had an affair with a man named Frank. (Dodd never denied sending the texts. She later said she sent these to get a reaction out of her spouse and that she didn't actually have an affair.)

Members of the Dome coordinated an effort where they would all call *WWHL* during her appearance and tell the producer screening calls they had some benign question. If and when they finally got on the air, they would each ask Kelly about the affair and mention Thunderdome. Three members got through that night.

"This was the real first triumph of the Dome and the event which made us known/feared," the glossary entry for #KellyGate states. "This is what began our real split from the OG [original group, i.e., Whispering Alenes], when they fervently denied any involvement and basically tried to suck Casey and Danielle's assholes while throwing us under the bus and not taking any responsibility."

Kelly Dodd responded to the events on Twitter (read this all with one giant [*sic*] because it is Kelly Dodd on Twitter so there is little regard for proper capitalization or punctuation.) "Got my phone hacked with the fraud Dept. Going to get a private investigator and I'm going to sue & press charges!! Good luck Thunderdome," she posted on November 2, 2016. No charges were ever filed.

Thunderdome was doomed, finally, by internal politics. Apparently, after one member traveled from the United Kingdom to New York City, he posted pictures of himself meeting up at a bar with other members on his personal page, not on the group's page. The admin of the group saw these pictures and, realizing she was not invited, was hurt. I heard a few different versions of this story from former members.

One attendee of the New York City bar night was a former friend of the admin with whom she had a present online feud. That night, she posted something on that woman's personal Facebook page referencing a very personal story she had once shared in confidence. Things spiraled from there, and, really, the whole incident is straight out of a *Housewives* show.

"That was the beginning of the end," a former member told me.

"People were rightfully disgusted and called the admin out on her actions, which she joked about and defended but never truly showed remorse for . . . People had just had enough. Nobody was comfortable being in a space where somebody would maliciously go after another person like that." The Thunderdome shut down in 2018. Some of its splinter groups still survive, like BaaBaDOME, which is dedicated to *Southern Charm,* and one named Tater Tot Casserole is God BTW, for discussing the show *Sister Wives.* That's not a warning, just a statement of fact.

Bitch Sesh has hardly cornered the market on crazy fans. When I asked Twitter for stories about insanity on the *Real Housewives* boards, several people got in touch about a popular group that started with fans of *Watch What Crappens.* One of its moderators was accused of making up a house flood in an attempt to get free stuff from other members; when a former federal agent posted a research-heavy claim that the flood didn't exist, chaos erupted. The post with this exposé has more than 1,600 comments.

Things like this can even happen on the *Bravo* page itself. Someone alerted me to a particular exchange between two of its 1.2 million members. Let's call them, for the sake of this argument, Jill and Bethenny. Bravo posted a picture of Sonja Morgan and Ramona Singer dressed in vintage '80s aerobics gear from when they took Dorinda Medley's exercise class during season 11. The point of the post was to prompt people to watch the season 11 reunion.

Under the post, Jill wrote, "OMG, they look gross. They need to stop drinking vino . . . their guts are gross looking in those leotards." Jill's definition of "guts" and my definition must be different because Ramona and Sonja look tauter than the khaki around Jon Hamm's bulge.

"Do you feel good about yourself for writing that?" Bethenny replied.

"Yes. I feel great. But I want to help them and they're too young to look like that. Hell, I'm 67 years old and I don't allow myself to look like a swollen wine stomach."

"I'm sure your comments on a random post they'll never see are helping."

"Bethenny, you, too. Stop the beer drinking. You have a beer belly."

"You are skinny. Good for you. Your skin on the other hand . . . [gritting teeth emoji]."

"Thank you for stalking my social media page and looking so hard for a fault of mine. Haaa! Too funny!"

"I just love to see women supporting other women," Bethenny finally says, rounding out the thread.

Not all *Housewives*-related Facebook groups are bad; some are filled with women supporting women. (I also guarantee there are Facebook groups about soccer, Civil War reenactments, and macramé crafts full of awful people saying awful things to each other.)

The only *Housewives* group I'm a part of is one called the Vulturinas, which was started by a group who used to gather in the comments section of my *Housewives* recaps on the entertainment website Vulture. As such, I was invited as an honorary member to the private group, and honestly, I don't participate that much.

When I asked the group if they had any Facebook shenanigans to report, one member, Jeanie, had this to say: "We are pretty tight and have supported each other through all kinds of tragedies and deaths and births and adversities and have come out the other side loving each other no matter what. We (at least I) feel we can say just about anything in here and there is never ever judgement, only support. The ridiculous House-wives are now just the nearly inedible pink fondant on the marked down Walmart cake we guiltily binge. And it is still FUN!"

A fan who has been in and out of *Housewives* fan groups of all stripes told me that they start with talking about the shows but devolve into people taking swipes at each other, the airing of grievances and recrim-inations, apologies that aren't apologies, and factions going to war with each other over their alliances. As with Thunderdome, you get *Real Housewives* role-play, where every day is a reunion episode with names to be called out and receipts to be pulled out of a couch cushion.

⛛ ⛛ ⛛

Of all the fans who take their love of *Real Housewives* to a dramatic ex-treme or turn their hobby into a full-time job, none are quite like David

Yontef. The opening to his podcast, *Behind the Velvet Rope,* plays "Eye of the Tiger" as he intones, "This is the true story of a New York City boy with big-town hopes and small-neighborhood dreams of becoming best friends with the Real Housewives and other Bravolebrities. Then, one day, that dream came true. Kinda?"

That's right: his podcast is all about his real-life interactions with Bravolebrities. Yontef told a reporter for *New York* magazine at Bravo-Con that he's spent upward of $250,000 over the past several years going to events to hang out with and possibly meet the Housewives. When I spoke to him on the phone, he said that number might be a little bit inflated, but perhaps not. The day before we talked, he had just flown to Michigan to attend a live taping of *Vanderpump Rules* star Kristen Doute's podcast and hang out with her afterward. He spent the night in a hotel room and then flew back to his home in New York City the next day. He said the week before that, Real Housewives of Dallas Stephanie Hollman and Brandi Redmond asked him to come to their live taping at the last minute, and he shelled out for another plane ticket and hotel stay.

If you follow Yontef on Instagram, where he only posts pictures of himself with famous people and in particular Real Housewives, his whole life revolves around this pursuit. "It really started very organically," he says. "There was never a crafty plan. I don't know who it started with, but I would just DM Housewives. I would say, 'Great episode last night,' to Luann and then she would respond to me. We were far from best friends. Then I was like, 'Let's DM Tamra,' and, 'I have something to say to Kandi,' and they would DM back. That is one way it started . . . You eventually get a DM and then a cell number. There really is a way to go about it."

Yontef says he also put himself at events where he knew he would run into the women and made sure to talk to them to build familiarity. "That's not access. I'm just putting myself in that situation," he said, citing specifically his recent trip to hang out with Kristen. "You just keep chipping away, and you get access when you didn't have before because you keep running into the same people." The access and the friendships seem like an end in themselves, a way for him to wrap his favorite shows around him like a blanket.

Eventually, that turns into something like a friendship, and sometimes the real deal. "There are housewives I am friends with. If you ask [Real Housewives of New Jersey] Dolores [Catania] or Margaret [Josephs], they would say I'm family," he says. "I'm really good friends with a lot of those Housewives and that is of my own doing, and that didn't happen overnight."

There is another tier of his famous friends that Yontef says invite him to join them at events, but "if I was dying in the street would they reach out to help me? Probably not." He says that he is still doing things like hanging out at the door to the stage entrance after Erika Jayne performs in *Chicago*, and he describes himself as A-list and D-list at the same time.

"Dolores had an appearance with Ramona and Kelly Dodd, and then we're at dinner with them afterwards," Yontef says of a recent night out. "The average person is like, 'You were out drinking with Kelly and Ramona to all hours. That's amazing!' People are curious as to what happened. I don't understand how you can keep hanging out with them and they know you're going to talk about them the next day. If there is really confidential stuff, well, obviously, I'm not going to talk about that. I'm not an idiot."

Yontef grew up in New York City and the tonier suburbs of Connecticut, where he attended the same high school as Dorit Kemsley. He attended the University of Connecticut and eventually got his law degree and did corporate tax law before founding Advertising Executives Inc., a staffing company for the pharmaceutical advertising industry. In 2011, he tried his hand at reality fame himself, appearing as a bachelor on Bravo's *Millionaire Matchmaker* in the show's fourth season. According to a post the same year in the blog *Guest of a Guest,* Yontef said that he is richer than many of the other people who are also on that show. He said he owns a $5 million property with no mortgage and has another $1 million on hand. "Yontef is a lively personality who has made a habit of pursuing reality fame (he's made it to the final round of similar Bravo shows and has his own VH1 show on the cutting room floor)," the article reads.

He sold that company a few years ago, which is how he affords his high-flying, Housewives-courting lifestyle.

"I would live this life regardless of if it's related to *Housewives*," he says, in regard to the travel, the nights out, and the lavish spending. "I'm single, and I would do it anyway. I travel, and this is not my whole life, but it does consume quite a bit of it . . . It's fun to hang out with these women. It gets you access to things, it gets you into the *OK!* magazine party, and it's just a fun night out. When you're in the mood to have fun, it's a lot of fun."

He admits that there are drawbacks. "The thing about hanging out with a lot of them all the time is that it's all about the Housewives," he says. "I play a little game with myself: I was hanging out with [a Housewife] for forty-eight hours, and I was like, 'I'm going to play a game and see if she asks me one question about myself.' I think for forty-eight hours and I was not asked one thing about myself . . . I feel like that's where it's a full cycle of 'careful what you wish for.' I'm evolving to a different level. I'm coming out the other end of it with certain people." To be fair, he is somewhat fetishizing these women. Why would they want to ask about him when they know he's there to be in their orbit?

In our conversation, Yontef deflected criticism by musing on what he thinks other people think of him. "The people I don't know think I'm crazy, and I have no life and all I do is this," he says. "They think I'm a grifter trying to befriend all these women. Let's be honest, they're not all wealthy. I don't need anyone's money."

Later, he said, "A lot of people in the outside world, not that I give a shit what they think about me, but they are like, 'How pathetic, he has no life. He just follows all these people around, and his whole existence is getting the eight hundredth selfie with Erika Jayne.'" His voice is mocking. "The Housewives that know me don't feel that way. I feel like that is the perception of the outside world. But it is more about me, in that it could be laying the groundwork for something in the future. I don't know what that is, and if that might not happen, it's okay, too."

Yontef is currently working on a book about how to befriend famous people, but I also suspect he's hoping to star in his own reality show.

What Yontef is searching for, his ultimate quest, is the same as all the other members of the Real Housewives Secondary Economy: a connection. It's continuing a conversation, whether between fans on Instagram accounts, between a host and a listener on a podcast, between a bespoke pin maker and her customer, or between fans at odds over Lisa Vanderpump in a Facebook group who might also be calling each other fat to prove a point.

It's bringing fandom out of our living rooms and into the real world.

It's not a crime to talk about *Real Housewives* all the time. Even the women themselves do it, a secret Yontef has unlocked. "Believe it or not, when you hang out with a Housewife, all they do is talk about each other the whole time," he says. In my experience, hanging out with Housewives outside of the show, I've found the same thing to be true. "They talk about the show and filming and this one and that one. Most of the time, we spend talking about *Housewives*. This is what I would be talking about anyway. I might as well be talking about it with someone who is on the damn show."

YOU HAVE A LITTLE FAMILY VAN!
MY VACATION WITH VICKI

arrived at the Hyatt Ziva Puerto Vallarta on a Sunday afternoon in early December, a day later than everyone else who paid somewhere in the neighborhood of $2,000 to spend a long weekend with Vicki Gunvalson, the OG of the OC. That meant instead of Vicki Gunvalson waiting in the lobby to greet me, as with all the participants who arrived on Saturday afternoon, I was greeted by hotel staff wearing the shiny gold name tags and starched shirts that are supposed to signify good service but really make you feel like you're about to have a bad experience renting a car.

The lobby was large and airy, with the ocean lapping against the shore just beyond a group of people half drunkenly doing the Macarena as a DJ egged them on. Since I was there for the inaugural Vacation with Vicki, I was given my complimentary gift bag, a short-handled jute tote that said LIFE'S A BEACH, or RESTING BEACH FACE, or 99 PROBLEMS BUT A BEACH AIN'T ONE. Some sort of pun like that. I can't look it up now because at the end of the vacation, I left it in my room for a housekeeper to repurpose as she sees fit.

Inside the bag was a light blue lanyard attached to a convention-style name tag. On the back was the schedule of events for this weekend of Housewife interaction, beginning with a beach party with Vicki starting promptly at 6:00 p.m. There was also a blue bracelet I was supposed to wear to signify that I was part of the group, a pair of transparent sunglasses with reflective blue lenses, and, the crowning glory, a black-brimmed trucker hat that said #whoopitup on a white field with gold sparkly letters. That, alone, seemed worth my $2,000.

With time to kill before beach partying with Vicki and a group of absolute strangers, I sat down for a disappointing spaghetti bolognese and a soak in one of the several pools. Yes, this one had a swim-up bar. Would you even bother to go on a vacation to an all-inclusive resort with a Real Housewife if it didn't have a swim-up bar?

While in my trunks, I met a pair of bears (the beefy, hairy, homosexual kind, because I don't think they have the other sort at Mexican resorts). They were two of many escapees of the Canadian winter, one a handyman and one an airline pilot. They asked what I was doing at the resort all alone. I told them about Vacation with Vicki, and they were completely amused and befuddled. Not only had they never heard of her, they couldn't imagine why anyone would pay a premium to hang with a reality star. Hey, if you're looking for some beach time in the middle of the winter, why not get someone famous to watch you pickle your liver in unlimited rail liquor? Upon comparing the prices of our rooms over a similar time period, I was paying about $800 more for the pleasure of Vicki's company.

By 6:30, as I arrived at the beach in front of the hotel's south tower, the sun was already setting. There were around fifty people—mostly women, mostly middle-aged, almost entirely white—gathered on the sand listening to upbeat pop hits like it was a bachelorette takeover of a Hawaiian-themed gay bar. There was a bonfire burning. It seemed like a scene out of a *Real Housewives* group trip. Specifically, when the Real Housewives of Atlanta went to Anguilla with their husbands and Kenya twirled *Gone with the Wind* fabulous by a poolside.

I sidled up to one of the cocktail tables erected on the beach (you could tell this was a common setup for the staff) and waited to see who would talk to me. I met Vicki's PR team, a husband-and-wife duo who do mostly corporate work in Orange County. Vicki is their only celebrity client. They were both attractive and had the placid smiles of people always listening for their way into a situation.

As I surveyed the crowd, it became apparent that most everyone in the group had spent the day availing themselves of the free alcohol. Vicki came over and introduced herself. As you would expect of the hard-partying Housewife in Puerto Vallarta, she was carrying a tray of tequila shots and wearing a sleeveless black halter top, flowing black pants, and no shoes. After some small talk, where she listened attentively and asked me where I was from and what I did for a living, she went into the crowd to pass out the rest of the tequila shots. Everyone was enjoying themselves.

"You look fun, come talk to us!" a voice behind me said. Two attractive women in their thirties sat on a low, white tuffet placed on the smoothed-out sand. They were Lindsay and Sarah, best friends and coworkers from Lake Tahoe (well, Sarah is actually Lindsay's boss at a real estate management company), both well lubricated and ready to have a good time. I sat down and chatted with Lindsay, who is a Bravo superfan and a Vicki Gunvalson fan in particular; when she saw the vacation advertised on Vicki's social media, she signed herself and Sarah up immediately for one of the "girls' trips" a *Housewives* watcher hears so much about.

Sarah was really only fluent in speaking about *Real Housewives of Orange County,* the only Bravo show she watches, but she was plenty fluent in having a good time, flitting from group to group with nonstop dance moves.

Unlike the refrain we hear so often on reality TV, all the women on the trip, and even a couple of the men, were there to make friends. I met another couple of women, Melissa and Jennifer, cousins from Sacramento who, like me, were happy to stand a little bit on the sidelines and watch as the sun set and the group danced in the darkness.

Doing her job to keep the party going, Vicki charged to the sidelines and dragged people, me included, in front of the speakers set up in the sand, which had been cleared as a dance floor. Everyone complied, dancing like it was a favorite cousin's wedding while the whoops floated along the ocean breeze. Vicki's boyfriend (now fiancé), Steve Lodge, stood on the sidelines with a few other husbands and drank a beer looking like the retired lawman that he is. The crowd really started screaming when someone put on a playlist of Bravolebrity dance singles: Kim Zolciak's trailblazer "Tardy for the Party," Countess Luann de Lesseps's banger "Money Can't Buy You Class," Melissa Gorga's underrated "On Display."

I finally walked back to the tables and started chatting with Suzanne, who wore a maxi dress cinched with a Gucci belt and strappy sandals. She looked like she was dressed to go on a shopping excursion in Mexico with Ramona Singer. Suzanne (some of the names have been changed) owns a boutique in Columbus (or Cincinnati or Cleveland, I didn't want to be so rude as to take notes at a party) and her college-aged daughter kept trying to FaceTime without success. She handed me her phone and told me to text her daughter. "Leave your mom alone. She's wasted on the beach and trying to have a good time," I wrote because, seriously, unless it's an emergency, why bother your mom on her vacation?

"CALL ME IMMEDIATELY," her daughter replied. Suzanne hit me on the arm for alarming her daughter, which, honestly, I deserved. Once she was assured that her mother was fine (though wasted), she agreed to leave her alone. In this life, we must take even the smallest victories.

Suzanne's friend Melanie barged over, kicking sand the whole way toward our table. She had that wedge-cut helmet of streaky hair that one assumes to be the entrance exam for every beauty salon in the Midwest that caters to middle-aged women and is probably named Shear Delight. Naturally, talk turned to the one thing we all had in common: Bravo. Melanie, who is so slight I had to bend down to hear her over Simon van Kempen's "I Am Real," said, "I would make an excellent Housewife. I would be perfect. I say it like it is. I bring drama. I stand up for myself. Andy should really call me. I would be perfect on the show." I told her I would let him know in case he were casting *Real Housewives of Columbus* (or *Cincinnati* or *Cleveland*).

As the level of frenzy in the crowd approached Tamra Judge break-ing her leg climbing out of a hotel hot tub topless, the jet lag hit me like low-level, time-released LSD. I decided to rest up for the next day's events, which started off with a Q&A between Vicki and Dave Quinn, *People* magazine's *Real Housewives* expert. The event was held on the pa-tio of a large, empty ballroom. With a napkin full of mini muffins (the only thing I love more than *Real Housewives* is a continental breakfast, although this one proved disappointing), I settled in.

We heard all about Vicki's connection to Puerto Vallarta, how she went down there with her parents for the first time because they had a condo there. Vicki said she doesn't feel her mother's spirit at home in OC, because her mother never lived there, but she does feel it when she goes to Mexico. Dave delved into her early life in the Chicago suburbs, where her father owned a modestly successful construction company. She didn't go to college because she told her father she just wanted to be a wife and mother, and he didn't think she needed an education for that. She did a year at junior college and then beauty school.

Vicki also got a job as a checkout girl at the Jewel supermarket in Rolling Meadows, Illinois. "That's where I actually met Mike [her first husband], and he was my bagger, and couldn't keep up with me because I was the fastest checker in all of the store," she said. "I knew all of the codes by heart because that's how we rang up the groceries; there was no bar code."

We heard about Vicki's high school boyfriend, whom she dated even while she was at the grocery store. "We dated freshman year [of high school] all the way through freshman year of college, and then he said he wanted to go date others to make sure I was the one." Shortly thereafter, she met Michael Wolfsmith, who is her children's father. "I was at the grocery store, and he was bagging for me, and I'm like, 'Wow, you have a nice butt and a car.' And that was it."

After she got married at twenty-one, her father told her he needed her to work in the accounting office. He had his CPA teach her every-thing she needed to know to do the books and fill out the three hun-dred paychecks for the workers by hand every week. He also gave her husband, Michael, a job. After seven years together, things weren't going well.

"I was here in Puerto Vallarta with my parents for a couple months, Mike was supposed to be running the jobs, and he wasn't, and I had two babies," she said. "Briana was just born, Michael was one, and I could never find my husband. Literally, he was always missing.

"We were here in Puerto Vallarta and it was pouring down rain and I was crying, and my dad said, 'Your mother and I will support you and help with your children, not financially, but we will support you. You need to get divorced.'

"I went home and I asked him if he wanted to get divorced. He said, 'Yup.' I said, 'I didn't just ask you if you wanted to go get ice cream, I asked you if you wanted to get divorced.' He said, 'Yup.' And six weeks later, we were divorced."

Vicki says she never thought she would live a prosperous life, that she would always struggle through raising her children as a bookkeeper when she met the true love of her life: insurance. "So we were divorced and I was scared out of my pants and my friend sold me a life insurance policy on my ex," she told the enrapt crowd. "She told me I could buy life insurance on your husband or your future ex-husband-to-be and you become the owner, you become the beneficiary, and so I did. Then I asked her what she made, and she said six hundred dollars. I have to work a whole week at forty to fifty hours at my dad's construction company to make six hundred dollars. So she said, 'Go get licensed,' and I did, and then I became the bestselling agent because I had to make money." As for Mike, according to Vicki, he lives in his mother's basement and hasn't worked a day since she divorced him.

Vicki tells the crowd that they need to become "stewards of money," something she'll echo throughout the weekend. For her, a stable life means being financially sound, and she makes sure that she, and everyone around her, takes care of their fiscal responsibilities first. "Every season when I start, I send Tamra and Shannon an Excel spreadsheet," she said. "When we get paid from Bravo, it's typically on a monthly basis, don't put that money in your account right away. You go pay your state and your federal taxes right away and be done with it. Then you only end up with 50 percent of it. Shannon's like, 'Well, that's not fair.' I'm like, 'It's not your money. Half of it is the government's and the states.'"

Who knew that Vicki, a woman we've seen screaming on a ski slope about having "multiple partners" and screeching in Slade Smiley's face while dressed in an '80s-inspired costume could be so utterly sensible? If I had an accountant who treats me like Vicki treats the other House-wives, I might actually put some money into my retirement account.

Vicki says that her financial worries changed once the show started airing and her business took off. "I got my own internet server for my website for insurance services," she said. "The server shut down. People are going online to buy insurance? Here we go!"

She also addressed some of the harder things about being on the show, like her fight over her boyfriend Brooks Ayers (whom she claims "murdered her bank account") with her castmates and her children. They had all figured out that he was after her for money and fame and that he was only pretending to have cancer. It took her several years to swallow those hard truths. She also relived the famous incident when she was caught on camera screaming about getting a "family van" sent to her house—one of the first viral moments of the franchise.

She tells Quinn that the biggest regret of her time on the show was that she divorced her second husband, Donn, so publicly. "I got eaten up a lot because everybody loved Donn. They didn't know what I had experienced; we seemed to live fun and happy. He's a great guy, but we weren't great together," she said.

She also explains that renewing their vows, a kiss of death for any Real Housewife's marriage, was her idea. On a trip to Turks and Caicos, Vicki surprised Donn at dinner one night by having the waiter deliver their wedding album to the table. Just that made Donn emotional, but when she said they were renewing their vows at the resort the next day, he became teary-eyed. "You have a wedding planned?" he asked.

The next day on the beach, under a white tent affixed with tropical flowers that matched the bouquet Vicki carried, they both cried when talking about their love and their future together. Yet after that, Vicki's love tank was notoriously empty.

"It was my last-ditch effort," she said. "I knew it was over when we got up to [our hotel] room with the big heart on the bed and trail of candles and he goes, 'That'll be good for TV.' I knew it was over. I just cried. He's like, 'Stop crying. It'll be good for an episode.' And I knew he was checked out." The saddest part of all is that part of their trip didn't even make it to the episode.

Vicki did claim to exercise some power about casting, saying she got Lauri Peterson, her onetime employee, kicked off the show for alleging on camera that she had a three-way ("I told them we couldn't film with liars"). She also claimed to have axed Quinn Fry, a season 3 addition whom she thought was boring.

"I want to believe I have some power, but at the end of the day, the viewers really have the power," she said. "If the viewers are tired of me or tired of my story or tired of the yelling or tired of me going to work, then I'm off . . . I don't believe my story is over, but if Bravo and the viewers think it is, then it will be." About a year later, they would come to that very decision.

While it seemed like everyone was enjoying Vicki spilling her secrets, the sun was beaming into Vicki's and Dave's eyes, which not only forced them to shade themselves with their hands but was making visible sweat circles on their respective shirts. We're next to the ocean and about seven different pools, so why should anyone sweat so much? They decided to call an end and move everyone over to an enclave of beach chairs set up for Vicki and her friends to hang out.

I sat around with all my new friends for a casual day on the beach, sort of like being on Fire Island but with less screwing and Britney Spears dance remixes. Everyone was gossiping and chatting, talking about all the new people we'd met on the trip as well as Vicki and her castmates.

Dave Quinn and I went on a little walk in the water, and Vicki came over to chat. She asked me what I was hoping to get out of this vacation. I told her, "I really just want you to try to sell me some insurance." I didn't actually want insurance, but she's talked about her business for so many years on the show and obviously has an affection for it, yet we never get to see her in action.

"Oh, oh," she said, frazzled with excitement, like a dead iPhone that finally gets plugged in and vibrates with a barrage of messages. "What kind of insurance do you need? Are you a freelancer? Do you need health insurance?"

"I have that through Obamacare."

"So, is there anyone dependent on you, or are you dependent on anyone? Are you married? Does your husband make more money than you do?" she asked.

"He does. Yes."

"What happens if he dies? Will you be protected? What size policy would you need?" We got into some specifics, and she told me that if I was serious, I should get back in touch after vacation.

This was a woman clearly in her element. All these fans were here to hear about the show, to find out the gossip about who is really nice off camera and who Vicki secretly hates, and all she wants to do is to make sure that I'll be financially stable in the sad event of my husband's untimely death. She was being a steward of her own money by helping me to be a steward of mine. Sensible, boring Vicki, a Vicki underneath and outside the pursuit of fame, was somehow the most intriguing Vicki of all.

She told Dave and me that there was going to be an off-book trip that night after dinner to Andale's, her favorite bar in the center of town, where she and other Housewives have been known to dance topless during their Mexican exploits. She said it couldn't be on the official calendar for liability reasons but that she was going to be there and she would love all of us to join her. "And wear your #whoopitup hats."

Dave and I joined up with Lindsay and Sarah, the fun girls from Tahoe, and decided to make our way over to the swim-up bar. As we eased into the surely-to-be-peed-in water and pretended not to care, Sarah told us about Desiree and Chuck. They were a Canadian couple on the trip that I had met briefly at the beach party. Desiree, who seemed to be about sixty and owned an entire wardrobe of animal prints, promptly told me that she used to be a stripper, that Chuck was twenty years her junior, and that she had forced him to take her to Mexico for their anniversary.

According to Sarah, Chuck had approached her, and just about every other woman in the entourage, asking if she would be interested in joining him and Desiree in a threesome. As she shared that fact, her mouth opened wide and her eyes glowed like ice cubes in the sun, faking surprise but mostly amused. Lindsay pursed her lips and nodded her head to say, "Can you even believe?"

They also told us that Chuck was going around grabbing all the girls' butts under the water, so they had started avoiding him. Sadly, as fans of *Real Housewives,* we are not unaware of men behaving badly. There have been plenty of garden-variety cheats, like Mario Singer, David Beador, and Joe Giudice, but also some much nastier characters. It's hard to forget that scene on *RHOA* when Phaedra Park's husband, Apollo Nida, comes into their home and stands threateningly in front of her wielding a power drill. There was also the time Kenya Moore's boyfriend broke the windows in her house in a fit of rage. The worst case, though, is Russell Armstrong whose wife, Taylor, talked openly about her abuse on *Real Housewives of Beverly Hills.* Chuck wasn't as bad as that, but it seems like we had our own Bravo-level creep in our midst.

We nursed our drinks and gossiped in the gorgeous Mexican afternoon, and Suzanne came over to regale us with her own tale of Chuck trying to get her in the sack. Suddenly, standing on the edge of the pool was her friend Melanie holding an armful of towels and other beach supplies. "Why did you leave me?" she shouted, trying to keep the tears out of her voice.

"We didn't leave you. We told you we were going to the pool," Suzanne said.

"No, you didn't. I went to the bathroom and I came back and I was all alone. You were all gone. Why did you leave me alone?"

We peeled away from the fight as Melanie dropped everything in her arms on the pool deck, some of them landing in the water, and pointed down at Suzanne, still marinating in the heated pool and holding her head and her drink just above the surface. Even as Suzanne apologized and tried to explain, Melanie seethed and continued her tirade.

"This is amazing," Lindsay said to our little clique. "It's like *living* in Bravo."

That, right there, was the money shot. Vicki and her organization banked on the fact that people would pay for access to one of their favorite television celebrities. What they didn't realize they were selling was the lifestyle in toto—the boozy, drama-filled vacation with a bunch of friends, new and old, whom one both adored and couldn't stand. Getting face time with Vicki, and Chuck groping them all at the swim-up bar were both just bonuses, one more awful than the other.

I could really see the Bravo lifestyle that night after everyone ate dinner separately and got together at 10:00 p.m. in the hotel lobby to head to Andale's. The hotel's largest conveyance pulled up to drive us all down, a fifteen-seat van that prompted every guest to shout, "A family van!"

After a ten-minute drive, during which Sarah told me Chuck had walked into town earlier that evening looking for Mexican Viagra and left Desiree all alone on their anniversary, we arrived at the bar. Wave after wave of Vicki's new friends livened the place up on an otherwise sleepy Sunday evening. Out front, Vicki introduced me to the owner of the joint, who thanked her for bringing so much business to his bar over the years. To a small subsegment of the population, she turned this bargain-basement TGI Friday's into a destination. It would never earn a Michelin star for its watery margaritas in fishbowl-size glasses with multiple straws, but the Bravo seal of approval is the next best thing. His staff, well inured to drunk people screeching through their vacations, was dutifully tolerant.

With their #whoopitup hats in place, everyone drank, danced, and vibrated at the fact that we were in Andale's with Vicki Gunvalson, though we were told that dancing on the bar, topless or otherwise, would not be allowed that evening. Andale's is, objectively, not a great bar. It's much smaller and more cramped than it appears on TV. Though Vicki told me she loved the music, there was nothing played that had been recorded after 1993. It was like the best option for a drink in an airport in a second-tier city, like Columbus (or Cincinnati or Cleveland).

But there was an aura there, an energy of people living their best lives. Maybe it's like that all the time, with all the vacationers. It felt different, though. As I watched the women taking turns to pay a man a few pesos to ride his donkey into and then back out of the bar, I felt the strange urgency of people visiting a place for the first time that had immense meaning for them, the mecca of a pop-cultural pilgrimage.

After a couple of hours, as the buzzes started to coagulate into something sloppier and more aggressive, I peeled off from the group and headed to a gay strip club a few blocks away, where all the buff, shirtless dancers called me Pablo Escobar, either because I have a mustache or because I actually spent money on a couple of the boys and tipped in dollars. It was certainly not because I was doing coke. I swear! I wasn't.

The next day, everyone recovered on the beach and by the pool. Vicki came down from her suite and spent time with the group when she wasn't scheduled to, which spoke either to her narcissism or her need to give people their money's worth. Maybe it was a little bit of both. That evening, there was a closing cocktail party in the too-large ballroom where we had the Q&A session. This time, there were pigs in a blanket and other mini hors d'oeuvres, which were equally disappointing as the mini muffins.

What was not disappointing was the company. No one needed their name tags anymore. Mostly, we talked about Bravo, what our favorite shows were, which characters we loved, and which we hated. Those with inside knowledge shared what gossip they could or recounted things they heard from Vicki and Steve over the weekend. ("Steve told me Eddie and Tamra are only nice to them when the cameras are on," someone said.)

Vicki took time to speak to everyone, myself included. She told me how the show had been key to her success as an insurance agent and how she was shocked at the response she had gotten to showing off her "black box," a plastic organizer full of all her investments, insurance policies, and other important papers. People were already calling to ask her to set up black boxes for them. It could be another revenue stream.

At the cocktail party, she knew everyone's names. She thanked them all personally. She mingled with the efficiency of an underdog politician at her first fundraiser. The rest of us, while waiting our turns, followed each other on Instagram and promised we'd see each other next year, if there was a next year. She told me she'd love to talk to me for this here book and to get in touch with her people when I was home. By the time we coordinated it, she had been fired from the show and told me she wanted to save her best stories for her new podcast, *Whoopin' It Up with Vicki.*

Vicki was not in the lobby to see us off the next morning. I left alone, after another disappointing breakfast, and made the ten-hour flight back to London. A few days after I landed, I got a note in the mail. Inside the cream envelope was a matching cream note card with a navy blue border and *Vicki Gunvalson* embossed across the top in a matching hue. "Dear Brian," it said. "Just a quick note to thank you *so* much for taking the time to join us in Puerto Vallarta for the 'Vacation with Vicki.' It was so good meeting you and spending time with you! Wishing you a Happy Holiday! Warmly—Vicki."

Regardless of what I thought of her on the show, and she's had some awful moments, she proved herself to be a very kind and classy lady. Either it was her midwestern upbringing or her decade plus of being on *Real Housewives,* but she knew all the right moves to make people like her.

As I stashed the letter away as a keepsake, I thought of a moment from the second-to-last day of the trip, when a bunch of us were hanging out on chaises by the pool. A man we didn't know came up to try his luck with some of the ladies. He went around introducing himself, trying to strike up conversations. The women weren't giving him the time of day. They all paid good money to be around someone whose life they had been following and imitating for years. To them, she was the reason to be here, the planet around which all other moons orbited.

Finally, the man turned to Vicki and said, "What's your name? What do you do?"

"Hi. I'm Vicki," she said, extending her hand and giving a slight shrug. "I sell insurance."

THE SEXIEST MEN OF
THE *REAL HOUSEWIVES* UNIVERSE

Objective, definitive, and based on physical appearance only.

Joe Gorga:

> His supplements may have killed all his sperm, but it was worth it for a physique no one's husband can match.

Apollo Nida:

> Yes, this felon doesn't have a great personality, but you can't deny his beauty.

Mauricio Umansky:

> Kyle Richards's husband is successful, low-key, and looks amazing in a bathing suit. Truly the full package.

The Milkman:

> Kelly Dodd only dated this milk salesman for a hot second, but that second was really, really hot.

Donnie Edwards:

> The most memorable thing about one-season-wonder Kathryn Edwards was her stunning partner.

Mario Singer:

> Yes, he might have cheated, but no one does silver fox like Ramona Singer's ex.

Romain Zago:

This Miami-based club promoter was the only man pretty enough to keep up with Joanna Krupa.

Evan Goldschneider:

We don't see much of RHONJ Jackie Goldschneider's husband, but when we do, we all want to drown in this tall drink of water.

Frankie Catania:

Sure, Frank Sr. is built like a brick shithouse, but someone really needs to give his and Dolores Catania's son a modeling contract.

Aaron Phypers:

Denise Richards is always crowing about his finer attributes, and we can see why.

Juan Dixon:

This former basketball star and his ex-wife, Robyn Dixon, have a complicated relationship, but why she's attracted to him is fairly simple.

Harry Hamlin:

There is only one former Sexiest Man Alive on this list, and it is the one Lisa Rinna only refers to with both names.

Adam Kenworthy:

Carole Radziwill was worried about how many good summers she would have with this dish of a vegan chef.

Shane Keough:

The son of a *Playboy* Playmate was sure to turn into a perfect specimen.

Don Juan:

Anyone ever notice that Kandi Burruss's business partner is a bit of a babe?

Cedric Martinez:

Lisa Vanderpump kicked her gay BFF out of her house after season 1, but we've always missed him.

David Beador:

Shannon Beador's ex was athletic and handsome, if you don't mind that dead-behind-the-eyes look.

I HANG OUT WITH
QUEENS ONLY

LOVING LIFE AT BRAVOCON

You could hear it before you could see it, the line of thousands of white women ages roughly thirty to sixty huddling together on West Thirty-fourth Street in the brisk Manhattan evening. There was a chirping of excitement. The line snaked all the way down Thirty-fourth Street and around the corner up Ninth Avenue. Its tail grew as more and more women arrived, but the head stayed pointed squarely at the Hammerstein Ballroom.

On this day in early November 2019, this was ground zero for Bravo-Con, the first-ever fan convention put on by the network that has given us everything from *The Real Housewives* and *Below Deck* to *Project Runway* and *Inside the Actors Studio*. James Lipton was not the draw that Friday. Everyone was lined up for the largest-ever live taping of *Watch What Happens Live,* Andy Cohen's ten-year-old talk show and *Real Housewives* feud generator. The evening promised seventy-seven Bravolebrities on the same stage all interacting across casts. It was the closest thing a *Real Housewives* fan would get to experiencing something like one of Cohen's all-time favorite shows: *Battle of the Network Stars*. Sadly, for lovers of the male form, the best we would get is *Vanderpump Rules* star Tom Sandoval in revealing drag, not *St. Elsewhere*–era Mark Harmon in his Speedo.

This was my first event of BravoCon weekend. While many had been attending panels and other events all day, I didn't secure a pass for Friday, only a $150 ticket to *WWHL,* which was a separate paid event not included in the price of fans' wristbands, which ranged in price from nearly $1,500 for a three-day VIP pass to $124.50 for a one-day general admission ticket, the lowest available tier. Though I had shelled out extra for a seat on the floor of the ballroom, I was worried I would be at the back of the house with the first-come, first-served seating.

Luckily, as I was approaching the line, I heard someone shout my name. "I love your recaps!" a redhead in a leopard-print fur jacket and a ball cap said. Her name was Lauren, and we struck up a little conversation, and then I asked if I could cut in line. No one seemed to mind, or at least said anything, so I cheated all the women (and a handful of gays) behind me. Hey, they, too, would do anything for Bravo.

As much as I worried about the wrath of the fans, I also wondered what I would find when I finally got into the Hammerstein Ballroom. All early indications made it seem like BravoCon was going to be a mess. Just two weeks before the event started on Friday, November 15, the Bravo gossip blog *All About the Real Housewives* published a post saying the conference was going to be a total flop. Exhibit A was that Real Housewife of New York Sonja Morgan had announced on Instagram that she would be hosting a wellness retreat in Florida the same weekend.

The report also said that Bravo was scrambling to find Bravolebs willing to attend, because they weren't paying enough money. It stated that NeNe Leakes and Kandi Burruss would not attend (which turned out to be true) but that Dorinda Medley and Tinsley Mortimer were going to be no-shows as well (which turned out to be false). Some were already likening the three-day convention to the Fyre Festival, the notorious concert scam where thousands of people expecting luxury accommodations and gourmet food arrived in the Bahamas to find soggy mattresses and white bread with cheese served in Styrofoam containers.

It didn't help that Bravo hadn't announced the schedule or list of attendees until just eleven days before things were kicking off in Manhattan. Until then, fans had bought their tickets (and booked their hotels, planned their flights, and purchased GOODBYE, KYLE T-shirts on Etsy) on empty promises. I'm sure the thought of being granted photo ops with only B-list Housewives entered more than a few heads.

There was also all the drama surrounding tickets going on sale in August. The three-day passes sold out in less than a minute. Thousands of fans waiting by their computers to purchase them were shut out. A similar thing happened a week later when the one-day tickets became available. Irate fans blamed scalpers and bots swiping up tickets to gouge people on the secondary market for keeping so many people out of their happy place. Roughly ten thousand tickets were sold overall.

I was lucky enough to score a mid-tier VIP ticket for Sunday and a ticket to *WWHL*. Oh yes. My $234.50 didn't get me into many of the events, which required additional purchases, like Andy's big show, a *Vanderpump Rules* dance party, a *Southern Charm* brunch, and a *Top Chef* food event.

The reason I was buying tickets at all is because unlike many other media outlets, bloggers, meme account runners, and podcasters who were covering the event, I was not granted a press pass. I had my editor at Vulture reach out to Bravo PR to see if I could get a pass to write an article about it for them. My editor was told by Barry Rosenberg, the vice president of communications for Bravo, that it would be a "conflict of interest" if I were to attend because I was, at the time, working on this very book that you now hold in your hot little hands.

To back up a little bit: research for this book turned out to be a lot more difficult than I had hoped. A Real Housewife loves to talk about nothing more than herself, but they can only do that with Bravo's stamp of approval. After I sold my book, I got in touch with a junior PR staffer at Bravo (who has since left the company) and told her what I was planning. I had always had a rosy relationship with the network and decided it was best to keep it that way. Shortly, I was in touch with Barry Rosenberg himself, and chatted with him and Jennifer Geisser, now the executive vice president for communications for Bravo and NBC's other "lifestyle networks," about collaborating together. They asked for a proposed outline and a list of people I wanted to interview, and in good faith, I sent it.

This was a mistake.

Jill Newfield, a lawyer from Bravo's business affairs department, got in touch with my then editor and offered him a deal. They would set up interviews with the Housewives, Bravo execs, and producers I was interested in talking to and help me promote the book by using their official platform. The price was 10 percent of every book sold—and complete control over the editing and marketing of the book. My editor at the time balked less at the profit sharing than the lack of control, which would make this book just another house organ for Bravo, sanitized of anything approaching bad PR. They wanted to turn me into merch.

After the deal was scuppered, Bravo did me the favor of contacting every single real Housewife, past, present, and possibly future, and told them they were not allowed to talk to me. I figured for sure Brandi Glanville or Aviva Drescher would love to dish, but both of them turned me down, like many other Housewives. Aviva, like several others, initially agreed and then mysteriously became unavailable or unresponsive, possibly after they attempted to clear the interview with Bravo and were told no.

Bravo also blocked me when I was writing an article for *The New York Times* about how reality shows were handling reunion specials during the COVID-19 lockdown. They told my editor at the *Times* they would not participate in the article if I was writing it. The same held for a panel at the online Vulture festival, where the network said I would not be able to moderate a discussion between two of the Housewives because of the book.

In the late stages of writing, I decided to put out one last plea on my social media channels, telling anyone who had worked on the shows to get in touch with me. The next day, I got an email from one of Bravo's lawyers. "We noticed your Instagram post about the book," an email from Justine Beyda, senior council for litigation, read. "I am not sure if you are aware but our contracts with Bravo talent and production employees include standard confidentiality agreements that are necessary given the unique realities of the television industry. Now that you are on notice of these provisions, we respectfully request that you refrain from conduct that may encourage or induce violation of those agreements."

Well.

I was not about to let any of that stop me from getting in on Bravo-Con.

※ ※ ※

I bought tickets like any other member of the public who refreshed her web browser fast enough when they went on sale. Still, I was worried that Barry, or one of the other members of the Bravo PR team, several of whom I'd met over the years at various events, would recognize me and ask me to leave. Because I watched Robyn Dixon on *The Real Housewives of Potomac* dress up like a pizza deliveryman to drop a pie off on Karen Huger's doorstep to ascertain whether or not she actually lived in her house, I knew what I needed: a disguise.

As handsome as I might be, the most distinctive feature on my face is a mustache that I have cultivated through gibes and jeers for more than a decade. The easiest way barring a wig (and there are several *Real Housewives* wig lines to choose from) to escape easy detection was to get rid of my mustache, which I did on that sad Friday afternoon in my hotel room with a brand-new razor I purchased at the Duane Reade.

I have also been wearing a self-imposed uniform for the past five years. In the winter, it is a gray wool suit, white shirt, and dress shoes. For BravoCon, I bought myself a navy blue sweatshirt, took out the jeans I wear on more casual days, and popped on the Detroit Tigers ball cap I had just used as part of a *Magnum, P.I.* Halloween costume two weeks earlier. It wasn't much. My mother still would have picked me out from twenty paces, but I figured a busy Bravo PR rep wouldn't notice me as she picked her eyes up from her clipboard as I passed by.

Luckily, no one spotted me as I walked into the Hammerstein Ballroom, which had been transformed into a Bravo-branding fantasia. There was a huge wall of fake greenery with *BravoCon* spelled out in seven-foot-tall, Instagram-friendly sans serif font. There was a swing laden with flowers, like the one Lisa Vanderpump has set up in her backyard, where people could take pictures. It was sponsored by Pepsi Rosé, which is some kind of cola that tastes like rosé wine, or maybe it's just rosé wine made by Pepsi. I don't know. I wasn't going to sit in that swing if it meant taking a swig of that devil juice.

The crowd, however, was the selling point. There was a vibration in the room, like the atoms in your potatoes after you take them out of the microwave or children trying to sit still at an ice cream social. While there were different tiers of tickets, everyone was helpful about finding each other seats and making sure all could be accommodated.

I sat next to two women, one in a leopard-print coat and the other in a fur jacket, who seemed like they were longtime friends. I found out they had just met in line. That is what the atmosphere was like: everyone was here to bask in the thing they loved, and that love transferred to everyone else in the room.

I chatted with Margaret, the one wearing the fur jacket, and it turned out she was there with her best friend from West Hartford, Connecticut, just a few minutes away from where I grew up. She bonded with her eighteen-year-old daughter over Bravo and, since her daughter had been diagnosed with non-Hodgkin's lymphoma, she hadn't really been allowed to leave the house. That meant more Bravo for the two of them. Elizabeth told me she had to beam all her photos from her iPhone to her Apple TV so that her daughter could share in the fun from the couch. We swapped phone numbers, too, in case she got any great pictures and needed to text me. Here I was, five minutes in, and I already made what seemed like it could be a friend for life.

I've been to plenty of tapings of live shows in the past, and usually there is a comedian who comes out to warm up the crowd and make sure they're in the laughing and clapping mood. They also give instructions about when to cheer and applaud and give them the lay of the land. The live *Watch What Happens Live* did not need that. As soon as Andy Cohen was announced, everyone leaped to their feet and screamed like the Beatles, New Kids on the Block, NSYNC, One Direction, and BTS had all showed up at once.

The audience could have used coaching, for while they screamed for Andy and anything *Housewives* related (surprise guest Lisa Vanderpump got the biggest ovation), the reception for shows like *Married to Medicine* was tepid at best. The biggest negative reaction came when Tinsley Mortimer announced that she was back together with former boyfriend Scott Kluth, which elicited a rumble of discontent like someone just said the bar was out of everything but Pepsi Rosé. (This may foreshadow why Tinsley left the show halfway through the twelfth season after she and Scott got engaged.)

The episode was really just a bunch of introductions punctuated by feverish elation from the crowd. There were two distinct highlights. The first was when Andy pointed out that Lisa Vanderpump and New Jersey matriarch Caroline Manzo left the stage where all the Bravolebrities congregated before the casts of their franchises could be introduced, showing the audience that the squabbles we have been watching on TV certainly carry over into real life.

The second highlight was a game called Squash That Beef, where Bravolebrities from different shows who ran afoul of each other in the press or on social media were brought together to see if they could settle their differences. On the stage, there was a screen where two spinning wheels, like those in a slot machine, spun with faces of different Bravolebrities; the two it landed on had to come sit on the two stools in the middle of the stage to hash out their problems.

The best string occurred when Ramona Singer, in a sleeveless chain mail of gold sequins, was called up with *RHOP*'s Gizelle Bryant. At issue was a photo taken at a party in the Hamptons, where it looked like Ramona was telling Gizelle to get out of the frame.

"I said I would take a picture with her after I took a picture with the host," Ramona explained.

"Who did you say that to, though?" Gizelle shot back to the crowd's delight.

Ramona then offered the classic *Real Housewives* non-apology. "I'm sorry if I hurt your feelings."

"You didn't hurt my feelings, you were just rude," Gizelle said, and the crowd erupted.

After that, Ramona refused to apologize, and Gizelle sat down just as mad as ever. Then it was time for the next beef, and while the wheel with Ramona's head stayed where it was, the second wheel moved on to *RHONJ*'s Dolores Catania.

Ramona laughed as she sat back down. At issue this time was one of Ramona's appearances on *WWHL,* where Dolores's ex-husband, Frank (who is still her best friend), was there and Ramona refused to take a picture with him, upsetting Dolores.

Ramona is notorious for not wanting to take pictures, especially with fans on the street. "I don't like to take pictures," she told the crowd.

"Then what are you doing here?" Dolores asked to great applause. "Get out of the business."

Ramona said, "I learned that when I do these public events I need to be better and take the pictures." Everyone cheered.

Dolores said, "This is what we sign up for. These people deserve a picture." Ramona walked across the stage and hugged Dolores.

"It looks like we squashed that beef," Andy said. "Let's see who is next." Again, Ramona's wheel stayed where it was, and the other pinned to reveal Vicki Gunvalson. The crowd was incredibly amused while Ramona, turning back from returning to her seat, pretended to be upset.

"I saw her in Greece!" Ramona shouted at Andy. "I met her fiancé. I have done nothing to Vicki. Oh my god." Andy explained that Ramona has said multiple times that *RHONY* put the Housewives on the map even though *RHOC* was first.

"One of the head people at Bravo told me that *Real Housewives of New York* put *Housewives* on the map," she said to Andy, who seemed like he didn't believe it.

"No, I put you on the map," Vicki said, defending her position. She got a standing ovation, and continued to make faces at Ramona like she was crazy.

"*New York Housewives* put Bravo on the map," Ramona said, now out of her chair and confronting Vicki. "*New York Times, New Yorker,* the *Post, Daily News,*" she said, ticking off each outlet on her fingers.

"Are you kidding me?" Vicki said, getting to her feet to meet Ramona.

"No," Ramona said. She waved her hands in front of her face like she was swatting away a swarm of gnats and sat back down. "I'm not kidding you." The beef was not squashed, and Andy ushered each woman back to their seats as they continued to rant their points under their breaths as they sat back down.

This segment really was the promise of BravoCon fulfilled. It wasn't just the chance to see all our favorite Housewives but to see them interact outside the silos of their individual cities. It was to be floating in a space where these different planets, constellations, and comets were colliding into each other and careening off in new directions. Even better than seeing a panel with the cast of *Real Housewives of Beverly Hills* was seeing one featuring the show's OGs, the women who had remained on their shows since the first season (in parlance borrowed from hip-hop culture, perhaps the pop-culture sphere furthest removed from Bravo's core brand). There Kyle Richards, Teresa Giudice, Vicki Gunvalson, and Countess Luann de Lesseps sat Botoxed cheek by liposuctioned jowl talking about how they and their shows had changed since they started.

Panels were what I was in line for almost the rest of the weekend, starting Saturday morning. As I was back in the cold waiting outside the Hammerstein Ballroom, a shocking juxtaposition became apparent. Clumps of people in garish, fantasy-inspired garb kept walking by. There were hundreds of people in costume for an animé convention down the street at the much larger Javits Center. I thought for a minute that, for all their insane devotion, at least Bravo fans weren't crazy enough to dress in costume.

Then I looked around at the crowd. There were multiple women wearing variations on the felt fedora Kyle Richards wore when Lisa

Vanderpump kicked her out of her kitchen. (My husband and I officially call that style the "Goodbye, Kyle!") Plenty of others were in fur or feather vests, which, for a while, seemed to be issued to every first-year Housewife along with her initial contract. There was animal print as far as the eye could see, sky-high heels on the Manhattan sidewalk, Gucci insignia belts—all the modern signifiers of Housewifery at its finest. If I saw someone wearing a Sky Top, I don't know whether I would have rolled my eyes or bowed down to her dedication to cosplay.

These women *were* in costume. The looks were more quotidian than Comic-Con, but maybe more powerful because of it. If these women wanted, they could stay in Housewife costume all the time, and probably some of them did. While you can't show up to your job as a real estate agent dressed as one of the heroes from *Attack on Titan,* you can show up dressed like Kyle Richards. That might even get you a job at her husband's real estate company, The Agency. That ability to change people's daily behavior, not just what they wear to conventions, is truly powerful.

There was one woman waiting in line wearing a fur coat, leopard Louboutins, diamond earrings, a full face of makeup, and hair that was almost certainly professionally done. She wasn't thinking of BravoCon as a fan event; she was thinking this is an audition. She was getting so close to this with the hope that Andy Cohen would spot her in the crowd, reach out his wizard finger, and say, "You!" plucking her out from the sea of striving and placing her in an entry-level job on reality television.

None of that happened at any of the panels. Aside from a few brilliant fan questions—like the revelatory one about who pays for the cast trips—not much news was broken or lives changed. It was especially hard for the cast of shows like *RHOBH,* which was at the conference after the tenth season had filmed, but hadn't aired yet. When fans (and the moderator) asked questions about the previous season, the women seemed annoyed to rehash those events again. But when asked about upcoming seasons, they were happy to provide some variation on, "You'll have to watch and see!"

When a fan asked for a demonstration, Erika Girardi did get up and teach everyone how to do her signature move, "patting the puss," and it sort of made the whole thing worthwhile, at least for thirty seconds while she gyrated her hips in a circle and brought one hand to meet her crotch.

Proving me wrong about Q&As, the fans were the best parts of the panel, honestly. Heroic women (and gays) asked the types of questions—like whether Melissa Gorga had heard the smack Teresa, her sister-in-law, talked about her on stage at another panel—that made everyone else go, "Ooooh," waiting for the answer.

Shockingly, considering how brutal some *Housewives* fans can be on social media, everyone was well behaved. Well, almost. One woman verbally attacked Real Housewife of New Jersey Jackie Goldschneider, but the crowd quickly booed her into submission. Another asked Dorit Kemsley when she decides to put on her "fake accent" (which even Dorit jokes is hard to place) and was again shushed back into her seat.

In at least one event, I saw a Real Housewife in the audience. At a panel featuring four veteran producers of the show, Jill Zarin sat near the back of the crowd on the aisle. When producer Darren Ward was talking about his experience on Scary Island, he said, "I think we have a special guest somewhere here, Jill Zarin." Everyone immediately started looking around the room for her.

"Yeah, I'm like, 'What are you doing here?'" she yelled from her seat, talking about when she arrived at the airport in St. John to surprise the women and saw Darren and Kelly headed back to New York before the trip was over.

"There she is, everybody. There's Jill. Jill Zarin! Hi, Jill," he said as the crowd erupted in applause.

That was really all she said, but her friend, the podcaster Heather McDonald, did ask the producers if they thought about having Jill back on the show. They all demurred because the answer, as Andy has said many times, is no.

Most in attendance weren't reality stars, but they deserve no less attention. Everyone I met was so excited to be there. Chelsea, from Chicago, told me in the balcony of the Hammerstein Ballroom before the *RHOBH* panel that this was like her Disneyland, though she grumbled about the lack of good food options. Then she catapulted right back to excitement: "Have you ever been around so many people who thought like you before? Because I haven't. It's amazing."

Mara, Sally, and Meghan, from Atlanta, Nashville, and D.C., respectively, are old college friends who text predominantly about Bravo in their group chat. They decided this was the perfect opportunity for a little class reunion, with some Housewives on the side.

Surprisingly, nearly everyone I met was from outside of New York City and almost certainly the tristate area. That means people weren't only ponying up for tickets but also plane tickets, hotels, dinners out, and surely prodigious bar tabs. All of this so that they could be part of what is essentially a branding exercise, not just for Bravo and (ugh) Pepsi Rosé but Lay's Poppables (a strange combination between a potato chip and a Corn Chex) and Pure Leaf tea, which gave out special BravoCon bottles that said, "Elegance is sipped, my friends," a spin on lyrics from "Money Can't Buy You Class," obviously.

Almost everyone I asked said they just bought their tickets online, so scalping seemed to have been minimal. Then again, nearly everyone was rabid enough to have been refreshing the BravoCon website when tickets went on sale. One woman said she told her boss what was going on and ducked out of a meeting at her law office to buy tickets. Another woman had a tech-savvy neighbor set up a bot to buy her tickets, much like scalpers do, but just for her. It wasn't a very scientific poll, but it was the best I could muster.

Only two people I talked to used scalpers. One woman said her boyfriend paid $500 for two tickets for her and a friend so that he wouldn't have to go with her. Mara, Sally, and Meghan bought their tickets through a scalper, too, but the QR code they were given was fake. When they arrived at the BravoCon ticket office on Saturday to pick up their wristbands, the staff took such pity on them that they forked over three general admission passes.

The most shocking revelation was that Bravo made its own employees pay for tickets. I sat next to two nice women from the research department who said they were given early access to buy tickets, or they could work as volunteers at the event and then get free tickets. Shifts were not guaranteed, though, so the only way to assure attendance was to pay for it.

As one would expect, the tiers of tickets became a problem at some events where demand was higher. Those with SVIP and VIP tickets were allowed to sit closer to the stage, which was great in the two-thousand-plus main venue of the Hammerstein Ballroom, where a seat in the balcony reduced even the biggest-headed Housewife to nothing more than a smudged thumbprint. (There were monitors for a closer view.)

In most cases, fans weren't turned away, except when panels were held in the smaller venues, which closed out general admissions guests when they were at capacity. The only time I saw someone get testy was at one of the photo ops. Held before and after panels, these allowed people their opportunity for a selfie with their favorite Housewife. When a fan got to the front of the line, she would hand her coat, purse, and other belongings to one attendant and her phone to another. She would then take her place next to a single Housewife or in the center of a whole cast. "One, two, three," camera phone click, and the subject would be hustled out of frame and her belongings restored.

On Sunday, I got in the VIP line (I treated myself, and Bravo, to about 150 more of my dollars) to get my picture taken with the cast of *Real Housewives of Beverly Hills*. I immediately ran into Jennifer and Melissa, two of my friends from Vacation with Vicki, who were in town from Sacramento for this event. I was glad for the company, because after about an hour of waiting in the queue, we were still about twenty people shy of the front. I was standing so close to Lisa Rinna that I could see the microfibers on her QVC duster. (Just kidding, she wasn't wearing QVC, she was wearing a hot pink blazer with no pants like an even gayer Judy Garland.)

The allotted photo time had passed, but there were still hundreds of people crammed into a smaller venue boasting a kitted-out shed that was somehow selling State Farm Insurance (what, Vicki's COTO Insurance wouldn't pony up to be a sponsor?) and a tiny replica of the *Watch What Happens Live* clubhouse to take selfies in. As several women from the general admissions line were let in before the VIPs, a large (most likely gay) man a few bodies in front of me yelled at the attendant. "Excuse me, why are you letting them in?" he asked with the disdain usually reserved for someone speaking to Danielle Staub at a reunion special. "We paid a lot of money for these tickets. We should go first."

Eventually, all the VIPs were accounted for, right before the women were ushered off to their next engagement. The disappointed, pictureless fans shuffled around the venue while things were set up for *Vanderpump Rules* star DJ James Kennedy's set on the turntables. He got behind the decks looking like 10:00 a.m. was too early on a Sunday morning to be bothered, and by the time he complained that the music wasn't loud enough for fans, most of them had already dispersed.

Some went into the Bravo Bazaar, which was the best place to get a picture with other Bravolebrities, granted you were willing to pay for the privilege. Carl Radke and Kyle Cooke from *Summer House* were taking pictures for anyone who bought a four pack of their sparkling alcoholic iced-tea brand, Loverboy. Dorinda Medley stopped by several times to greet fans who were buying her aerobics-inspired T-shirts.

I didn't see Jill Zarin hanging out at the Jill Zarin Home booth, but there were some nice women there with carpet samples and a big bowl of candy, which I think might have been more appealing than the rugs. "You can buy a rug here?" I asked the women attending the booth.

"Yes, you can," one of them replied.

"But is anyone here buying an actual rug?"

"You *can* buy a rug here," she replied in a shrewd bit of misdirection that means she earned every penny that Jill was paying her.

There were a handful of non-Bravo booths at the event as well. Kerrin Piche Serna, the owner of Eternal Flame Candles, which sells candles with images of Housewives in faux-religious poses, was invited by Bravo to sell at the exhibition, but she had to pay $5,000 for the booth. She came up with twenty-four exclusive designs and launched them at BravoCon.

Leslie Carrier, an artist with a line of greeting cards inspired by the Housewives, talked the fee down to $3,000 for the booth. Both women said that, with the expenses of traveling and shipping, they just about broke even, but it was worth even more to them to be at the convention.

Piche Serna had already bought tickets to BravoCon, so she left her husband attending the booth while she went to panels. She gifted people like Cynthia Bailey and Shannon Beador the candles she made in their likenesses. "It was surreal," Piche Serna said of her time in the bowels of reality TV capitalism. "Cynthia Bailey was there selling stuff and signing stuff. Captain Sandy [from *Below Deck*] was across from us. Dorinda's booth was right there, and she walked over and said hi to us. It was crazy, and we lost our minds. Next time, we wouldn't buy tickets, we'd just work the booth."

I wondered if the Bravolebs had to pay for booth space. The completely unsubstantiated rumor was that everyone was getting $5,000 a day for their attendance, and travel and lodging paid for. (Some gossip rags reported that Ramona Singer tried to get more money out of Bravo for her and the fellow New York ladies, since they didn't get the travel bonus.) If that figure is true, maybe some were given a booth in the bazaar instead, a chance to make possibly more money selling T-shirts, branded eyewear, and accountability coaching than they might in just an appearance fee.

As I was getting ready to leave BravoCon on Sunday, I got another text from my new friend Margaret. We had peppered each other with pictures and updates throughout the weekend. She sent me pictures she got of herself with Captain Sandy and Ariana Madix from *Vanderpump Rules*. "I feel so incredibly fulfilled," she texted me. "I'm not saying that in jest!"

That got me thinking a lot about something that happened at the *WWHL* taping on Friday. Andy Cohen said that Lisa Rinna knew that BravoCon was an excellent idea as soon as she heard it. When she was a regular on *Days of Our Lives,* she would attend Super Soap Weekend fan events, which were very similar and always a hit as big as her lips.

But there is something different about BravoCon and a Super Soap Weekend, or even the animé convention happening down the street. Yes, they're all rooted in fans' desire to be around people who love the same thing as them and share the same fixation that, in other contexts, might be deemed embarrassing or unworthy. But there's something else at play as well. With animé, fans go to see the people who created their favorite characters. At Super Soap Weekend, fans go to see the actors who play their favorite characters. At BravoCon, fans go to see the people who actually *are* their favorite characters.

When watching two people who play rivals on a soap, a beef isn't going to happen right there in front of everyone. Fans know and accept that there is a veil of fantasy over the entire enterprise. At BravoCon, fans gossiped about how Teresa Giudice and Melissa Gorga, her long-suffering sister-in-law, were talking trash about each other on different panels, rekindling not just a feud but actual family strife. There are actual stakes here. This is fans living in the thing they love the most, like a virtual reality game that shades into real reality. It's *Housewives* as gladiatorial combat.

Here everyone clamors to see Kyle Richards do the splits, as she did during one of her panel appearances, to the rapturous applause of fans. The ultimate promise of BravoCon is the reassurance that the fandom we've all spent so much time and devotion nursing, is valid. It is worthwhile, and tangible. Every panel, every celebrity interaction, every selfie taken, every piece of merchandise purchased was like the universe whispering, "This is real. This is real. This is real."

12

PRETTY IS SMARTER THAN YOU THINK

HOUSEWIVES GONE HIGHBROW

Brenda R. Weber, a professor of gender studies at Indiana University, has an anecdote in her book *Reality Gendervision: Sexuality and Gender on Transatlantic Reality Television* about talking to a lawyer at a university function. The lawyer, a muckety-muck on the university board, told Weber in a bit of party chitchat that he worked on cases involving the eradication of toxic sludge. He then asked what she studied at the university. She said that she researched reality television.

"So we both work in toxic sludge," he responded.

Any fan of reality television in general, and *The Housewives* specifically, can see the look on his smug face. It's the same face you get from people at cocktail parties who say things like, "I don't even own a television," or "I'm not vegetarian, I'm actually vegan." The hardest part about loving *The Real Housewives* is the judgment received from people who are not fans or, even worse, are passing judgment on us for our obsession with the franchise when they haven't seen an episode. Remember, these are the kinds of people who don't even own televisions.

Because of those reactions we couch our love of these shows as a "guilty pleasure" or admit that we know that they're "dumb" or "silly," but we love them anyway. I honestly think it's time we stop doing that.

"I wish that people would stop saying it's a guilty pleasure and admit it's a passion pursuit," says Sarah Galli, the host of the *Andy's Girls* podcast. "The judgment some people pass on it is ridiculous."

If you're reading this book, you probably know there is nothing wrong with being an out-and-proud *Real Housewives* fan. People that think the shows are harming the world or making us dumber or setting their favorite cause back twenty years are probably wrong. So wrong that many academics seriously disagree with them. The next time you're eating hors d'oeuvres and staring down the nose of a smug jerk who just said, "What is a Lisa Vanderpump?" here are some arguments and facts you can throw back at them to prove your passion is just as valid as anyone else's.

◻ ◻ ◻

June Deery, the head of the media studies department at Rensselaer Polytechnic Institute and a frequent author on topics relating to reality television, says, "People are very proud of the fact that they are big sports fans and they're watching a lot of sports. But if you say, 'I'm a huge fan of *Real Housewives* and I'm watching a lot of *Real Housewives*,' it's not the same prestige value. I think there's a lot to do with gender there. It's clearly a more feminized form for most people."

Weber questions why people think less of reality television in the first place. "We think of high culture as needing some high priest or professor or a translator to help us understand T. S. Eliot or *The Odyssey* or something like that. But nobody thinks that you need to have crib notes to *People* magazine, right?" she says.

She explains that the cultural gender binary tends to confer authority on all things associated with maleness. Things that are associated with women or gendered female are in the weaker and more submissive position. "High culture gets put into the masculine zone, the more powerful, the more elite, the more respected," Weber says. Conversely, "feminized art forms like gossip, celebrity, and popular culture" are looked down on. "[Reality television is part of that.] That's what I mean when I'm talking about the genre is gendered."

Whatever your television taste, dismissing *Real Housewives* out of hand while greeting *Breaking Bad* as serious art plays into the sexist binary that infects our world order. A love of reality TV—even something as macho as *Deadliest Catch* or *Ice Road Truckers*—is a tiny stab in the heart of the patriarchy.

"Take the *Breaking Bad* example. It does tend to be fascinated by masculine authority, breaking the rules, and pushing the boundaries of ethical codes," Weber says. "It's always interesting to me that the show has been saddled with this 'Housewives' idea because if you think about a traditional housewife who's at home, not working, submissive, and relying on a man, a lot of the women on the shows are breaking those rules in the same way. They're fully employed, single, and out in the world, but we don't see them breaking the rules in the same way that we see Walter White is."

Yes, that means that Ramona Singer may not be making meth in her backyard, but she's definitely living life on her own terms. For my money, she's also no less deserving of an Emmy nomination than anyone else. You want to talk Method acting? How about living your actual life on-screen, walking the tightrope between high drama and real emotional stakes, knowing that if you don't do it right your days on camera are numbered?

Feminist scholars have their own critiques of the franchise. Nicole B. Cox has published several academic articles critical of the *Real Housewives* franchise. In the introduction to "'Femme Dysfunction Is Pure Gold': A Feminist Political Economic Analysis of Bravo's *The Real Housewives*," her 2012 doctoral thesis at Florida State University, Cox says, "I argue that the *Real Housewives* franchise targets and exploits the female audience, selling them 'images' of themselves that are deeply problematic and indicative of the contemporary epoch of postfeminist media culture."

A similar argument was made in the high church of the Real

Housewives, Andy Cohen's *Watch What Happens Live* clubhouse. In 2013 while on the show, feminist icon Gloria Steinem said, right to Andy's face, "It is women—all dressed up and inflated and plastic surgeried and false bosomed and incredible amount of money spent—not getting along with each other. Fighting with each other. It is a minstrel show for women."

These women do have a bit of a point, and it reminds me of my old "friend" Chuck from Vacation with Vicki, grabbing ass in the pool wherever he could. The *Housewives* franchise has shown plenty of women being mistreated by the men in their lives. We've also seen the producers (many of them men) manipulating the women's behavior. And while it is mostly women at the top of Bravo's corporate structure, the fans all see them answering to a man: Andy Cohen.

Still, there are plenty of feminist interpretations of the show. Roxane Gay, public intellectual and author of *Bad Feminist,* got her own chance to hit back at Steinem on the very same stage, saying, "I think that the *Real Housewives* franchises allow women to be their truest selves. We see the mess, we see their amazing friendships and everything in between. When women are allowed to be their fullest selves, that's the most feminist thing we can do." Gay even added that she once personally challenged Steinem about her view on *The Housewives* when she ran into her at a fundraising event, a conversation I would have paid real money to witness.

If you don't believe Roxane Gay, maybe you'll believe one of the Real Housewives herself. In 2018, Kyle Richards promoted the premiere of the short-lived comedy *American Woman,* based on her life, in which Alicia Silverstone played a version of Kyle's mother, who left her husband and got a job so she could support her children. It also showed her best friend fighting misogyny in her career working in a bank.

A reporter for *The Daily Beast* asked Kyle if the feminist values of *American Woman* jibe with what's on *The Real Housewives of Beverly Hills.* "All the women on our show are incredible women," she responded. "I think all these women are empowering. They're all incredible businesswomen. They have solid marriages. They're mothers. They're juggling.

They're doing it all. I think all of them are inspiring, honestly. If you look across the board at all these women, I think they're all inspiring. People say this to me on a daily basis, all day long, on Instagram and Twitter. So that's what I have to say about that." Amen, Kyle. But we *have* seen enough vow renewals and subsequent divorces to know that maybe those marriages aren't so solid.

Weber thinks that, regardless of how people feel about *The House-wives,* it is a viable field for feminist study. "There's a lot for a feminist to learn about gender and sexuality from the Real Housewives," she says. "I think the Real Housewives are very savvy about this new edge of the economy that we're in, in terms of how you make yourself visible and keep yourself relevant and the kind of work that you do in order to sustain those forms of value. Now, whether we like that or not, that's a whole different question. But I think they're very skilled at doing it."

The best defender of the Real Housewives' feminist honor I've found is Yael Levy, who teaches film and television at Tel Aviv University, in her article "Serial Housewives: The Feminist Resistance of *The Real Housewives'* matrixial structure." She takes umbrage with a quote in an article by Cox and Jennifer Proffitt saying that the franchise is "problem-atic from a feminist political economic perspective" because it promotes "consumption, emphasis on appearance and perpetuation of gender roles." Basically, they think the Housewives shop too much and look too pretty.

Levy's defense is that most people are looking at *The Real Housewives* as a linear text, like a movie, television show, or a novel. Scholars analyze the shows individually and in a self-contained manner, reading them from start to finish. Anyone with a DVR clogged full of Bravo content knows that this is not the way that the shows are aired or how they are consumed by most people. There is always more than one franchise of *The Real Housewives* on at any given time, sometimes more than one on the same night. That means the shows shouldn't be seen as a straight line but as a matrix, where one show can correct the bad impressions made by the others.

"The show's structure conceals subversive instances that undermine the very normativity the show perpetuates," Levy says before getting all academic about it. "Seeing as the majority of the franchise's episodes are followed by episodes of a different installment before their consecutive intra-installment episodes are aired, I contend not only that seasons resist closure, but also that each installment 'absorbs' the narratives of its horizontally coextensive installment (airing during the same weeks), internalizing its deviations and suspending any possibility of a 'return to order.'" There's never a "patriarchy wins" happy ending; the Housewives contain too many multitudes for that. While this simultaneous story structure may be accidental on Bravo's part, it is the way that many fans absorb the franchise. And even if a viewer watches only one city, there are instances of this effect within the show.

The best example Levy gives compares an event in the third episode of the third season of *RHOBH,* where frequent-marrying dried-up desert lizard David Foster makes a comment about his wife, Yolanda, who was new to the series that season. Foster, in his inimitably endearing way, says, "Yolanda as a hostess is nothing short of stunning and spectacular; I'm shocked now at how many women don't know how to be a great homemaker and hostess. She just gets everything right without being froufrou, because I hate, hate, hate froufrou."

Levy says of that comment, "Read vertically, the Beverly Hills scene presents a traditional gender role commentary, ostensibly perpetuating patriarchal rule." Basically, she means that Yolanda is stuck in the role of hostess, pleasing her man without being so feminine as to offend him. The TL;DR is something that *Housewives* devotees know very well: David Foster is a jerk.

She then compares that scene to one in the fourth episode of the fifth season of *RHOA* that aired later the very same week as the *RHOBH* episode. That scene is the famous one where Kenya Moore, also a first-season Housewife, orders takeout, places the food on plates, and passes it off to "boyfriend" Walter as her home cooking. "It took me forever to make this meal, but I'm just trying to focus more on, you know, family life, and trying to get myself more accustomed to being wifey, being at home, being a mother," she tells him. She is saying this to woo Walter, but she's also being sarcastic, because if she did care more about these things, she might have actually bothered cooking. Also, we know Kenya; she's almost always sarcastic.

"The Atlanta scene plays against the Beverly Hills scene, intertextualizing with David Foster's comment by which women must perform femininity (in this case as homemaker and hostess) just 'right,' and in a sense satirizing Foster's words," Levy writes. "Read independently, the Moore sequence is framed as comic, but read alongside Foster's sequence, it becomes a tale of unintentional feminist criticism regarding the binds of femininity."

I bet if you asked Kenya Moore, she would tell you that's exactly what she was going for.

Levy's point only extends as more *Housewives* episodes accrue; there is a critique or counterbalance for just about everything somewhere in the great Bravo oeuvre. Take, for instance, Carole Radziwill's relentless campaigning for Hillary Clinton in the 2016 election and compare that with Alexis Bellino submitting herself to the will of her ill-fated husband, Jim. The ostensibly liberal is critiqued by the ostensibly conservative. Since many *Real Housewives* aficionados hold all these events in their heads at the same time, it becomes possible to interpret the world through a million lenses at once.

That's also true if you look at how consumerism plays out on *The Real Housewives.* Many have accused the franchise of promoting conspicuous consumption, and to those critics, I can only say—yeah, you're totally right. I mean, one episode of *RHOBH* features Erika Girardi and Dorit Kemsley going to drive Pagani cars at a dealership in Beverly Hills under the auspices of Dorit who is going to buy one for her husband's birthday gift. The cars start at $2 million. They did not buy one, but the show gives the impression that if you really want to honor your spouse, it will take a car worth about six suburban homes. (Or sixty Suburbans.)

But to live in a late-capitalist society is to be confronted with glorified consumerism at every turn. Are Real Housewives any different? Speaking of Dorit Kemsley, remember when she spent exactly $18,481.98 on a set of Hermès china and how ridiculous everyone thought it was? "That was crazy," Reddit user CheckMeBooo posted online of that incident. "I impulse-buy dark chocolate peanut butter cups from Trader Joe's. She buys HERMÈS PLATES WTF I DID NOT EVEN KNOW THEY MADE PLATES."

Viewers watch for the extravagance of the lifestyles, but they're often rejecting that lifestyle as well. Cox and Proffitt recognize that in their article "The Housewives' Guide to Better Living: Promoting Consumption on Bravo's *The Real Housewives*." "Exploring how fans seek participation in—or rejection of—consumerism, research suggests that fans are actively negotiating the meaning and value of the consumerism propagated by the show," they write. "Although online comments illustrate acceptance of consumerism, these comments exist alongside a questioning of the Housewives' spending habits and misappropriated values."

The thrill viewers get from watching Phaedra Parks order twelve cakes for her son Aden's first birthday—one for every month—isn't in the ludicrous amount of money she's spending on baked goods for a child who won't even remember the event. The thrill is in being able to shake your head at her, at the ridiculousness of her consumption. Sure, plenty of people want a lavish birthday party, but let's be honest, none of us know enough people for twelve cakes.

The consumerism is also critiqued by what we know about the women's lives. We know Vicki has a successful business and a great house with a backyard, including a pool with a crazy water feature that belongs in a Disney park. But no matter how much she has, her love tank is never full. Sure, Dana Wilkey had $25,000 sunglasses, but it didn't keep her from falling afoul of the law. For that matter, not one of Phaedra's twelve cakes kept her marriage to Apollo Nida from dissolving or him winding back up in jail. If anyone thinks that money can buy you happiness, the easiest way to be disabused of that notion is by checking Bravo about three times a week. (As long as *Below Deck* isn't on. That makes it look like luxury yacht vacations really can solve all your problems.) If someone really wants to yell about conspicuous consumption, try turning the dial to HGTV, where shows literally tell you if you can afford a house or a home makeover or a backyard with a firepit, then you'll finally be happy.

The money these women spend is not just supposed to give viewers a vicarious thrill but also to signal that rarified quality: class. As we saw, the show was initially intended to give us a view "behind the gates" of what it is like to live in a wealthy, gated community. But class doesn't always play out in such a straightforward manner. Or as a spiritual troubadour might say: "Money can't buy you class."

"One of the things that's interesting about the *Real Housewives* franchise is how often class is an actual topic," says Deery. "They talk about things like, is it okay to be a gold digger or should I have my own career? As the show goes on, they have their own income and, more importantly, they have a brand opportunity, because they're on the show and the media exposure can be translated into dollars." That sometimes translates into elevated status, thanks to a country where class more often equals money than in a closed system like Britain, where class is determined by breeding. Just look at someone like Bethenny Frankel, who, throughout the course of the show, went from a scrappy upstart in a dingy apartment to buying and selling properties all over New York (even if the house she was selling in the Hamptons was a little too close to the highway for Ramona's taste).

To illustrate her point, Deery looks at two of the other New York women. "More recently, it's been the Sonja Morgan narrative about class," she says. "To what degree she claimed to be part of the upper class, the elite of New York, and the slipper incident . . . Sonya came into quite a bit of criticism from cast members about her pretension about being a Morgan." She is, of course, talking about when Sonja started making slippers with a stag on them because it was part of the Morgan family crest, even though the Morgan family was one she married into rather than was born into. Dorinda Medley, and some of the other women, took umbrage at her appropriating the symbol as her own.

Deery calls this *class delusion* and says that the women often catch each other and criticize each other, calling into question the very notion of class themselves. She points to what she sees as Dorinda's dubious claims to a higher class as well. "There's also Dorinda Medley's story where her father was a mason on the big house, and then she dreamed one day of having the big house," Deery says of Blue Stone Manor, Dorinda's self-named and notorious Berkshires hideaway where she's hosted many drama-fueled weekends. "She married the money that got her the big house that she dreamt of as a girl. There's a question if she is really among the elite in the Berkshires, and of course, she's absolutely not."

Whether or not that is true of Dorinda's neighbors, viewers know that the class delusion is real. Sonja may own a $10 million town house on the Upper East Side, but we can clearly see that the elevator is broken, the ceilings are leaky, and the whole thing needs a complete refurbishment. The women of *The Real Housewives of Atlanta* have enormous mansions, but we all know they're off in the suburbs. The women of *The Real Housewives of Beverly Hills* are wearing designer clothes, but they might be borrowed from stylists or designers.

We know that many of these women are playing at being rich, and we're okay with that. We're also aware that the show is sort of a self-perpetuating cycle of money. One has to appear to have money to get on the show, to make even more money, which then needs to be used to look like one has money. And if the money can be a bit of an illusion, then maybe that means class is, too. If all that separates these hoity-toity women from us at home is them being cast on a reality show, maybe class differences are equally unimportant.

There might be some class distinctions that not all viewers are keen to. "[Real Housewife of Potomac] Gizelle [Bryant] comes from a very old money, prestigious sort of like Black lineage but none of those things are legible, I think to Bravo's white audiences," says Racquel Gates, a professor at the College of Staten Island who wrote about race and *The Real Housewives* in her essay "Keeping It Real(ity) Television." "They don't know what Hampton University [Gizelle's alma mater] is, right? None of that stuff is legible even though it's very legible to me and a lot of other African American viewers . . . The minute that I saw the cast photos of Robyn [Dixon] and Gizelle, I thought, 'Oh, this is what they're doing.

They're doing that kind of old, old money, old lineage Black folks. OK. Got it.'"

It's not only the representation of class that might be above some non-Black viewers' heads, but also the problems with representation on the franchise's shows with predominantly Black casts: *RHOA* and *RHOP*. *RHOA*'s sixth season, which aired in 2013 and 2014, was especially a problem. It featured both the famous pajama party brawl between numerous castmates (but especially Phaedra's husband, Apollo, and Kenya's assistant, Brandon DeShazer) as well as the notorious altercation between Kenya and Porsha Williams at the reunion. You don't even need to see the YouTube clip to remember when Kenya pulled out a bullhorn and called Porsha a "dumb ho" across the couch, which led Porsha to drag Kenya to the ground by her hair and punch her. Porsha's lawyer remembers it, too, since it led to official assault charges.

After the hair-pulling incident, Black civil rights group Color Of Change issued this statement. "After weeks of promoting the RHOA reunion altercation, on Sunday executive producer Andy Cohen finally condemned the violent behavior of cast members—completely ignoring the staged hostile environment that provoked the altercation and the troubling pattern of violent, stereotypical portrayals of Black people across many of Bravo's Black reality franchises," it read. He seems to be referring to incidents like when Shereé Whitfield tugged on castmate Kim Zolciak's wig, when Kim and NeNe almost came to blows in the back of a tour bus, or when Shereé and Marlo Hampton screamed at each other during a cast trip to South Africa. There have since been other incidents—namely, 2020's physical altercation between Monique Samuels and Candiace Dillard on *RHOP* that led to each woman filing assault charges against the other, but no jail time.

Part of the problem isn't the behavior, though, it's how it is received between different casts. "I'm watching Lisa Rinna in Amsterdam," Gates remembers of the scene in season 5 of *RHOBH* when Lisa threatened Kim Richards with a broken glass for insinuating Lisa's husband was up to something dirty. "I'm like, did this woman just break a glass like she's about to come across the table and cut her? Can you imagine if that had happened on Atlanta?"

Kristen Warner, an associate professor at University of Alabama and author of "'Who Gon Check Me Boo': Reality TV as a Haven for Black Women's Affect," feels similarly. "There's all of this frantic discourse about Black women acting like the stereotypes and how we just keep being angry and fighting with each other," she says. "But white women do it, too. You know Teresa Giudice and Danielle Staub? She shoved that table at that girl and pulled that woman's hair. How are we not reading them in a way that we are reading ourselves as doomed to always fit these stereotypes?"

Warner sees the idea of arguing against negative portrayals of Black women in reality TV or searching for good portrayals there as somewhat futile. "I teach my students that it's like there are all these warehouses. It's like all those stereotypes that have existed, that have been created over three or four hundred years. All those things exist in a warehouse and they don't go away," Warner says. "You can't burn them up. That's not how representation works. It's an accrual of types. It's an accrual of images. Just because you have a so-called good one doesn't mean that a bad one was eliminated. It just means you overlapped the so-called good one on top of the bad one. So if that's the case and if these things are always going to be with us in this warehouse and that they can be taken out around us, always, will we ever be able to be free of them?"

Warner argues no, so it doesn't matter if Michelle Obama decided to take up a peach and join Andy Cohen's stable of women, people will still think negatively of Black women and people will still think negatively of reality television and people will especially think negatively of Black women on reality television.

But there is an alternative. "We might as well come to Jesus on it and figure out a way to deal and figure out a way to grapple with our insecurity and our discomfort with the fact that white people will think badly of us," Warner says. "I would rather indulge the pleasure of watching these women on-screen doing things I can't do because I'm supposed to be professional. I'd rather watch them do it and live vicariously than try and fret."

Nor would the problem of race and representation on *The Real Housewives* be fixed by integrating the casts. Up until 2020, there was only one Black woman on one of the predominantly white shows, Stacie Scott Turner on the ill-fated *RHODC*. In 2020, Garcelle Beauvais, a Black actress, was included in the cast of *Real Housewives of Beverly Hills,* an event that sparked a deeper investigation into race and casting on the franchise by *The New York Times*. In 2020, Bravo also announced that Eboni K. Williams would be the first Black cast member on *RHONY.*

There has been a little diversity across the franchises in terms of Latina Housewives, particularly on *RHOM* but also on *RHOD* and *RHOBH*. Peggy Sulahian was born in Kuwait and featured on one season of *RHOC,* and Jennifer Aydin is Turkish and currently on *RHONJ.* There have been Asian Housewives on *RHOA* and *RHONY,* Lisa Wu Hartwell and Jules Wainstein, but they were short-lived. In 2020, *RHOBH* added its first Asian cast member, Crystal Kung Minkoff, to its eleventh season.

To Gates, it's a move that rings hollow. "Diversity doesn't mean adding one person of color to a predominantly white cast," she says. "Diversity should not be like the seasoning that you add to the main dish. Diversity would mean that you changed up the main dish. Diversity would mean that it's a stir fry, that you have some of everything. If you want to diversify [*Real Housewives of*] *New York,* you'd have to overhaul the cast."

Though it had yet to air when I spoke to her on the phone, Warner was skeptical of how Garcelle's inclusion would make much difference. "I think that's the problem with just putting one. One doesn't really allow you conversation. One creates a sense of how to integrate and assimilate into the group, one must figure out how to find friendship and not be isolated," she says. "So unless you're going into showing that kind of labor, the labor of how do you make yourself fit . . . Unless she can sort of describe that in a confessional, is she actually anything other than a visual placeholder?"

Warner says that instead of asking whether one scene or character is good or bad representation, viewers should be asking why these shows delight or disgust us. "I think the answer is reorienting how we think about what these characters and what these shows mean to us," she says. "Rather than it be limited to good or bad representation, it's how do these shows reflect on how we feel as a community? What did we learn from these shows? What kinds of joys and agonies do we have while we watch these shows? I think changing the questions shifts the way that these shows can continue to progress and allows for a continued spectrum of types."

Warner is talking about representations of Black women on television and among the Housewives specifically, but she could just as well be talking about the franchise as a whole. If we stop fretting about one production choice or another and start asking why we feel compelled to watch at all, we may get some new and interesting answers.

Many critics and fans alike will point out that the Real Housewives franchise is, for better or worse, one of the only places in television (outside of *Grace and Frankie* or *Golden Girls* reruns) where you will see women between the ages of forty and sixty interacting. If it's not happening in scripted shows, we might as well look for the truth about how groups of women of these ages interact.

That sociological excavation isn't the only benefit of a steady diet of trashy reality television. I asked all the scholars I talked to what is the benefit for people of watching these shows, and several of them made the same point, which is that, in some ways—no matter what the haters will say to the contrary—*The Real Housewives* is making us smarter and more critical as consumers of media.

This point was perfectly elucidated by Brenda Weber. "I think [the Housewives are] making attentive viewers more critically engaged in what they're watching," she says. "For instance, if they're watching an episode and then they're watching *Watch What Happens Live,* and then they see that there's a distance between what happened on the show and how it's being described. And then they're watching a Housewife's Twitter feed at the same time, they can triangulate the truth, right? And they become sort of media critics, and they start thinking about, 'Well, how can that be true? How can what happened on the show be true if what I saw on Twitter or in this other show don't map onto that?' That's doing intellectual work that the show alone doesn't. But it's like media across platform that's creating these new spaces for critical engagement."

So the next time someone at a cocktail party has something to say about your passion pursuit, just let them know that you're actually an amateur media critic and feminist critical theory observer. They're just some asshole who thinks they're cool because they don't own a television.

FIVE ESSENTIAL EPISODES FOR THOSE
WHO HAVE NEVER WATCHED *REAL HOUSEWIVES*

I assume this applies to none of my esteemed readers—but if you're looking to round out your fluency, or just trying to get a friend or romantic partner hooked, here are five episodes to get them started.

"The Dinner Party from Hell" (*Real Housewives of Beverly Hills;* season 1, episode 9):

This is what they would call in the scripted world a *bottle episode,* since almost the whole thing is about one event: a disastrous dinner party thrown by Camille Grammer with the psychic Allison DuBois as her guest. Camille picks a fight with Kyle Richards's friend, the "morally corrupt" Faye Resnick, and DuBois comes for Kyle while sucking on an e-cigarette at the other end of the table. Did this episode invent vaping?

"Finale" (*Real Housewives of New Jersey;* season 1, episode 6):

Much televised and much parodied, one really needs to see Teresa Giudice's table flip (/ table shift) in context to understand it.

"Sun, Sand, and Psychosis" (*Real Housewives of New York;* season 3, episode 12):

The epic that fans refer to as "Scary Island" is really a trio of episodes, all of them fabulous and best when viewed together. However, this wins gold for prominently featuring Kelly Bensimon's bizarre beachfront photo shoot and her subsequent nervous breakdown while chomping on gummy bears. Tennessee Williams never wrote a psychological drama as compelling.

"Bringing Up Old Ghosts" (*Real Housewives of Orange County;* season 11, episode 16):

For a late-season wonder, check out the OC ladies' trip to Ireland, which features Meghan King Edmonds trying to find her roots, Kelly Dodd being isolated from the group, and a 4:00 a.m. trip on a bus to the airport with a fight so vicious that it should be classified as a natural disaster.

"Pillow Talk or Pillow Fight" (*Real Housewives of Atlanta;* season 6, episode 13):

The reason to list this episode is not just the epic brawl that erupts at NeNe's lingerie-themed pillow talk party (though it is a scrap for the ages) but also because it includes one of Phaedra's outrageous birthday parties for her oldest son, where he is dressed up like a prince and the whole family is announced as if they're royalty before descending an elaborate, marble staircase. This is also the highest-rated *Housewives* episode of all time.

THAT'S MY OPINION!

WHY WE WATCH

Now that we have the "guilty pleasure" conversation out of the way, and all the anti-reality TV snobs are out of the room, let's get down to brass tacks: Why do we watch?

I think the easy answer for many fans is, "Because I like it," which is as valid a reason to do anything that isn't illegal or immoral as there is. But there must be something deeper than that. There must be something about these shows specifically that has made their fans so dedicated, loyal, and borderline psychologically unsound.

It seems to me there are two kinds of *Real Housewives* viewers. I like to call them *sincere* and *ironic* fans. The sincere fans are all the people who identify with the women and really want to be on the show. They're the type that say their life is so full of "drama," and when you ask them what kind of drama they're talking about, they say, "Oh, just drama." I don't know if they're already like that or if their yen for conflict has been stoked by watching too much Bravo, but they're right, they are always ready to get up in arms about something.

I don't know that these fans are analyzing the Housewives in the way some others are. They really aspire to be like them. They see them as actual role models for how to behave and get ahead. Who knows, some of them might even try to become rich insurance brokers like Vicki. I don't think they are right or wrong; that is just how they relate to the show.

Then there are the ironic fans. Those would be the ones that say they would never go on *The Real Housewives.* I include myself in this camp, even though I did make a brief appearance on two episodes when I was working with Erika Jayne. (I don't know if you saw it, but there was a hair flip at the end of that sentence.) I would hate to give up my privacy to be on television, and I would certainly hate being in some of the situations the women find themselves in. If one of my friends was shouting, "Clip! Clip! Clip!" and standing up in the middle of a busy restaurant in the Bronx like Dorinda, that is the last time I would ever have lunch with that person.

I watch the Housewives to see what makes them tick, to unravel their complex psychologies, like each one of them is playing Nora in *A Doll's House* or at least Neely O'Hara in *Valley of the Dolls.* I don't court "drama," but, then again, cut in front of me in line at the movie theater, and find out just how ready I am to stand my ground. I might not want to be like the Housewives, but I am fascinated by them and I love them. I want the best for them and, yes, I can empathize with them.

With two different ways of viewing the same thing, how can we both enjoy the same show? Why is this where we're all getting our kicks?

§ § §

There is little academic research about why people watch *The Real Housewives* specifically, but there is a slim, vital brief of research about the genre in general. The most comprehensive study attempting to get to the roots of why we watch was done in 2007. In "An Exploratory Study of Reality Appeal: Uses and Gratifications of Reality TV," Zizi Papacharissi and Andrew L. Mendelson isolated six factors that makes reality TV interesting to its fans. They asked 157 college students how much reality TV they watched in any given week. They discovered that the students watched seventy-six minutes on average, which is really a paltry two *Real Housewives* episodes, so it's far less than most of us consume. The students were then asked questions about their motives for watching these programs.

At the end, Papacharissi and Mendelson isolated six factors that made the genre appealing to people: "reality entertainment, relaxation, habitual pass time, companionship, social interaction, and voyeurism."

The first of those factors is a bit of a cop-out: the reason people like watching reality shows is because it's reality. The study did find that the more realistic viewers thought the show was, the more they were entertained by it, so maybe there's some merit there. I wonder if, now that we're fifteen years further into the reality TV revolution, that would still be true. We know that *Housewives* (and certainly things like *The Hills*) are deeply produced, but that doesn't lessen our engagement. The more real = more popular finding also held true for scripted shows, though, so it would seem those viewers may not be differentiating between what they're watching on TV, just that it's TV and it's realistic. (Unless it's HBO, which we are told is not TV, and Netflix, which is TV except when it's trying to win Oscars.)

The relaxation of reality TV would make sense to any fan, particularly those that like to put on some *Real Housewives* after a long day to "shut off their brain." I think this is why I have found, anecdotally, that the show appeals to so many people in high-pressure or high-profile fields. They deal with problems all day long that they have to fix. When they get home, they can watch the Real Housewives have ridiculous problems that they barely need to care about. So what if LeeAnne Locken didn't serve any dinner at her wedding on *RHOD*. Let her deal with the caterer and the wrath of her guests.

"There's very little complexity to what they have to do, and I think that's got an appeal to it," says TV historian Robert J. Thompson. "And it doesn't matter if you miss an episode, if you fall asleep during an episode, if you wander in and turn on the TV and there's only ten minutes left, you can understand that show at any time you happen to wake up on the couch and start watching it again."

He's absolutely right. *Real Housewives* is totally engaging except when it's not, so maybe that's actually the engagement viewers are look-ing for. Watching the show is like lowering your body into a bath, where the bath is both a means to relaxation and the end in itself. You're relax-ing because you're with your favorite show and with your favorite show because you're relaxing.

I'm much more fascinated by "habitual pass time," which means that reality TV is just the thing that these people do to pass the time. It ap-pears to have a compounding effect, in that the more you get into the habit of using reality TV to pass the time, the more likely you are to use it to pass the time.

The appeal isn't just the frittering away of the moments before our death; there's something deeper. "The habitual statements, however, sug-gested that this pass time activity was integrated into the daily routine of the individual to the point where it became a ritual," the study reads. I think this is especially true of *The Real Housewives,* which now blankets the calendar year.

"I think Bravo really spearheaded the idea that a franchise could be on TV all year round, but that you're changing the cast so you don't get franchise fatigue," says Ben Mandelker, one of the cohosts of the *Watch What Crappens* podcast. "It's sort of like, it's always getting a refresh just when I'm getting a little sick of this show . . . boom, the show wraps up and you get a new cast. You're still watching *Real Housewives,* but it's dif-ferent people, which is kind of brilliant and it gets you really addicted."

It also feeds into this sense of a habit. I see this in my own husband who comes home from work every night and asks, "Which *Real House-wives* do we have tonight?" It's just another part of our day. We do it because it's what we *do.*

That might be the "companionship" that is also one of the factors, although the study suggests that the companion is the television itself or the people within it. One of the appeals of reality TV is that for lonely people, it can sub in for personal interaction. Well, at least it gives you another voice in the room, which sometimes is all you need.

I think this is true of *Housewives* especially. Not only is there the sound of other people filling your den, but it is a show about social interactions—how they can go right and certainly how they can go wrong. It's a show about a group of friends (or coworkers, depending on how you view it). We are being let in on their most intimate moments over long periods of time, which makes it feel like catching up at brunch with long-lost colleagues—I mean, friends.

This bond seems to only intensify as the years go on and we get more and more enmeshed in some of these women's lives. Just think about our decade plus with Luann de Lesseps. We've been through her first divorce, her breakup with Jacques, her kids leaving the house, her second divorce, the loss of the capital A in *LuAnn,* several hit dance singles, arrest, sobriety, and what seems to be in season 12 like a relapse. There are soap opera characters who have been on for just as long who have been involved in less.

I also like to think about Gia Giudice, Teresa's daughter, who was just a tot when the cameras first turned on her. Now we see her going to college. It's the secondary thrill of seeing your actual friends' kids grow up, mature, and become interesting adults but, you know, on television. Growing up on TV might not be the best for human psychology, but it's what she experienced, and we were there along with her. The longer this goes on, the more and more we'll be interested. (Especially when those kids go from gawky teens headed to prom to some of the most popular supermodels in the world, like Gigi and Bella Hadid.)

"It's almost like we have a maternal feeling over these women," podcaster Sarah Galli says. "We've watched them go through marriage, divorce, death, kids, bankruptcy, federal prison, and at a certain point you're watching their kids grow up and you want to see what happens next. There is the actual investment of the time and the emotional investment of how this story plays out."

No amount of time with our "TV friends" can substitute for time with actual humans. Lucas Mann wrote the book *Captive Audience: On Love and Reality TV* about how reality shows (including *The Real Housewives*) brought him and his wife closer together. He says that on his book tour, he would always meet people who would say they weren't fans of reality shows but then add something like, "There was a weird time in my life where I had to move back in with my sister, and *she* watches the Housewives, so we would watch it every Wednesday and it became our show."

That is the social interaction that is one of the joys of watching reality TV in action. The authors of the study found that people would watch programs just because they knew their friends were going to talk about them, so they wanted to get in on the conversation. Either that or there were viewing parties where consuming this cultural artifact together and then talking about it was the excuse for getting together. Couple that with the ritual of it happening every week and "habitual pass time," and it only compounds the joys of watching reality TV with friends.

Mann talked to me about how something that is so societally condemned as reality TV became important to his relationship regardless of how other people feel about it. "If there is a certain amount of time spent every week watching these kinds of shows, that is shared time. I don't know if that time could have been spent in a better way or a worse way, but it's inextricably important time," he says. "I feel like the dumb knee-jerk reaction about reality TV or any sort of cultural form that people seem to think lowly of is like, 'Why are you watching that?' That implies why aren't you doing something else, but it's the thing that you're doing together."

Every *Real Housewives* fan has friends that fall into two camps: those who watch and those who don't. It is a danger to mix them because those who don't watch never want to sit through a brunch were all you talk about is Meghan King Edmonds's divorce and whether or not NeNe was fired. (A. He always seemed like a jerk. B. Jury's still out.) That is the secondary pleasure of the show, not only watching it but then having someone to revel in that pleasure with.

While at Vacation with Vicki and BravoCon, I so often heard people talking about "being with their people" or "all speaking the same language." After decades spent in the company of these women and their fans, what we're getting out of the shows is not just something to chat about around the watercooler, it is something far greater. It is acceptance in a society that was hiding in plain sight, one where the password is something like, "We see each oth-er," while making darting motions at your eyes with your index and middle fingers à la Kandi Burruss at an *RHOA* reunion.

The final factor in the reality assessment is voyeurism. Ah, good old-fashioned voyeurism. This is what all the detractors of reality TV try to tell us is the ill behind all our watching, but I've never really bought it. Yes, it's fun getting a peek into other people's lives, but I don't think it's as pernicious as the word *voyeurism*—which we all associated with some dude in the shrubs in a trench coat secretly watching a woman undress—would lead us to believe. (Also, I learned the word *pernicious* from Camille Grammer when she used it on season 1 of *RHOBH*.)

The universal appeal of voyeurism is what so many people assume is the driving force, including *The Housewives*' creator. "The whole country seems to be wrapped up in fame or faux fame," Scott Dunlop said just before the season 2 premiere. "Though it's a form of entertainment, I think the reason people watch it is that they want to judge other people more than anything else."

The first part of Dunlop's assessment, about people being obsessed with fame, doesn't carry as much weight with me. There are plenty of places for a modern audience to see how the elite live; you can fill countless Instagram feeds with them. Also, it's not like the Real Housewives are famous in a way that Jennifer Aniston is. Yes, we're obsessed with her fame and want to see into her world, but the reason we want to see in is because she won't let us. She is rich and famous enough to shelter her private life from mass consumption (at least until she has a movie to hawk and appears in a *Vanity Fair* cover story). Ramona Singer, on the other hand, wasn't famous until she invited us into her life, and we don't want to continue to see into it because that made her famous. It's something else.

"Judgment" I can buy. After all, one of the great joys of watching the shows is deciding who is right in any argument. Should Dorinda just admit that she heckled Luann at her cabaret show by continuously shouting, "Jovani!" so that everyone can move on? Like a Choose Your Own Adventure etiquette book, the answer is up to all of us at home.

When talking to people about reality shows, they often cite the status thing—that we get to feel like we're better than the people on our TV screens, whether it's the drunken shenanigans on *Jersey Shore* or the medical danger of *My 600-Lb Life*. I think that can be true of *The Housewives*. Remember when Teresa Giudice and Melissa Gorga didn't know what anti-Semitism was or how Porsha Williams thought the Underground Railroad was an actual train? Yes, I was definitely feeling superior in those moments. Maybe that is one of the "ingredients-es," as Teresa would say, to their success.

I think that a sort of voyeurism and judgment is definitely at play when it comes to the drama of the shows, and by "drama," people usually mean the fights. Who hasn't hated someone so much you want to flip a table at them because they dismissed your intelligence? Who hasn't gotten so pissed that you wanted to run out on the sidewalk and shift their wig a little bit in front of Michael Lohan like Shereé Whitfield did to Kim Zolciak-Biermann?

But is our judgment of the women in those inevitable moments what drives their appeal? I would say no. It's the thrill of vicariously doing something we want to but can't. "Most of us spend all our days working to control our thoughts and feelings," Dr. Douglas Gentile, a psychology professor at the University of Iowa, explained to the website Bustle. "We don't say everything we think or do everything we want to, and this is part of the stress most people feel, the feeling that they can't quite be themselves. And so when you watch someone not being able to control themselves, that's interesting to people because we know how it feels to want to just say the things we're feeling [. . .] This is a way of vicariously feeling that adrenaline rush. Getting to see what would happen if you just let loose."

The thing about describing this appeal solely as voyeurism is that it sounds like we are benefiting from and enjoying these women's humiliation. It would be as simple as a case of schadenfreude, a German word for the pleasure in someone else's downfall, as Dorinda explained to everyone several times reading from the Wikipedia definition on her phone, during her final season on *RHONY*.

But it's more complex than that. In 2016, Michael Hershman-Shitrit and Jonathan Cohen from the University of Haifa in Israel published a paper called "Why Do We Enjoy Reality Shows: Is It Really All About Humiliation and Gloating?" In their experiment, they showed 163 college students twelve different reality shows, most of which were Israeli versions of American formats like *Survivor, Big Brother, Super Nanny, The Amazing Race,* and others, as well as a few reality shows native to Israel. (Sadly, no *Housewives.*) They then gauged the students' willingness to be a participant on these programs or to have a family member participate in one. A majority of respondents said they would participate in one of the shows, and an even larger majority said they would want a family member to be cast.

"Scholars have likened reality shows to the Roman Coliseum where early Christians were thrown to lions as entertainment and gladiators fought to the death for cheering crowds," they wrote. "The present study sought to provide an innovative and critical test of the role of humiliation as a motive, and found that it is not central. Returning to the Roman Coliseum metaphor, it is hard to imagine that the joyful Roman viewers would report that they, or their loved ones, would like to be thrown to the lions."

The motivation they found to be the driving factor to enjoyment of the shows was not humiliation but its opposite: empathy. So many fans say which Real Housewife they are like, as if putting ourselves into their shoes. Because that is what we do every week while watching the show. As an extension of that, we weren't actually delighted when Luann got arrested. Well, we might have paid attention because of the drama, but I think all of us felt a little bad. Here is a woman who was getting out of a bad marriage and behaving horribly. We weren't chuckling at her downfall; we were all hoping that she would get better.

Or maybe the first and then the latter. As producers of the shows say, *Real Housewives* is all about conflict and conflict resolution. We want Luann to be a mess, but we want her to heal so that she can be a mess for us all over again.

Chris Oliver-Taylor, who developed the Australian versions of the

Real Housewives, learned a powerful lesson from *The Real Housewives of Sydney,* which was all fights all the time and audiences hated it. "I think, with *Housewives,* if you lose all sense of empathy or connection, it's a bitch fight with no redemption," he says. "For some die-hard fans, that's totally fine, but for the most part of the audience, it doesn't work." If it were all fighting all the time, *Housewives* would look like Thunderdome, the Facebook group that was always bullying its own members. Thunderdome didn't last long either.

Dunlop, the *Housewives'* creator, eventually changed his stance that people love the show only voyeuristically and told *The Orange County Register* in 2011, "There are a lot of relatable stories. There are a lot of blondes, for sure. But there are a lot of relatable stories that cut across the financial, marital, challenging and humorous aspects that occur in life." As much as the Real Housewives aren't us, they are us as well. There is a great leveling between their perceived status and their behavior or things that have affected them. They are continually brought down to our level, and that makes us love them, want to be them, and embrace them in a hug that won't be over until Brooks Ayers is in jail for faking cancer.

"I think people like to be reminded that the Real Housewives are just like everybody else," says Shane Keough. "You could have the nicest cars, the nicest house, all this money, and a beautiful family, but there's still going to be drama. There's still going to be death. There's still going to be sadness. There's going to be business problems. People are going to lose their houses. That transcends any walk of life, if you're a farmer or a hedge fund manager. We're all on the same roller coaster." Or, in at least one case, on the same Ramona coaster.

⚇ ⚇ ⚇

I don't think either the sincere or ironic fans are right or wrong. When it comes down to it, we all love the same thing. We all have the irony and the sincerity inside of us at different times and in different measures. At the end of the day, a fan is a fan. No amount of emotional or intellectual distance between myself and this phenomenon can stop me from needing to tune in. Taking in the irony and the sincerity is sort of like loving

Reese's Peanut Butter Cups. Some come for the chocolate, some come for the peanut butter, but it's the combination, the fusion of the two, that makes it irresistible.

We're all individuals, and we all react to the women differently. That's sort of what is amazing about the fandom. Take any of the cast members, and there will be people who will defend them to the death and people who will loathe them until their eyes flutter shut and they go to that "For more information on the Real Housewives go to BravoTV.com" in the sky.

We don't love a particular woman, a particular city, or the whole franchise for any one of the reasons in this chapter; we love them for *all* these reasons at different times and in different concentrations. (I think the one thing these studies leave out of our love of the Real Housewives is how truly funny some of them are, and I don't just mean when we're laughing at them for being fall-down drunk.) What makes the show so great is that it can accomplish all these things at once and yet completely defy categorization. It's constantly evolving, commenting on itself, and enmeshing itself further in our lives.

So many times when talking to people for this book, they referred to Bravo in general, and the Housewives especially, as "our sports." They are absolutely right. We care about the players, as well as the game and the health of the league. The motivations for hirings and firings can fuel countless hours of discussion. Maybe why people watch sports is also why they watch *Housewives*? "There is no single answer to why people watch sports, because the answer doesn't lie in the game, it lies inside the individual," Eric Simons wrote in "What Science Can Tell Sportswriters About Why We Love Sports." "It's complicated in the same ways all our relationships are complicated."

It's also complicated in the way our relationship to *The Real Housewives* is complicated. A suite of reality TV shows isn't given the same cultural importance or heft because, well, it hasn't been around nearly as long, which is a fair point. But I think the other reason it hasn't been given that importance is because it is sports for women and gay men, two marginalized groups in society. It is also still stuck with the erroneous stench of "voyeurism" that can't be washed off, even if it's not especially relevant to the enterprise.

Professional sports, though mostly filled with men, is seen as being for everyone. Why can't *The Real Housewives* get the same respect? "I think that the shows really offer sort of these multilevel, multilayered pleasures for audiences. And I think particularly when you have ensemble casts, there's always something for everybody," says media scholar Racquel Gates. "I feel my allegiance is changing for every single franchise, every single season. I think there's something that's very pleasurable about a text that is at once familiar and always a little bit new."

Each new season of *Housewives* brings familiar pleasures: the taglines, the hazing of new castmates, the inevitable blowups, the reunion looks. It's always the same, but it's also always a little bit different. I think that's a credit to Bravo, to the companies that produce these shows, and to the women who know that the moment they take their eyes off the ball, it will roll away from them.

EPILOGUE

THE FUTURE OF *HOUSEWIVES*

So, more than a decade into it, where do the Housewives go from here? Can they keep evolving or, like the TV westerns and daytime soap operas before them, have they seen their last golden age? There are those who argue that the balance has gone off for good. "It's a tired franchise, in my opinion," says reality TV scholar June Deery. "I wish somebody had the initiative to do it a little differently."

Some of the problem might be in the women themselves. If casting new people is what keeps the show fresh, what happens when those women are too clued into the game? "It's tricky because the new Housewives are too in on it," says a former Bravo exec. "They're too savvy. I think it takes away the storytelling, because they won't be cool with stuff. They won't let themselves be drunken messes for our amusement."

Kristen Warner, who has written scholarly articles about *The Real Housewives,* also wants the women to change. "The things that worked for *Real Housewives of Atlanta* five years ago may not work now," she says. "Audiences might desire different kinds of things. The cast needs to find something else to fuss about. Be honest about the difficulty of finding a job, NeNe. You thought you were going to be a big star. It's not happening. Be honest about that. Be honest about the difficulties of maintaining wealth and assets. Shift gears so that you can grow. We all grew up. Everybody grows up. You need to grow up, too."

Some think that Bravo might also see the writing on the wall. Andy Cohen always jokes that when the ratings get really bad, he'll just take eight to ten of the women and put them on an island together. Maybe that's not that far off. (In early 2021, there were rumors that such a project was under way.)

"My hunch is that Bravo thinks that the end might be coming sooner or later, so they're, like, bleeding it, dry," says Andy Dehnart from reality news site Reality Blurred. "That's based on the fact that they in the past year or so have tried many more types of shows than they've had." Bravo has tried its hand at scripted fare, to little avail, and also attempted an HGTV-esque Friday lineup, bringing back *Queer Eye* gurus Carson Kressley and Thom Filicia and kicking off a show called *Backyard Envy* about hunky landscapers.

Dehnart allows that *Housewives* is like a human soap opera, so as long as the women keep delivering story lines, it could keep going on. Just when you think things have gotten as crazy as they're ever going to get, we get the Boat Ride from Hell or Denise Richards's possible lesbian affair, and it's just as dramatic as ever.

I agree with this view, and I also think that for diehards who have watched all the franchises at one time or another, we dip in and out. I have given up on *RHONJ* about fifteen times, only to be drawn back in because people kept telling me that it had gotten good again. I also took up *RHOP* after getting the same advice. In both instances, they were correct. But it might now be time to give up on *RHOC*.

Andy's Girls podcaster Sarah Galli thinks that fans need to stay with it, even in the seasons when it gets really boring. Otherwise, how will they know when it gets good? "I've thought it was peaking and people were tired of it, and then *Potomac* comes along and they're new women, and it's such good TV that I can't imagine that not going on for another five years," she says, adding that every one of the shows eventually delivers. "I don't believe in God, but I have faith in *Real Housewives.*"

I have a similar faith, but the numbers aren't in our favor. The very open secret is that ratings have been slowly eroding year after year. *RHOA* has always been the highest-rated franchise, and all the shows follow a similar trajectory to their ratings.

Season 5, which aired from 2012 to 2013 and introduced Kenya Moore and Porsha Williams, had an average of 3.12 million viewers. Season 6 was the show's apex at 3.86 million on average. It's been slowly downhill since. Season 7 scored 3.11, season 8 (when *Facts of Life* star Kim Fields replaced NeNe) scored 2.9 million, season 9 averaged 2.62 million, and season 10 scored 2.25 million, despite NeNe's return. Starting with 2018/2019's season 11, the average season now scores under 2 million viewers with season 11 averaging 1.95 and season 12 averaging 1.79.

As of late 2020, the last complete season of *RHOBH* averaged 1.49 million viewers, *RHOC* averaged 1.31 million, *RHONJ* averaged 1.24 million, and *RHONY* averaged 1.13 million. All of them were down from their previous seasons—except *RHONJ,* which managed to gain 20,000 viewers on average. It must be because of Margaret Josephs throwing someone in a pool.

As of 2019, *RHOA* was still Bravo's biggest show in the eighteen-to-forty-nine demographic, which is really all they care about, because that's where they make their money. In that demo, it was tied for fifty-sixth most popular show on broadcast or cable. However, two outposts of TLC's blockbuster *90 Day Fiancé* franchise had more viewers. *RHOC* was tied for Bravo's second-highest-rated show among the youngsters, along with upstairs-downstairs yachting shows *Below Deck* and *Below Deck Mediterranean.*

Yes, that's a lot of numbers, and numbers are boring, so the takeaway is that the show loses a few hundred thousand pairs of eyeballs every year. The same is true not just for *Atlanta* but across the board.

Some of this erosion is due to fatigue with the franchise. Any show that's been on the air for more than a decade sees plenty of people moving on to the newest fad (which appears to be *90 Day Fiancé*). But some of that erosion is also keeping pace with the number of viewers, particularly young people, who are leaving cable altogether.

According to MoffettNathanson Research, in 2019, cable networks saw a decrease of 10 percent in overall viewers, most of those the young viewers that advertisers think they can cajole into buying their new line of conditioner. This has to do, of course, with the rise of streaming and the change in viewership patterns that the streaming services, like Netflix, ushered in. Many viewers now prefer to have all the episodes of a season banked so they can binge it all at once—a method I know anecdotally some Housewives fans enjoy.

The ratings figures only account for those who are watching *The Housewives* either live or within a few days on the DVRs. It does not take into account all the people who buy them from Apple TV or Amazon or wait for the season to end so that the whole thing will be available on Hulu, which currently streams the entire *Housewives* back catalog. These numbers also don't include those watching old seasons on a streaming service or rewatching their favorites over again in the same way. Again, anecdotally, I know many fans love a retro binge.

Those viewing figures also don't count me. Ever since I moved to London in 2018, I've watched all my *Housewives* on Hayu, a streaming service owned by NBCUniversal that makes Housewives available for an international audience. It's the best four pounds I spend a month.

More and more, when I think about its future, I liken *Real Housewives* to professional wrestling. Not only are they extreme personalities in crazy costumes engaging in overblown fights for our amusement, its fans are what could be considered a deep niche. There are plenty of people that aren't into it and can totally ignore it, but there is also an immovable base of diehards. It would take a lot to get the ratings back to 2010 levels, but Bravo can count on a certain viewership until the world ends in a nuclear holocaust or ecological disaster.

At BravoCon in 2019, Andy Cohen announced on stage the tenth city to welcome (or at least tolerate) the franchise. "We've always tried to choose a city that has completely unique personalities, and we also try to throw a little curveball now and then, pick somewhere you weren't expecting," he said. "We are very excited to travel to Salt Lake City."

Knowing Andy's thoughts on expansion, I thought he was kidding, but his "Psych!" did not come. He continued, "You didn't see it coming but I have to tell you, in Utah, you have the majesty of the mountains, the Mormon religion, an exclusive community of people who have very successful businesses who live in their own universe. It is gorgeous, and I think you're going to be really surprised and intrigued by the group of women we've found."

The series is made by InventTV, the production company that makes *Southern Charm New Orleans* for Bravo as well as all of Andy's hero Oprah Winfrey's reality shows for Apple TV. There were rumors before the show's 2020 launch that Bravo had fired the original production company (sound familiar?) and hired Shed Media (the new name of Ricochet, which still produces *RHONY*) to take over, reediting the footage into a new show.

Within a few weeks of Andy's announcement, the now-rampant Bravo blogosphere sussed out almost the entire cast list and even spotted them filming with native Utahans and *Vanderpump Rules* cast members Lala Kent and Katie Maloney.

My old shirtless friend Shane Keough isn't at all skeptical of the franchise's longevity. "Nobody knew that from that pilot, this was going to lead to fifteen years and different runs in different cities. That's crazy," Shane told me over lunch, his face as handsome and his hair as thick as the first time I saw him beaming out of my TV set while he lounged alone in Southern California in a bean-shaped pool. "We've watched dreams happen and dreams be crushed. Lives have ended and relationships ended. It's just so much has happened, but you look back, and twenty years of the show is not far off. I don't see it ending."

I don't see it ending either, mostly because it seems like Bravo, Andy Cohen, the production companies, and all the worker bees on the ground that contribute to this great franchise keep finding women who will make us cry and make us laugh, make us jealous and make us cringe, make us fall in love and make us love to hate.

Take a moment to think about your favorite Real Housewife. You must have one by now, if you've made it this far. Because I consider Erika Jayne a friend and collaborator, my favorite Housewife is Sonja Morgan, but don't tell the others. Think of your favorite. Think of her in the opening credits, holding the insignia of her city. Think of her as she pivots around against a glittering background, her name swishing across the screen like a magic comet. Think of her at lunch, ordering a salad with the other women. Think of her in a fight, think of her at home alone, think of her dog and her children, think of her failed fashion line (because she probably has one). Think of her in a reunion dress, and then another, and then another. Take all these images and hold them in your mind, your heart, your memories. Hold the Real Housewives close to you, and they will become something like a prayer.

ACKNOWLEDGMENTS

I n the summer of 2018, I had just turned forty, left my entire life behind in New York, and did two things I swore I would never do: get married and move somewhere for a man. I had to do the first to follow that man to London, which made it that much more complicated logistically and emotionally.

On the plane ride across the Atlantic I read *Bachelor Nation* by Amy Kaufman, a book about the history, behind-the-scenes antics, and cultural impact of *The Bachelor* / *The Bachelorette*. I had never watched either show, but as a scholar of the reality television arts and sciences, I figured it was my job to keep up with the latest scholarly publications. The whole time reading it I thought, "Why has no one done this for *The Housewives*?"

A few weeks after landing in London, while strolling through a John Lewis (it's like a Target but bigger and everything is in pounds), I got an email from my friend Michelle Collins asking me if she could introduce me to Nicole Tourtelot, a literary agent. She was Kaufman's agent and apparently was also thinking, "Why has no one made *Bachelor Nation* but for *The Housewives*?" So, with an assist from Michelle, these great minds thinking alike finally came together. And if you love this book remember that it was all my idea. If you hate it, please direct all of your correspondence to Nicole Tourtelot.

We sold the book to James Melia at Flatiron Books who, apparently, I had a lunch meeting with years before while in the midst of a panic attack that was so bad I didn't remember meeting him at all. I hope he paid. James is a huge *Housewives* fan and did such great work helping to shape the book. Sadly, he left Flatiron before a first draft was completed. So, in the middle of the pandemic, Flatiron saddled Zack Wagman and Meghan Houser with me and my little reality television project. Though neither had really seen "the shows" I couldn't have asked for a better pair. They whipped my meandering, too-long manuscript into lean, mean, fighting shape. They were basically like Martin, Tinsley Mortimer's boxing coach on *RHONY*, except there are two of them and they probably wouldn't put up with Tinz for very long.

The whole team at Flatiron has been amazing, especially Marlena Bittner, who was born to publicize this book, and marketing gurus Nancy Trypuc and Katherine Turro. Also "kadooze," as Ramona Singer would say, to Maxine Charles, John Morrone, Meryl Levavi, and Emily Walters.

Of course, there wouldn't even be a book without all the content in it, so I would like to thank everyone who talked to me—on the record and off—and indulging all of my probing questions about what it's like to make one of these shows, be on one of these shows, or care so much about one of these shows you decide to make it your livelihood or area of academic expertise. All of these people really are doing the lord's work. And by the lord, I mean our dark lord, Andy Cohen.

A huge thanks to Caity Henderson, a super journalist and super fan, who came in at the last minute and did some clutch reporting that was absolutely essential to getting this book done on time. She's still in college, so please give her a job. Amy Kaufman, Mx. *Bachelor Nation* herself, gave me a lot of great advice in the formative stages of research and was invaluable. Also, thanks to my legion of interns who did some grunt research work for me as well. Erin Grant, Gleason Rowe, Ariana Lang, Julia Fairorth, Susan Dawson, Kyle Perry, Katelyn Kirk, Laura Lynch,

Peter Davidson, Lindy Regan, and especially my Vacation with Vicki buddy Lindsay Harden. You all get the Pickles Award for Intern Dedication.

Kate Smolinski is the best sister-in-law that any boy, especially a *Housewives* fan, could ask for. Thank you for being my first reader, fact checker, copy editor, sounding board, sometimes transcriber, and all-around champion. I would buy you something nice, like a hot dog in a Thermos, if you would let me.

Christian Vesper, my darling husband, you have always been supportive no matter what I wanted to do and calm me down when I'm freaking out, pick me up when I'm discouraged, and keep me on track when I'd rather just play Best Fiends on my phone for the majority of an afternoon. You're also great to watch *Housewives* with.

My parents, Jim and Jan, have also always been excited about this project and always encouraging, even though they have never watched an episode of the *Housewives* that I haven't been featured in. But I'm still pissed at Jan for retiring as my accountant. Luckily Jim served as my personal accountability coach when I needed it the most. Everyone in the Moylan clan has always had my back and I love them for it, same goes for my dearest sisters the "F.G.s"—Dee, Forte, Riunite, Will, Fabien, and Bitzy (even though Will is the only one who will read this book).

Don't let me forget the little people, like Laura Lewis who took my very stylish author photo and Geoff Clement who got me skinny enough that I wasn't embarrassed to have it taken. Also Dr. Deidre Barrett, my therapist, swooped in and got me in the right place mentally when I thought this whole project was about to fall to shit. This really has been a culmination of a career, so thanks to Kristina Campbell, Lyn Stoessen, Will O'Bryan, Kevin Naff, and the other people at *The Washington Blade* who gave me a start, Gabriel Snyder and Nick Denton who hired me at *Gawker* and put me on the map, and every editor since then who has dealt with my awful spelling and turning in assignments without the file actually attached to the email.

Let's take a moment for the Housewives themselves. They have given us all so much joy and drama, so many GIFs, catchphrases, and memes that we can be entertained for a lifetime. It's not easy work that any of you do and your sacrifices do not go unnoticed. I know that Bravo pays you handsomely to do this, but I would like to think that even without the paycheck, without the platform, you would all go on continuing to do it just to keep the fans happy.

Oh, the fans. My fans. Oh, thank you. Thank you all. Seriously, you can stop applauding. I have never met a greater group of people in the world than the *Housewives* fans. Every time I have run into someone who likes my work or just watches the shows, they have always been fun, wonderful, intelligent people. I would rather be seated next to any of you at a dinner party than Madonna, Michelle Obama, or RuPaul Charles herself. I am honored to have served you all of these years and to be among you. You are all cool, not like, uncool, and don't ever let anyone make you feel bad for loving this completely ridiculous thing of ours.

ABOUT THE AUTHOR

Brian Moylan is the president and founder of the completely fictitious Real Housewives Institute. He started writing about the Real Housewives in 2011, though his episode recaps have been on *New York* magazine's culture website, Vulture, since what seems like the dawn of time. His work has also appeared in *The New York Times*, *The Guardian*, *Vice*, *Gawker*, *Interview*, *Time*, *W*, *Men's Health*, and at least one pornographic website. He lives in London with his husband.